Islands in the Sky

Islands in the Sky

Bold New Ideas for Colonizing Space

Edited by

Stanley Schmidt
and
Robert Zubrin

WILEY POPULAR SCIENCE
John Wiley & Sons, Inc.

New York • Chichester • Brisbane • Toronto • Singapore

This text is printed on acid-free paper.

Published by John Wiley & Sons, Inc.

Library of Congress Cataloging-in-Publication Data

Reaching for the Stars : Analog's book of space exploration / edited by Robert Zubrin and Stanley Schmidt.
p. cm.
ISBN 0-471-13561-5 (pbk : alk. paper)
1. Outer space--Exploration. 2. Space colonies. I. Zubrin, Robert. II. Schmidt, Stanley.
QB500.R33 1996 95-32914
919.9'04--dc20

Printed in the United States of America

10 9 8 7 6 5 4 3 2 1

Contents

Introduction

At the 1989 International Space Development Conference in Chicago, one of *Analog's* writers advised me to be sure to hear a talk by someone named Robert Zubrin, on a scheme for greatly reducing the cost of traveling to other planets. It sounded at least casually interesting, but the program showed that the paper was being presented shortly after my departure. Since at that time I knew nothing about Bob Zubrin or his ideas, I simply shrugged off his talk. It was too bad I'd have to miss it, but there were plenty of others I'd also be missing, and I had no reason to assume this one would be any more of a loss than them—except, of course, that recommendation from our mutual friend.

What I didn't know was that the mutual friend had also told Bob about me. Late one afternoon, as I was passing through the hotel lobby on my way to something utterly unrelated, a visibly energetic young man accosted me and said, "Dr. Schmidt?"

"Yes," I confessed cautiously.

"I'm Bob Zubrin," he said. "I'm giving a paper tomorrow that I think you might be interested in for *Analog*, and I hear you won't be able to be there. I wondered if you might have a few minutes. . . ."

My normal reaction to such encounters is to cringe and start thinking about how to escape if, as often happens, the unsolicited exposition proves long, tedious, and fruitless. This time, though, something told me to listen, though I must confess I still started out with a *bit* of the usual skepticism.

That didn't last long. Bob Zubrin proceeded to give me, there in the lobby, what amounted to a private performance of the public talk he was going to give the next day. He gave it much faster than I suspect he did in public, perhaps because he sensed that I'd been on my way to something. (It may be significant that I no longer remember what.) He didn't refer to notes, except to point something out in a diagram or table. He never missed a beat and always had a ready answer if I had a question. I've seldom seen a speaker so thoroughly familiar with what he had to say.

And what he had to say was spellbinding. Why *should* spacecrafts spend much of their fuel lugging all the fuel for a round trip, when it's perfectly possible to refuel at your destination? It was the kind of idea that makes you say, "Why didn't *I* think of that?" and Bob made a detailed, thoroughly thought-out, compelling case for it.

As I've already hinted, my usual reaction when somebody collars me in a hallway to tell me about a story or article they want to write, is either to tell them why we can't use it or to say cautiously, "Well, if you want to send it in, I'll read it." This time I found myself saying, "How soon can I have the article?"

Only after we had gone our separate ways did I find the time and presence of mind to think, "What have I done?" But the article came in right when Bob had promised, and in such polished form that it needed very little editorial work. We published it, and our annual poll showed it to be one of our readers' favorites for the year. I have since come to regard Bob Zubrin as one of the most prolific and reliable sources of solid, imaginative ideas for space travel—an opinion widely shared in the aerospace field. Now, whenever he calls me to describe a new idea, I drop what I'm doing and listen. Usually I buy the article; you'll find several of them in this book.

Why are such ideas important? Humankind *needs* to get into space, for a wide variety of reasons. The most basic is survival itself. We *know* from the paleontological record that mass extinctions have occurred on this planet in the past. We know that they will almost certainly happen again; they could happen at any time, and *we* could be the subject of one. But disasters affecting a whole planet occur much oftener than disasters affecting an entire solar system or galaxy. We as a species will be far less vulnerable if and when we have outposts elsewhere.

Beyond that, there's the fact that Earth's human population is growing at such a rate that it's beginning to feel the pinch of limited elbow room and resources. This has several deleterious effects: the direct ones of trying to house and feed billions of people with fixed resources, and the indirect ones of the psychological impact of feeling that there's no more room to grow. Easy access to space can do something about both kinds of problems. It won't eliminate the need for people to exercise reasonable prudence in reproducing and using whatever space and resources they have. But it will provide more space for people to move into, more material resources for people both down here and out there, and the psychological and cultural boost that comes from the existence of a new frontier.

The key word there is *easy*. Access to space has seldom been seen as easy; indeed, it's often been used as a metaphor for the ultimate in difficulty. ("If we can put a man on the Moon . . .") But things often seem prohibitively difficult not because they *are*, but simply because we haven't yet learned to do them—and often we must learn the hard ways before we can see the easy ones.

When I was growing up, many adults seriously believed that space travel of any kind was quite impossible. That was true even less than five years before *Sputnik* and less than twenty before *Apollo 11*. Before that, people were just as skeptical about air travel, which is now routine on a very large scale. Not so long ago, the very concept of the telephone seemed like the wildest fantasy. A little later, people knew it could be done, but only the truly visionary dreamed of a time when every village would have a phone. Now, in many parts of the world, not only does every *home* have at least one phone, but many people have phones that they can use *anywhere*—even at the beach. So when somebody like Bob Zubrin tells you that a ticket to space may someday be as cheap and easy to get as a ticket to Chicago is now, there's a good chance he's right.

How do you get from "impossible" to "routine"? You need people who can look beyond what "Everyone knows" and see what we could do in the future. That's where *Analog* and the writers in this book come in. *Analog Science Fiction & Fact* was born in 1930 and has been published almost continuously since then. For its first thirty years its title was some version of *Astounding Science Fiction*, but science fact has always been an important part of its make-up, both as the basis for its fiction and as the subject of factual articles like those gathered here. Its stories and articles in past decades have played a demonstrably important role in getting us as far as we've come so far. Many scientists and engineers responsible for real achievements in space were originally drawn to their careers by the ideas they found here. Others saw them as wild imaginings. *They* thought, "I can make that happen"—and they did.

Recently space exploration has fallen on hard times. It has lost popular support; too many people have lost sight of why we need it. But we still *do* need it; and to get the huge benefits it has to offer, we need people who can see, and show others, the huge range of possibilities, and how we can bring them within our grasp.

Astounding in the past was a leading source of such people and ideas. Thanks largely to them, we have made some preliminary accomplishments. But the *real* payoffs still lie ahead, and *Analog* today is still pointing the way to them. In this book you'll find a treasury of imaginative suggestions from some of the brightest minds working in this field.

And remember: we're not kidding about any of this. These articles are not "just science fiction." They are things we *can do*—and with any luck at all, and vision and determination, we *will*.

Stanley Schmidt
Editor, *Analog Science Fiction and Fact*

Part One

Breaking the Bonds of the Earth

Chapter 1

G. Harry Stine

Comes the Revolution . . . .

In spite of crashes, politics, budget battles, and opposition from today's version of Jules Verne's Baltimore Gun Club, we're on the verge of having inexpensive, reliable, and responsive single-stage-to-orbit (SSTO) spaceships like the *Delta Clipper* DC-Y described in Dr. Arlan Andrews's science-fact article in the June 1993 issue.[1]

Given that we can build reusable spaceships that operate like commercial airliners, what is this *really* going to mean? In one word: *revolution*.

In the social context, the word "revolution" means a rapid and radical change in the way of doing things as opposed to "evolution" which is a slow and gradual change. And the introduction of the SSTO is indeed revolutionary, as you will see herein.

It's presumptuous to believe that anyone can fully assess the impacts of a truly revolutionary concept such as the SSTO. However, assuming that the basic technology to build SSTO spaceships exists, it's possible to look at how SSTO spaceships will (1) reduce the costs of space transportation, (2) change the way we conduct operations in the Earth-Moon system, and (3) impact allied areas that haven't been considered when operating with expendable space launch vehicles.

Although an SSTO spaceship hasn't flown yet, it's prudent to begin looking at the consequences of this space transportation revolution. It is *not* too early to look at the business economics of the revolution.

(The question was unreliably reported to have been asked in the Continental Congress, "Mister Chairman, as the delegate from New Hampshire, may I ask if this revolution is going to cost very much?")

And given the lightning speed with which our political, regulatory, and legal systems operate, is it wise to leave political, regulatory, and legal questions unresolved until the last minute? We may end up having the technology for a cheap, reliable, and reusable SSTO spaceship but be unable to use its services or even fly it!

THE TECHNOLOGY IS IMMATERIAL

First off, assume that the basic technology to build SSTO spaceships exists. Leave it to others to focus on technology; they love the technology. However, even after nearly two decades of people like me admonishing them, they still don't understand that technology alone isn't going to make it happen. Where specific technological problems presently exist, aviation history says that a reasonable number of flight tests with prototype X-vehicles can provide engineering solutions. Build 'em, boost 'em, and bend 'em . . . and name a few more streets at Edwards Air Force Base for courageous former test pilots.

Furthermore, the specific SSTO technology used is immaterial. For example, the exact operational modes—VTOVL, VTOHL, HTOHL, nose-first entry, tail-first entry, etc.—influence only the type of required spaceport facilities, not their extent.

Basic assumptions about a generic SSTO include:

- Propellants are liquid oxygen and liquid hydrogen with no auxiliary propellants.
- The airframe, propulsion, avionics, and other on-board systems are completely reused.
- Turnaround between flights is no longer than 72 hours.
- A ground crew of 50 technicians and mechanics per flight is required.
- Operations involve only aircraftlike procedures from austere "flight simplex" facilities.

THE ECONOMY, STUPID!

Listen up! The first lesson: The space transportation revolution will not occur unless someone can make money flying spaceships.

For the last 30 years, space transportation has been operated and controlled by the federal government as a part of national security. However, with the end of the Cold War, it's too expensive to continue doing it the old way. And this socialized space transportation system has retarded progress. It has been 35 years since NASA was established. This is the same period that existed between the first government air mail flight with DeHaviland DH-9 biplanes in 1919 and the first flight of the Boeing 707 prototype in 1954. Anyone who claims that space technology is more complex than aeronautical technology simply doesn't understand what went on between 1919 and 1954.

The federal government has shown it cannot operate a spaceline any more than it could (or did) operate a national railroad or a national airline. Private enterprise did and does. With the SSTO, it's going to make more sense to let private enterprise engage in profitable space ventures.

However, the bad news is: *Perceived risk* is high. The good news is: It has *always* been high! In the past, high-risk ventures with new technology have used a proven risk reduction procedure: modest government research funding and incentive programs to reduce risk. Railroads got government guaranteed loans and land grants. Airlines got airliners built using government research findings and air mail contracts to help them get started. The government is presently comtinuing this historic procedure by funding experimental SSTO test vehicles.

As we have learned in the past 35 years, few things get done well and economically without the profit motive. Before we go any farther, we must determine the attractiveness of the business opportunity of providing civil and military space transportation. Therefore, we must first answer the question: *Can someone make money doing it?*

The answer to this question rests with the size of the market opportunity. This is, in turn, dependent upon the nature and price of the service offered by spaceship operators. The market opportunity and the price of the service are interconnected by a feedback loop. One affects the other.

With this principle in mind, The Enterprise Institute, Inc., in Phoenix, Arizona, developed a space transportation economics model designed to answer the questions an investment broker or a banker would ask the organizers of a prototype spaceline who are raising capital to buy a fleet of SSTOs.[2] A banker or investor wants an answer to a simple question: *Am I going to get my money back?* In short, what's the risk? Can the service be sold? Is there a market? He will ask additional questions that will get him an answer to this first question.

WHAT IS THE MARKET?

The effect of introducing a new product or service into any market ranges from zero to revolutionary. An evaluation requires answers to several questions before the effect of a new product or market opportunity can be assessed. These include:

- *WHAT—What is it and what will it do?* For the purposes of this analysis, a first-generation SSTO spaceship will transport up to 10 tons of cargo and/or passengers into low-Earth orbit and back every 3 days.
- *LIMITS—What won't it do?* In terms of its limitations, a first-generation SSTO spaceship will not be configured to accommodate very large and bulky payloads. Payload support services for cargo will be limited as is the case with current cargo services provided by airline operators. Customers must supply their own specialized cargo support.
- *AVAILABILITY—When, where, and how easy is the product or service to obtain?* Each SSTO will provide service at regular intervals of 3 days. A full payload bay won't be required for a flight. Service will be provided from several spaceports. Weather will be no more of a problem than it is for subsonic commercial air transportation.
- *PRICE—How much will it cost?* This raises the key issue: How much will a commercial spaceship operator *need to charge* for the transport service? How does this price compare to alternative transport services to low-Earth orbit?

The *required revenue per flight* can be determined if the following performance and financial information is known.

1. *Capital equipment costs*—Spaceship, ground support equipment and facilities, spaceship life, and facilities life.
2. *Operating costs*—Marketing, G&A, insurance, spaceship maintenance, crew and ground personnel, and fuel.
3. *Financial costs*—Competitive return on equity and cost of debt.
4. *Capital structure of the business*—Debt to equity ratio.
5. *Performance data*—Weight profile, fleet attrition, and flight rates.

The Enterprise Institute financial model was designed to allow variation in inputs to determine factors having the most significant effect upon the required revenue per flight.

One other point about the financial model: It was assumed that, at the end of 5 years, the business was totally liquidated. The model shows no value for residual costs, market position, or used equipment.

For a first-generation spaceship, the differences between a commercial vehicle and a military vehicle converge. Thus, if a first-generation spaceship is designed to satisfy military and civil customers—as was done with the Boeing 707—a manufacturer can spread his nonrecurring costs over a wider base. This in turn will reduce the cost of a spaceship and make it even more economically viable in the commercial sector. Furthermore, satisfying both types of customers through convergence not only lowers development costs but also reduces the risk involved in developing the technology. The bankers will like that.

The most realistic run with the model used the following key assumptions: A spaceship costs $500 million (1993 dollars), has a life of 500 flights, requires 1,200,000 pounds of liquid oxygen and liquid hydrogen per flight at a cost of $0.50 per pound, and has an annual flight rate of 100 flights. In addition, a conservative debt to equity capital structure of 33% debt and 67% equity was assumed for the business. A competitive pretax return on equity requirement was pegged at 16%.

The results are impressive. The total required revenue per flight for placing 10 tons of cargo and/or passengers into LEO is $1.6 million (1993 dollars). In terms of passengers, this works out to be $14,500 per person for a round-trip ticket to low-Earth orbit. (If you want to go, you don't buy a new car that year.)

This represents a price about 1 to 3% of current launch services. But is this reasonable? What assumptions exert heavy influence on the competitive posture of a reusable spaceship relative to expendable and semi-expendable vehicles? Various sensitivity analyses identified those factors that have the greatest effect upon the required revenue per flight—that is, they identified the economic "drivers."

Financial model inputs of particular interest were spaceship purchase price, propellant cost, spaceship life, and number of flights per year.

The price of *anything* varies according to the number of production units over which development costs will be recovered, the recurring cost of production, and the associated production learning curve. The cost of propellants depends on the overall demand for them. The flight rate is determined by spaceship design. Spaceship designs that have a longer life and allow faster turnaround influence the revenue needed to provide an attractive return on investment.

The results of the sensitivity analysis are interesting:

- A five-fold increase in the price of the propellants from $0.50 to $2.50 per pound caused the required revenue per flight to increase to $2.2 million from $1.6 million, a 38% increase.
- When the propellant price of $0.50 per pound was maintained, but the price of a spaceship was tripled from $500 million to $1.5 billion, the required revenue rose from $1.6 million to $4.2 million, a 163% increase.

Of the two inputs, the purchase price of a spaceship clearly is the significant economic driver.

It is important to note that in the case of a fuel price of $2.50 per pound and a spaceship cost of $1.5 billion, the resulting required revenue of $4.7 million per flight remains a fraction of the cost of service using expendable and semi-expendable launch vehicles.

Other sensitivity analyses showed great flexibility between spaceship cost, spaceship life, and spaceship flight rates.

For those who believe that certification costs could seriously skew the model's results, these factors were taken into account. The increased development costs simply increase the basic spaceship cost from, for example, $500 million to $700 million, or from $1.2 billion to $1.4 billion. This means that the prospective operators will have to do a little more work when talking to the bankers. The model was run with a spaceship cost of $2 billion. In such an example, the financial community is likely to conclude that the venture is slightly more risky. Therefore, they'll want it to be more heavily equity oriented and with a greater after tax return on equity of 20+%. In this case, the required revenue became $10 million for 10 tons, still extremely competitive against existing expendable systems.

The sensitivity analysis underscores what every airline in the world knows: *Keep the airplane flying*. The primary economic driver is the cost of the equipment and the efficiency of its use. Operating costs such as fuel become more important only when all competitors are using vehicles of a similar nature.

Although further financial analysis of spaceship characteristics and economics will define the exact nature of the costs, operating profile and resulting required revenue, the basic conclusion will still stand: *A spaceship with performance and cost characteristics in the ballpark with those outlined will hold an overwhelming price advantage over any expendable or semi-expendable space transportation system*. The flexibility of operation inherent in an SSTO spaceship will extend this competitive advantage still further.

From an investor's point of view, the financial analysis shows that a space transportation service using SSTO spaceships can be brought to market at a price that can only be described as revolutionary.

Lowering the price of a valuable service to between 1 and 5% of current prices is not an event that goes unnoticed in the business community.

MARKET IMPACTS AND CONSEQUENCES

Whenever such a major change is brought to a market, market dynamics change to a degree that causes major ripples through other markets. A good example of this is the introduction of communications satellites and their effect on the television industry, television programming, and long-distance and intercontinental telephone service. The rapid decrease in the cost of high capacity integrated circuits allowed the development of the personal computer that, in turn, created major changes in the computer industry as a whole and the manner in which companies, both large and small, conduct business.

Similarly, the introduction of SSTO spaceships into commercial service will revolutionize the infant commercial space transportation industry. Regular and inexpensive transport services to low-Earth orbit will cause a major shift in the design and operating philosophy of satellites, space stations, space-based production facilities, Earth-lunar travel and interplanetary travel.

Present satellite design and operating philosophy is the result of three factors: (1) The high cost of getting to low-Earth orbit, (2) the lack of a significant human presence in space, and (3) the long and uncertain lead times in obtaining space transportation services.

Reducing the cost of reaching low-Earth orbit has the greatest impact. Robert A. Heinlein said it 40 years ago, and we should have paid more attention to him. When the cost of climbing out of the Earth's gravity is substantially lowered, the heavy emphasis placed upon the weight and redundancy of satellites, space stations, and other space facilities will be reduced. The decreased emphasis on very high reliability required by one-shot operating philosophies permits the utilization of less exotic materials and the application of modular spacecraft design. These factors will result in less expensive satellites and on-orbit facilities and, in turn, an increase in market demand for the services. Low cost access to LEO will also allow more energy-intensive flights for orbital, translunar, and interplanetary travel.

A greater human presence in space will also have an effect upon satellite design. The ability to reach orbit easily and quickly permits on-orbit repair and lowers the need for heavily redundant fail-safe space-based assets. The inability to reach an inoperative orbital asset means it's "dead" from an investment standpoint. The ability to reach it quickly to repair it turns on the cash flow stream once again and lowers the burden of capital and fixed operating expenses. This, in turn, allows a lower cost to the ultimate beneficiary of the space-based operation and a greater return on investment to the space asset owner.

Going back to the opening question: Does the operation of SSTO spaceships represent an attractive business opportunity? From a financial and investment point of view, the answer is an overwhelming YES!

Therefore, an excellent case for profitable space transportation can be made. The financial and economic numbers will continue to be persuasive, no matter what sort of space vehicles are used, as long as they are totally reusable single-stage-to-orbit types offering turnaround times of a few days. *The technology used to do this is immaterial.*

This is an important point to keep in mind. When a prospective space transportation company executive goes to New York City to talk to CitiBank, Prudential Bache, Morgan Trust, or whoever can put together the financing necessary to build spaceships or operate a spaceline, the banker doesn't care what the technology is. If McDonnell Douglas, General Dynamics, or Rockwell International needs a line of credit to build spaceships, they have a track record of making similar technologies work profitably. Thus, the financier assumes the company knows what it's doing with an arcane technology he doesn't need to learn about. It's also easier if the operator has a track record. However, Fred Smith at Federal Express had no such track record when he started, just an outstanding and convincing business plan, and a large inheritance.

By looking at just the economic numbers, one fact should be obvious. The first people who build and operate SSTO spaceships will dominate space for the first half of the next century.

SPACE MARKETS

Determining a market size for SSTO spaceship services is uncertain since the market demand curve is largely unknown. One can logically and reasonably assume on the basis of historical evidence that a sharp drop in space transportation costs will produce a proportional increase in the demand for space transportation services. An SSTO spaceship transportation cost that is 5% of existing services indicates a potential annual requirement of 40 million pounds to low-Earth orbit by the year 2010.

Many factors can affect this estimate for SSTO spaceship launch services. As the aircraft and airline industries learned during the 1930s, estimating errors are more likely to result from overconservatism when new technologies and major shifts of economics are introduced to a market.

A look at some present-day air cargo figures can help put the estimated 40-million-pound launch forecast of 2010 into perspective.

In 1988 the three major airports of the New York metropolitan area processed a combined total of more than 1.8 million tons of air cargo.[3] That's 3.6 billion pounds of cargo for just one region of the world. Assuming that the air cargo market continues to grow at its steady historical rate of 2.5% per year, by the year 2010 the air cargo volume for the New York area would be about 6.2 billion pounds. The estimated 40 million pound LEO launch requirement of 2010 represents less than 1% of the projected air cargo volume of only one region of the world.

Considering the historical perspective provided by air cargo, it's not fantasy to speculate that the annual space transportation services required during the first two decades of the next century would grow far in excess of the 40 million pounds of payload estimated initially. How much in excess? This is truly anyone's guess, but the numbers could be in the hundreds of millions of pounds. Obviously, this wide range of possible futures has a bearing on spaceship fleet size and the required ground infrastructure needed to support this magnitude of operation.

Assuming that each SSTO spaceship is capable of carrying 20,000 pounds to low-Earth orbit and has a flight rate of 100 flights per year, the total fleet size required to meet an estimated market demand of 40 million pounds of payload to LEO is 20 spaceships. It's unreasonable to assume that each spaceship will have a full cargo bay on every flight. For purposes of this analysis, the result is a fleet size requirement that remains at 20 spaceships.

For a market requirement several times larger—such as 120 million pounds of payload to LEO—spaceship fleet size would increase to 60. Does this sound unbelievable considering the level of space transportation today? Not really. Orbital space promises to be an ideal environment for the manufacture of many high-technology products such as electronics and pharmaceuticals.[4,5,6]

But some of the best products from an investment standpoint will undoubtedly turn out to be mundane or appear to be "frivolous." As the cost of access to low-Earth orbit decreases, the importance of the transportation portion of a space-based investment decision becomes less important. A look at the manifests of the air cargo carriers in and out of the New York area shows that they consist mostly of such "low-tech" items as clothes, toys, games, vegetables, fruits, and seafood.[7] To say that space will forever remain the domain of high technology is to ignore the business lessons of history.

When payloads heavier or larger than those capable of being deployed by a single spaceship are considered, the cost per ton is not a smooth curve. Figure 1.1 is familiar to people in the airline business. On the vertical axis is cost per ton where in the airline business it is normally cost per passenger. The spikes are caused by reaching the maximum payload capability of a single spaceship where a customer wants to put up 11 tons. This creates a spike in the curve because an additional spaceship must be scheduled either to lift the additional ton or to divide the payload equally between two spaceships. This obviously increases the cost per ton (Figure 1.1).

But when the cost per ton of orbiting large payloads in excess of the maximum payload of a single spaceship is compared to the same costs of lifting them on the existing fleet of expendable and semi-expendable vehicles such as the Space Shuttle, Titan, Atlas Centaur, Ariane, and Delta, the results are depicted in Figure 1.2. This dramatically indicates that any reusable vehicle anywhere in the neighborhood of the financial characteristics and operating char-

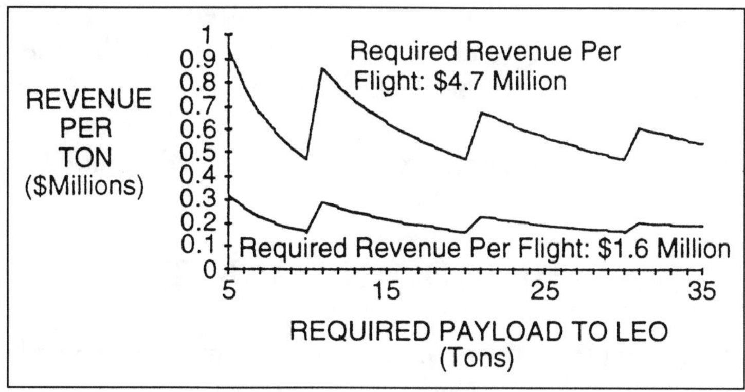

Figure 1.1. Required revenue per ton of payload.

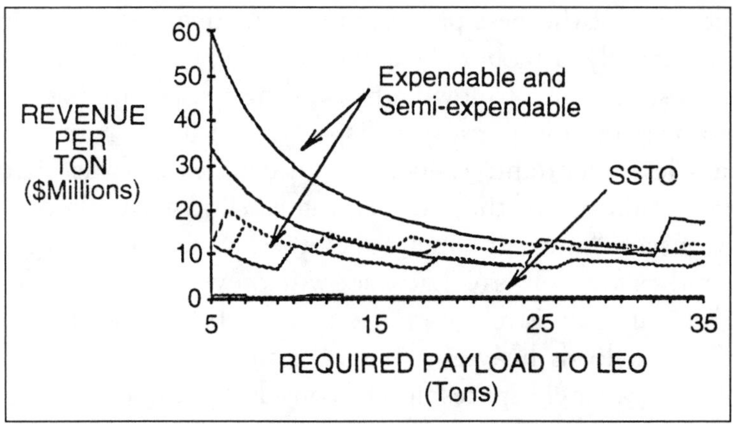

Figure 1.2. Required revenue per ton of payload for various vehicles.

acteristics of the SSTO spaceship used in the model is going to force a major change in the market.

Some people may object to this analysis on the basis that much the same sort of thing was claimed for the NASA Space Transportation System, the space shuttle. However, the major difference of the Enterprise Institute analysis revolves around the fact that the designers and builders of the STS didn't have to talk to New York bankers, but to people in Congress who are quite a different class of financiers.

As detailed earlier, the secret of making money with any machine is to keep it working. That's how airlines counteract the $150-million-dollar fly-away costs of a Boeing 747-400, for example. Because the NASA space shuttle has a multimonth turnaround time, requires a standing army of 40,000 or more people, and throws away a major part of the launch vehicle on every flight, it's impossible to fly it for less than ten times the projected cost using an SSTO spaceship. Now, more than 12 years after its first flight, the space shuttle is clearly seen to be an experimental vehicle that cannot possibly be commercially operated at a profit. However, like an airliner, an SSTO can be designed to be operated profitably.

THE HIDDEN MARKET

Initially, transportation of cargos to and from orbit won't be the most profitable or largest market (see Figure 1.3).

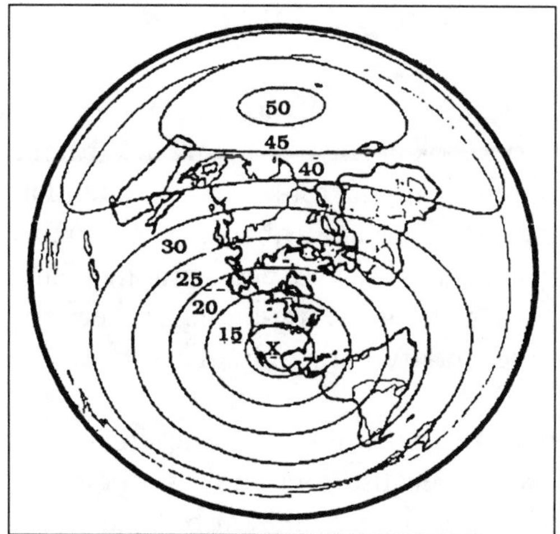

Figure 1.3. The hidden market. Here's the hidden market for initial SSTO Services. The World is shown in polar projection centered on a hypothetical U.S. Southwest Regional Spaceport. The numbered zones indicate how many *minutes* are required to reach any location in that zone from the Southwest Regional Spaceport at "X." Europe is about 25 minutes away, for example, while Japan requires a flight of only 30 minutes. Australia is between 40 and 50 minutes flying time for an SSTO.

Most space economists agree several years will pass before the space transportation markets adjust to the introduction of the new spaceships. While this is happening, however, the new spaceships will have a lot of work to do in another market that's usually overlooked.

Any SSTO spaceship that can take a payload to orbit can also deliver passengers and cargo to any place in the world in less than an hour.

A 15-hour subsonic flight to Tokyo becomes a flight of less than an hour using "Fractional Orbital Transportation"—take off, climb above the atmosphere, make a partial orbit, and come down to land at the destination. Furthermore, it's environmentally benign.

Again, Robert A. Heinlein told us that fast transportation will pay because it always has. Businesses are keen to beat their competition because time is money.

Very well, if operating SSTO spaceships can be a profitable business, thus justifying companies to design and build them, what then? Don't stop here or you'll miss other business opportunities!

THE NEW SPACEPORTS

The new SSTO spaceships will no longer be chained to existing launch sites. A brief look at the historical background will show why.

The original requirements for a site to launch large rockets were stated by Colonel Walter R. Dornberger in Germany in 1935.[8,9] He was an artillery officer who had been put in charge of the secret German project to develop a long-range artillery rocket with twice the range of the legendary Paris Gun. This rocket became the German V-2.

Dornberger wrote that a rocket launching center should be located on a seacoast because Germany didn't have open land on which these artillery rockets could crash. Since the German rocket program was secret and a lot of rockets blew up in those days, he wanted the facility to be in a remote location for security and safety.

Dornberger described the ultimate firing range for long range artillery. We're still wedded to Dornberger's requirements because present space launch vehicles were developed from long-range ballistic missiles (ICBMs), the descendants of the V-2.

Every space launch center in the world is nothing more than a super artillery range. When spaceships begin to operate like airplanes, they no longer need to be flown from artillery ranges. They will operate from true spaceports. The new spaceport requirements include:

- Transportation access by rail, highway, and air.
- A "noise-clear" zone extending about 10 miles around the takeoff and landing site.
- Clear airspace corridors for departures and arrivals of both vertical-takeoff-vertical-landing (SSTOs) and horizontal-takeoff-horizontal-landing (aerospaceplanes) spaceships.
- Proximity to other transportation nodes—rail, highway, and air.
- Proximity to existing natural gas pipelines; natural gas is a source of hydrogen that can be processed into liquid hydrogen rocket fuel.
- Proximity to a high-capacity electric power grid.

Note that remote locations are no longer considered necessary. But suppose these spaceships fall on our heads? People asked the same question about airplanes 60 years ago. The safety concern of flying spaceships over populated areas disappears with the advent of SSTO spaceships that don't drop boosters or lower stages in flight. They have engine-out capabilities and safe abort modes similar to aircraft. How often does a jet airliner lose all its engines leaving San Francisco International?

The prohibition of flying rockets over populated areas arose on May 29, 1947, when a German V-2 flew off the White Sands range in New Mexico and landed in Ciudad Juarez, Mexico. The present-day flight safety system for ballistic missile and space vehicle launch sites evolved from the policy and procedures developed immediately thereafter by an artillery test officer in the U.S. Army Ordnance Corps, Major Herbert L. Karsch.[10] These require that no rocket or missile be allowed to land beyond the range boundaries.

With SSTO spaceships, such flight restrictions are no longer necessary. The new spaceports will be located where they are needed, just like airports.

The new spaceships and spaceports will require services other than fuel supplies and the facilities for maintenance and repair. Look at any major international airport to get some idea of the services and supporting businesses that will, within 20 years, be clustered around the new millennium spaceports.

Such spaceports will become the industrial hubs of the twenty-first-century hydrogen economy because this is where large-volume liquid hydrogen production and handling facilities will be installed.[11]

THE LEGAL ISSUE OF TORT LIABILITY

The existence of a large civil SSTO spaceship fleet and extensive, growing spaceship operations also brings up some interesting legal issues. Tort liability is one of these. At this time, if a Northwest 747 airliner has an engine failure leaving Tokyo's Narita International Airport and crashes in the Ginza, the airline itself is responsible under the terms of international law.

However, if any space vehicle has a similar accident in which property is damaged or lives lost, the incident is covered by the United Nations Treaty of Principles. Under the provisions of this early-day space treaty, if a Northwest Spaceline's spaceship has an accident, the company is not liable. The U.S. government is *individu-*

ally and severally liable under the terms of that treaty.[12] Thus, the federal government has had to establish the Office of Commercial Space Transportation within the Department of Transportation.

The OCST regulations covering safety inspections, clearances, permits, and approvals is long and costly for each individual space launch operation, regardless of the type of launch vehicle used. These will become unworkable with frequent SSTO spaceship operations.

Therefore, the United States needs to investigate getting that treaty amended to reflect the reality of the coming age of commercial SSTO spaceship operations. Or the president must revoke the U.S. ratification of that treaty.

Ratifying a treaty requires the advice and consent of the U.S. Senate. But to revoke one requires only an Executive Order. This happened in the case of the Panama Canal Treaty. It led former Senator Barry M. Goldwater to sue the Carter administration in federal court and lose. Therefore, this set the precedent that the United States can back out of any treaty by a presidential order.

CERTIFICATION OF AIRWORTHINESS

Certification of spaceships is yet another issue that must be addressed under international law.

At this time, every airplane that crosses an international border must have a certificate of airworthiness (C of A) issued by the country of aircraft registry. It must also carry a certificate of manufacture and a cargo manifest.

This has been considerably muddied in the last 20 years because the NASA Space Shuttle orbiters originally didn't carry them. In 1981, an author named Lee Correy wrote a novel entitled *Shuttle Down*[13] that created a stir at NASA Headquarters. The plot centered around an orbiter that had to make an emergency landing on Easter Island. The Chilean military governor maintained that the orbiter was an airplane that, under international law, had to have a C of A and other documentation, including passports, for the orbiter crew of astronauts and mission specialists. In the early space shuttle program, the orbiters and crews had none of these. Now each orbiter carries all the necessary documentation except a C of A because

Federal Aviation Regulations Part 21 has no provisions for certificating a space vehicle.

The legal problem of certification remains unsolved. Again, this will change once commercial SSTO spaceships begin flying to orbit and back. Therefore, some effort needs to be addressed to drafting regulations in this regard.

DEFINITION OF AIRSPACE AND ORBITAL SPACE BOUNDARIES

Yet another legal and operational issue arises over the definition and establishment of boundaries for airspace and orbital space.

No accepted international definition of the interface between airspace and orbital space exists. Thus, the question arises: *Where does airspace end and where does orbital space begin?* Or will it make any difference? Indeed it does, especially from the standpoint of national security.

At the present time, over the United States and most of the rest of the world, controlled airspace as defined in various federal and international rules and laws ends at 60,000 feet above mean sea level. That is as high as the authority of the FAA and other national aeronautical agencies goes when it comes to air traffic control.

Who takes over from there? That's unknown at this time. The USAF awards astronaut wings to pilots who have flown above 50 miles, while the Federation Aéronautique Internationale with headquarters in Paris says that space begins at 100 km (62 miles). The Office of Commercial Space Transportation hasn't addressed the problem. It must be resolved in an international conference within 10 years.

SPACE TRAFFIC CONTROL

In the coming era of expanded and extended space operations with SSTO spaceships, space traffic control will be mandatory. It is an absolute necessity from the standpoint of national security (Figure 1.4).

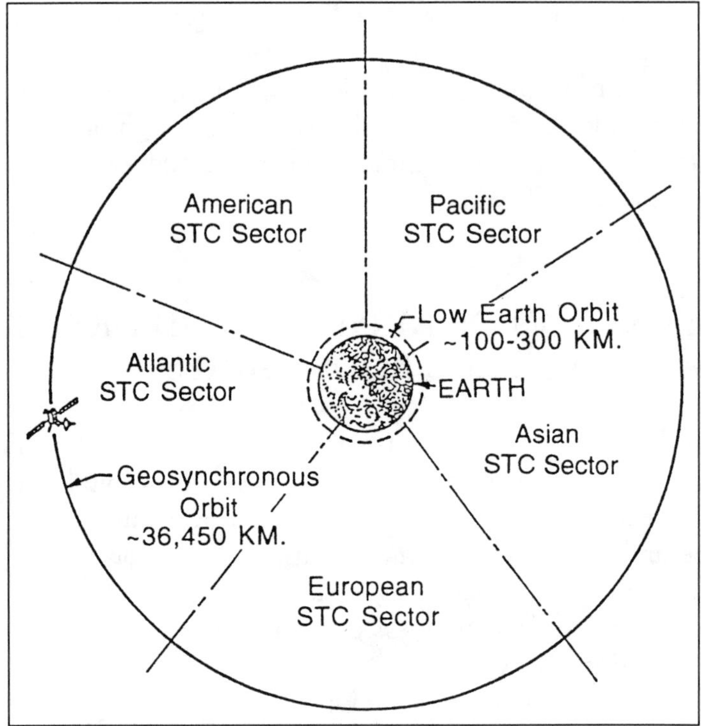

Figure 1.4. Possible LEO/GEO space traffic control zones.

Today, a nation launching a space vehicle is required to report the launch and the orbital elements to the United Nations after the fact. This poses a severe problem for national defense in the future when SSTO spaceships begin operations within and through the atmosphere.

For example, if you're on duty in the national aerospace defense command and detect *something* coming over the horizon at Mach 20, you won't have time to identify it and determine what action to take before it's passed and gone.

Does it have an announced flight plan? Is it the same vehicle that was flown on that flight plan? Is it the daily FedEx flight from Beijing that took off an hour late or a threat to someone other than UPS? Do you alert your ballistic missile defense system? Do you shoot or not?

You won't have time to make a telephone call to get more information. You must know in advance. The thing leaving that ionization trail must be squawking the proper code on its radar transponder. If it isn't, you must have rules and procedures to implement *immediately*.

The principles of air traffic control must be extended into orbital space. Space Traffic Control out to geosynchronous orbit and probably beyond will be required. And soon.

Again, science fiction author Lee Correy, wrote a novel, *Manna*—serialized in this magazine—in which space traffic control existed.[14] Don't say that science has outpaced science fiction!

CONCLUSION

Because the technology to create SSTO spaceships exists and can be shown to create a profitable business opportunity, we must assume that such spaceships will be built. The coming commercial space age has many facets that have been overshadowed by the effort to bring SSTO technology to operational status. However, a scenario exists where reusable, reliable, safe, responsive, and economical SSTO spaceships can be built but can't be operated because of political, diplomatic, or military concerns that weren't addressed in concert with technology development. It appears prudent to assume technological success and to address these other factors as quickly as possible.

Acknowledgments

The author expresses appreciation to Paul C. Hans and The Enterprise Institute, Inc., for permission to utilize the results of their space transportation economic model.

Chapter 2

Robert M. Zubrin

The Hypersonic Skyhook

Skyhooks. Many readers of science fiction and speculative astronautics have heard of such devices and why they can't possibly work. I think they can—but let's begin at the beginning.

Way back, in 1960, the Soviet newspaper *Komsomolskaya Pravda* published an interview with engineer Y. N. Artsutanov,[1] containing a description of a novel means for Earth to orbit transportation. In the Artsutanov scheme, a satellite placed in geostationary orbit would simultaneously extend cables down toward Earth and in the opposite direction, keeping its center of mass, and thus its orbit, constant. This procedure would continue until the lower cable reached the surface of the Earth, where it could be anchored and used to support elevator cabs. These cabs, in turn, could then be used to transport payloads up to the satellite where they could be released into geostationary orbit. Alternatively, if allowed to proceed out along the outward cable, the payloads could be released with greater than orbital velocity, so that at different stations along the outward cable, payloads could be released to proceed on trans-lunar, trans-Mars, trans-Jupiter and other trajectories of interest. This concept, while published in both Russian and English, was widely ignored and promptly forgotten, only to be rederived, and published by a group of American oceanographers[2] in 1966, after which it was forgotton again. The concept was then independently discovered for a third time in 1975, by Jerome Pearson,[3] of the Wright Patterson Air Force Base, who published a series of papers going into much greater detail than the earlier authors, including derivations for system mass, tether taper configuration, and allowable limits to the rates that payload could be moved along the tether without exciting dangerous vibrational modes. Subsequently, the geostationary skyhook concept was widely publicized by Arthur Clarke, who employed such a device as a central feature of his novel *The Fountains of Paradise*.

While offering the exciting prospect of a simple cable car-to-orbit system, the geostationary skyhook described by Pearson and the others suffered from one little flaw: It was impossible. The reason why it was impossible was this: If one places a load at the bottom of the geostationary tether, the bit of tether holding it must be thick enough to support that load. The next bit of tether must then be thick enough to support, not only the load, but the load plus the bit of tether supporting it. Thus, as it proceeds from the ground toward geostationary altitude, the tether must get thicker and thicker, and its diameter expands exponentially. Depending on the strength-to-weight ratio for the tether assumed, the final result would be that the cross-sectional area of the tether at the satellite would be 6 to 20 *orders of magnitude* greater than its area at its base, with similar fantastic ratios holding between the tether system mass and the mass of the payload it is required to lift. In answer to this problem, Pearson could only propose that in the future, ultrastrong materials, such as single-crystal graphite fibers, might become available with orders of magnitude improvement in strength-to-weight over current materials, resulting in exponential reductions in taper diameter ratio and system mass. Until such futuristic materials became available, skyhook applications would have to be limited to lower gravity bodies, such as Earth's Moon, where while the problems faced by skyhook engineering are greatly reduced, the imperative for an alternative to rocket transportation is correspondingly less compelling.

A potential means of bringing the skyhook back down to Earth was offered in 1977, by Hans Moravec,[4] who proposed that the skyhook be placed in an orbit lower than geostationary, and the two tethers extending from it be made to rotate, or "roll," so that during its descent through the atmosphere, the tether tip would be moving backwards at an equal speed to the skyhook's orbital velocity. This would cause the tether tip to briefly possess a ground-track velocity of zero, at low altitude, thus enabling a payload on the ground or on a slow-flying aircraft to be transferred to the tether for a ride into space. By bringing the skyhook to a lower orbit, the length of the skyhook is reduced, creating the potential for a large reduction in system mass. This idea was subsequently elaborated and improved upon by Rod Hyde[5] and Pearson.[6] The realization of the mass reduction potential in the rolling skyhook concept is restricted, however, by the fact that as the two tethers spin about the system center of mass, centrifugal force is generated, which is additive to gravity while a tether is in the downward position, and negative to it when the tether is in the upward position. This adds both static and dynamic loads to the tether system, requiring tether thickening and mass increases. The result is that futuristic materials are still required for the construction of a practical system. As an operational system, the rotating tether suffers in comparison to the geostationary tether by the brevity of potential access, and by the fact that while a payload can reach a stable orbit condition by climbing the tether to the skyhook center prior to release, and injection energies for interplanetary velocities are easily attained during release from the tether during its upward, forward-moving swing, useful injection orbits may be difficult to attain due to the lack of correspondence between the tether's motion and the proper orbital phasing for payload release (i.e., the tether will generally not be moving through its upward arc at the right moment to throw the payload where it is supposed to go).

In this article I present a third type of tether-skyhook system, which I call a hypersonic skyhook (Figure 2.1). As I show, the hypersonic skyhook has the potential of relieving the severe strength-of-materials demands, which have thus far prevented the implementation of a practical skyhook of either the geostationary or rotating varieties. The hypersonic skyhook accomplishes this by keeping the tip of the extended tether outside of the tangible atmosphere and allowing it to move at hypersonic velocities with respect to the ground. This allows the skyhook's center of mass to be lowered from geostationary altitude, reducing the length of the tether, and cutting its mass and taper ratio by many orders of magnitude. Unlike the rotating skyhook, however, the hypersonic skyhook does not spin about its satellite center of mass, but keeps both tethers aligned

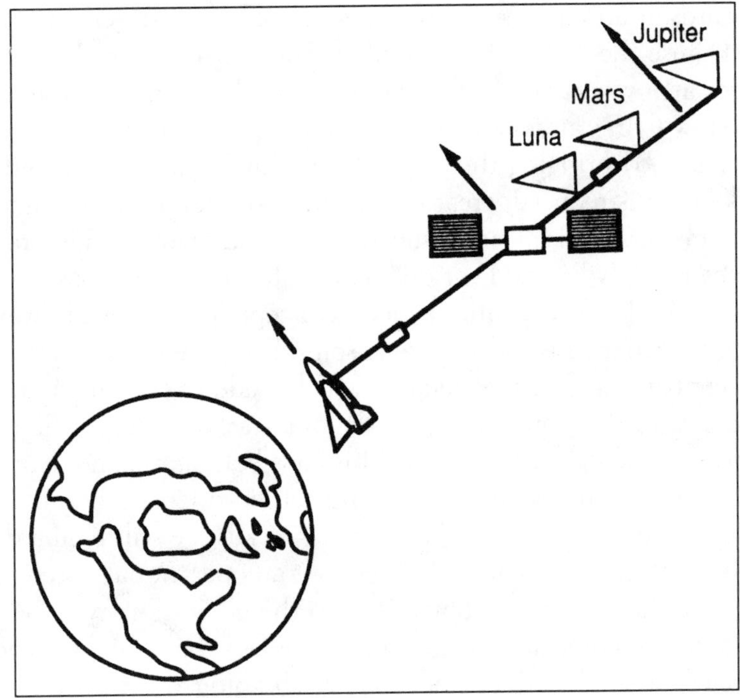

Figure 2.1. The hypersonic skyhook.

along a constant radial direction toward and away from the center of Earth. This causes the centrifugal force term along the tether to be constant in time and always antigravitational in nature This eliminates the dynamic stresses faced by the rotating tether and causes a further exponential reduction in tether mass, as the gravity term driving the tether mass expansion is negated more and more when the tether's orbital velocity increases. The result is that tether systems with masses only one or two orders of magnitude greater than the payloads to be lifted become possible using present-day or near-term materials, for hypersonic tethers moving with ground-track velocities in the Mach 10–15 range. Because the atmospheric drag caused by traveling through the atmosphere at such velocities is unacceptable, the base of the hypersonic skyhook must travel outside the atmosphere, perhaps at an altitude of about 100 km. Access to the hypersonic skyhook would have to be provided by transatmospheric vehicles capable of matching horizontal velocity with the tether and utilizing vertical rocket thrust to negate gravity during rendezvous. While the design of such vehicles is certainly a significant challenge, it is much less formidable than the development of transatmospheric vehicles with full orbital (Mach 25) capability. The hypersonic skyhook, moreover, allows the payload to be sent from suborbital trajectories, not only to orbit, but to any destination in the solar system without the further use of propellant.

SKYHOOK EQUATIONS

The relevant equations governing the performance of a hypersonic skyhook can be derived as follows: (If you have trouble with equations, don't worry about it. Just skip ahead to the bottom-line results, which are given in the following section.)

The amount of mass in a given segment of the tether is given by

$$dm = \rho a \, dl \tag{1}$$

where ρ is the density and a is the cross-sectional area. The amount of additional load added to the tether due to this segment is given by:

$$dF = g \, dm - \omega^2(R_1 + 1) \, dm \tag{2}$$

where g is the gravitational acceleration at the altitude of a given tether location, R_1 is the distance of the base of the tether from the center of Earth, 1 is the distance along the tether from the base, and ω is angular velocity (in rps) of the tether with respect to the center of a fixed (nonrotating) Earth.

The local gravitational acceleration, g, is given by

$$g = g_1 \frac{R_1^2}{(R_1 + L)^2} \tag{3}$$

where g_1 is the gravitational constant at the base of the tether.

Putting equations (1), (2), and (3) together and noting that the force, F, at any point along the tether equals σa, where σ is the tether material yield stress, we can obtain an equation for how the tether cross-sectional area, a, changes with respect to its length, L.

$$\sigma \frac{\partial a}{\partial L} = \rho a(g_1\left(\frac{R_1}{R_1 + L}\right)^2 - \omega^2(R_1 + L)) \tag{4}$$

The solution of equation (4) is:

$$a = a_0 \exp\left[\left(\frac{\rho L}{\sigma}\right)\left(\frac{g_1 R_1}{R_1 + L} - \omega^2\left(R_1 + \frac{L}{2}\right)\right)\right] \tag{5}$$

Equation (5) is the expression that yields the required taper ratio for an orbiting, nonrotating, tether skyhook of any given length, L. It can be seen that the tether taper ratio is an exponential function of the material density to system ratio, ρ/σ, multiplied by a the length of the tether, L, multiplied by a term that decreases strongly as the angular velocity, ω, increases. It can also be shown from the laws of orbital mechanics that:

$$(R_1 + L)^3 = \mu/\omega^2 \tag{6}$$

where μ is the mass of Earth times the universal gravitational constant. Until such time as either of those quantities should change, $\mu = 398600\ km^3/s^2$.

Now, as the velocity of the tether with respect to the ground increases, so does ω, which, as equation (6) shows, has a strong inverse relationship to the length of the tether from its bottom tip to its thickest (orbital center of mass) position. As equation (5) shows, *each* of these effects tends to reduce the required tether taper ratio *exponentially*, so it may be expected that taken together, the resulting reduction in required taper ratio will be extremely strong. As we shall see in the presentation of results given below, this is indeed the case.

A tether skyhook starts with a certain cross-sectional area, a_0, at its base, which increases to a maximum cross-sectional area at its orbital center of mass. The ratio of the maximum area to a_0 is called the tether's "taper ratio." The tether then continues outward beyond its center of mass, tapering off again as described by equation (5), or faster. In general there will be an upper strand to the skyhook system that will extend outward beyond the orbital center of mass by a distance at least as great as the lower tether strand.

DISCUSSION OF RESULTS

The strength-to-weight ratio of tether materials is ordinarily given in terms of the tether's characteristic velocity (U), which is simply the square root of the strength (in pascals) to density (in kg/m^3) ($U = \sqrt{(\sigma/\rho)}$). Kevlar with a U of 1.2 km/s has been available on the commercial market for some time, while state-of-the-art high-strength kevlar-type materials with a U of about 1.6 km/s are now becoming available. Advanced materials with Us of somewhat over 2 km/s will probably be available in the near future.

Figure 2.2 shows the taper ratios resulting from equation (5) for hypersonic skyhooks with Us of 1.2, 1.6, and 2.0 km/s. The case of a ground-track velocity of zero is simply the classic Artsutanov–Pearson geostationary skyhook. It can be seen that, postulating present-day or near-future materials, such devices require taper ratios that are astronomical, making their construction infeasible.

The merit of allowing the skyhook to move at hypersonic velocities can, however, also be seen. For example, assuming a U of 1.6 km/s, the geostationary skyhook requires a ludicrous taper ratio of 10^8, while one whose base is allowed to move at 4 km/s (Mach 12) only requires a quite reasonable taper ratio of 10^2.

Figure 2.3 shows the mass of a hypothetical skyhook system capable of lifting loads of 4 tonnes. The skyhook mass was estimated by integrating equation (5) from the bottom of the tether to its orbital center of mass (to calculate the mass of the lower tether

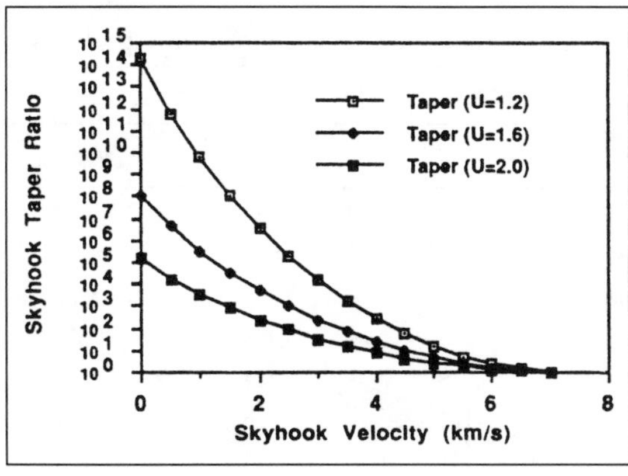

Figure 2.2. Taper ratio for hypersonic skyhooks.

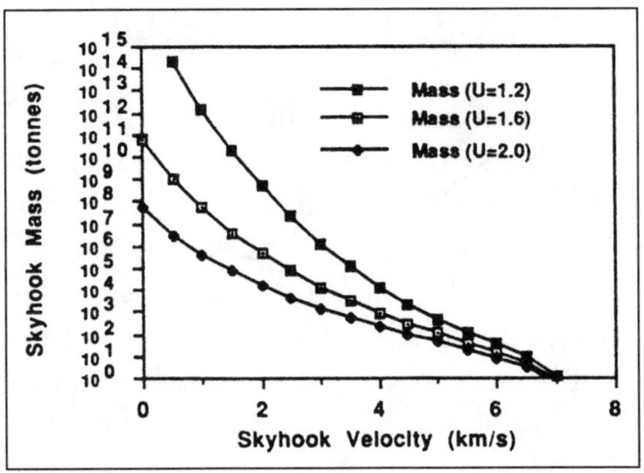

Figure 2.3. Mass of hypersonic skyhook tether lifting 4-tonne payloads.

directly), doubling this account for the additional mass of the strand of the tether beyond the orbital center of mass (this is an approximation—there is a certain amount of design freedom in the configuration of the tether upper strand), and multiplying the result by 1.25 to allow for margin. Once again, the drastic reduction in mass of the hypersonic skyhook compared to the geostationary variety is readily seen.

Table 2.1 gives the lower tether length (100 km less than the skyhook central platform orbital altitude) and the total tether mass (both upper and lower strands) for hypersonic tether skyhooks capable of lifting 1-tonne loads, again with a safety margin of 1.25. It can be seen that while a geostationary skyhook with a U

Table 2.1. Hypersonic skyhook performance for tonne payloads

Velocity (km/s)	*Lower Length (km)*	*Skyhook Tether Mass (tonnes)* U = 1.2	U = 1.6	U = 2.0	*Upper End C3 (km²/s²)*
0.0	35727	3.68×10^{16}	1.40×10^{10}	1.34×10^{7}	21.9
1.0	13275	3.23×10^{11}	1.26×10^{7}	102,250	32.1
2.0	7501	1.22 E 8	117,000	4200	30.0
3.0	4667	325,000	3,425	375	21.4
4.0	2936	3,575	224	55	8.1
5.0	1751	122	26	11	−8.8
6.0	880	31	3.8	2.1	−29.1
7.0	208	0.33	0.19	0.12	−52.4

of 2.0 km/s requires a total (upper and lower sections combined) tether mass of more than 13 million tonnes, a hypersonic skyhook with a ground-track velocity of 5 km/s only requires 11 tonnes of tether mass.

Also shown in Table 2.1 is the energy measured in units of "C_3" that the payload will have if released from the upper end of the tether, assuming that the tether is constructed symmetrically, with the upper strand identical to the lower strand. (The C_3 of an orbiting spacecraft is the difference between the square of its velocity and the square of the planet's escape velocity at its altitude.) Since a C_3 of 8 km^2/s^2 is about what is required for a minimum energy trajectory to Mars or Venus, after which a planetary gravity assist can be obtained, it can be seen that a hypersonic skyhook with a base velocity of 4 km/s or less can be used to transfer payloads from a suborbital condition to a trajectory to any planetary destination in the solar system. While it cannot achieve Earth escape, a payload released from the 5 km/s skyhook has more than sufficient energy to achieve an elliptical orbit whose apogee is at geostationary altitude (i.e., a GTO orbit).

HYPERSONIC SKYHOOK SYSTEM

Let's now take a look of what a sample early skyhook system might be like. Based on the results given in Table 2.1, we'll assume a 1.5-tonne payload delivery design with a ground-track velocity of 5 km/s and U = 2.0 km/s. The required tether thus has a mass of 16.5 tonnes. A power source will also be required to lift the payloads up the tether by a cable car mechanism; 30 kW should do it. This can be provided by either photovoltaic panels or a nuclear reactor. Assuming near-term space technology, this will have a mass of 2 tonnes for the power source and its power conditioning system. While moving up the lower strand of the tether, the 1.5-tonne payload has an initial weight of about 7800 N (the weight is reduced by centrifugal force), decreasing to zero at the orbital center of mass. If we assume an average weight of 4000 N, the average speed that the payload can be moved is (30,000 W/4000 N) = 7.5 m/s. Since the lower strand of the tether is 1751 km long, it will thus take about [1,751,000/(7.5*3600)] = 65 hr to move the payload from the tether lower tip to orbital altitude at the skyhook center of mass. Raising the payload beyond the orbital center so that it can be released at some point along the upper strand of the tether requires no power at all, as beyond the orbital center of mass, the outward centrifugal force term along the tether is greater than the inward pulling force of gravity. Effectively, a payload being transferred out along the tether upper strand is being lowered away from the Earth.

While the bottom of the tether has a ground-track velocity of 5 km/s, it has a velocity of 5.471 km/s with respect to a fixed (nonrotating) Earth (assuming a tether bottom altitude of 100 km.). The tether center of mass is moving at a velocity of 6.96 km/s with respect to a nonrotating Earth. Moving a 1.5-tonne payload from the tether base to its orbital center of mass thus increases the payload's angular momentum about Earth by (6.96*8229) – (5.471*6478) = 21,883 tonne-km^2/s. Since the angular momentum of the total skyhook-payload system about Earth must be conserved, thrust will be required or the skyhook will lose altitude. If we adopt the approximation that the total mass of the skyhook (about 20 tonnes, accounting for various miscellaneous subsystems and micrometeorite protection) is concentrated at its orbital center of mass, we find that a total ΔV of [21,883/(20*8229)] = 0.134 km/s will be required for the tether to maintain altitude. If this is provided by ion engines with a specific impulse of 5000 s, then 54 kg of propellant will have to be expended to enable the skyhook to maintain altitude after the lifting of each 1.5-tonne payload. Alternatively, part of the tether could contain an aluminum wire whose current, interacting with Earth's magnetic field, could be used to produce thrust without the expenditure of any propellant. Based on existing studies,[7] a 20-km-long electromagnetic (10 km above the orbital center of mass and 10 km below) tether operating in an equatorial orbit at a distance from Earth's center of 6778 km and consuming 30 kWe would have a mass of about 800 kg and be able to generate a thrust of 3.75 N. Our skyhook operates in an equatorial orbit at a distance from the center of Earth of 8229 km, and since Earth's magnetic field falls off as the distance from its center cubed, this implies that such a design would exert a thrust of 2.1 N if used to propel the skyhook. This amount of thrust would be sufficient to provide the required compensatory ΔV for the skyhook in about 15 days. If more frequent use of the skyhook were desired, part or all of the ΔV could be provided by lifting a high-thrust propellant to the orbital center of mass as part of the payload. For example, if hydrogen/oxygen propellant with a specific impulse of 450 s were used to provide half of the required 134 m/s ΔV, then 306 kg of the 1500-kg payload would have to be propellant, but the tether could provide the rest of the reboost electromagnetically in a period of 7.5 days, thus allowing it to be used about 40 times per year.

The skyhook system could be made safe from severance by orbital debris by using a multistrand configuration such as that recently proposed by Robert Forward.[8]

Payloads would be delivered to the skyhook by a transatmospheric vehicle, perhaps similar to the National Aerospace Plane (NASP) or Single-Stage-to-Orbit (SSTO) vehicles currently being developed. Vehicle performance requirements would be far more modest, however, since only suborbital (Mach 15) flight would be needed, instead of the Mach 25 speeds entailed for both flight to orbit and orbital reentry. The transatmospheric vehicle would match speeds with the skyhook bottom (which is hanging at an altitude outside of the tangible atmosphere) and use vertical thrusters to negate gravity during the period of rendezvous. During rendezvous the transatmospheric vehicle would hover below the tether, open its cargo bay and allow its payload to be hooked by a cable car mechanism, which rides upon the tether. After the payload is hooked, the transatmospheric vehicle would drop away, close its cargo bay, and return to Earth.

Assuming that 30 s of thrust-negated gravity are required for the hooking operation, and hydrogen/oxygen thrusters with a specific impulse of 450 s are used, then an amount of propellant whose mass is about 3.3% of the transatmospheric vehicle will have to be expended during rendezvous. The amount of fuel used is only 3.3%, not 6.6%, because a suborbital vehicle flying outside the atmosphere at a ground-track velocity of 5 km/s only experiences about half of Earth's gravity. (This suggests another interesting use for hypersonic skyhooks: Use them to suspend nonrotating, partial-gravity space stations. Such stations could be used to train crews or test equipment under simulated lunar or Martian surface gravity conditions.)

Using its own electrodynamic thrust capability, the skyhook could deliver itself from LEO to its design altitude of 1851 km in about 86 days, without requiring any propellant. The system's total initial mass in LEO would thus be the same as its operational mass, that is, about 20 tonnes, and either a Titan IV or a space shuttle could lift it to orbit in a single launch.

Each 1.5-tonne payload lifted to the base of the skyhook would be delivered not merely to orbit, but, by running out along the upper tether of the skyhook system, could be placed on a GTO trajectory. The delivery of 1.5 tonnes of GTO represents an equivalent capability to that represented by a Delta/Pam launch vehicle and upper stage combination, which has a ground liftoff mass of 220 tonnes, and a cost of $60 million. A single-stage suborbital rocket using $H_2/0_2$ propellant with a trajectory averaged Isp of 420 s and a stage dry mass fraction of 20% that could deliver the 1.5-tonne payload to the skyhook base (6 km/s ΔV assumed), hover for 30 s, *and land*, would have a ground liftoff mass of 25 tonnes. Thus, the skyhook-aided system would only have a liftoff mass of 11% of that of the Delta and could be fully reusable as well. Savings per mission would probably exceed $55 million, with financial breakeven against the $130 million required for the initial skyhook Titan launch exceeded on the third suborbital launch.

STORMING HEAVEN

The near-term hypersonic skyhook described previously can thus reduce the cost of launching medium-sized satellites by about an order of magnitude, but in the longer term, it represents something far more important. *The skyhook is a beachhead for the storming of heaven.*

Let's see how this could work. The skyhook described above has a mass of 20 tonnes and can assist in the lifting of 1.5 tonnes to orbit per suborbital launch. This means that in 14 launches of a reusable suborbital vehicle, the mass of the skyhook can be doubled. If the parts lifted to orbit are simply a parallel skyhook system, the two can be made to work in tandem, and we now have a skyhook capable of lifting 3 tonnes to orbit per suborbital launch. The skyhook's capability has been doubled, and the total ground liftoff weight of the 14 reusable suborbital launches required to double it, about 350 tonnes, is less than half that of the 850-tonne expendable Titan IV (or 2000-tonne partially reusable space shuttle) required to launch the initial system. Using 14 launches of a larger suborbital vehicle, with a ground liftoff weight of 50 tonnes, the skyhook can now be increased to a system with the capability of lifting 6 tonnes per launch, with similar savings. We could go on like this, simply using the leverage offered by the 5-km/s skyhook to double its capacity with every 14 launches, or we could use some of the mass lifted to extend the skyhook so that instead of requiring 5 km/s groundtrack velocity for the suborbital launcher, only 4 km/s will be needed. If the ΔV required to achieve orbit is dropped in this way, the payload delivery capability of the suborbital system will be doubled. This will cut in half the cost of delivery of all further mass to orbit.

This is only the beginning. As the skyhook continues to operate in support of its own expansion, the mass of payloads deliverable to orbit can be made to increase exponentially, while the costs of delivery drop in inverse proportion. As the skyhooks are lengthened to allow for flight to orbit at lower and lower velocities, the delivery of *large payloads* to orbit using hypersonic *airbreathing* systems will become increasingly practical. Within a comparatively short time, transporting people and payloads from Earth's surface to orbit could become as cheap as long distance jet travel is today.

The golden door to the high frontier will then be wide open—and not just for governments with billions to spend, but for anyone willing to fly. For the teeming masses of humanity, the Space Age will have truly begun.

Part Two

Stepping Into the Solar System

Chapter 3

Robert M. Zubrin and
David A. Baker

Mars Direct

A Proposal for the Rapid Exploration and Colonization of the Red Planet

Can the United States send humans to Mars during the present decade? Absolutely. We have developed a set of vehicle designs and a mission architecture that can make this possible. We call the plan *Mars Direct*.

The Mars Direct approach does not require any in-orbit assembly or refueling, or any support from the Space Station or other orbital infrastructure. However, despite this, the Mars Direct plan is not merely a "flags and footprints" one-shot expedition, but puts into place immediately an economical method of Earth–Mars transportation, real surface exploratory mobility, and significant base capabilities that can evolve into mostly self-sufficient Mars settlement.

In this article we present both the initial and evolutionary phases of the Mars Direct plan. In the initial phase, only chemical propulsion is used, sending four persons on 3-year round-trip Mars exploratory missions. Two heavy-lift booster launches are required to support each mission. In the second phase of Mars Direct, nuclear thermal propulsion is used to cut crew transit times in half, increase cargo delivery capacity, and create the potential for true global mobility through the use of CO_2-propelled ballistic hopping vehicles (NIMFs).

During the second phase of Mars Direct, as the exploration of the planet accelerates, a new strategy is also introduced, leading to the rapid establishment of a 48-person permanent Mars base. This base, in turn, acts as a construction team to prepare the economic infrastructure required to support a wave of colonists to follow.

We shall show that the potential exists to colonize Mars during the twenty-first century at a rate comparable to that of European settlement of North America during the seventeenth, and that the colony so established can not only survive, but prevail, ultimately transforming Mars into a world habitable by humans and much of our kin of the terrestrial biosphere.

MARS DIRECT: PHASE I

The implementation of the initial phase of the Mars Direct[1,2] plan is shown schematically in Figure 3.1. In 1997 a single shuttle derived "Ares" heavy-lift launch vehicle (Figure 3.2) lifts off from Cape Canaveral and uses its upper stage to fire a 40-metric-ton unmanned payload off on a minimum energy trajectory to Mars, where it aero-brakes and lands. This unmanned payload consists of the following:

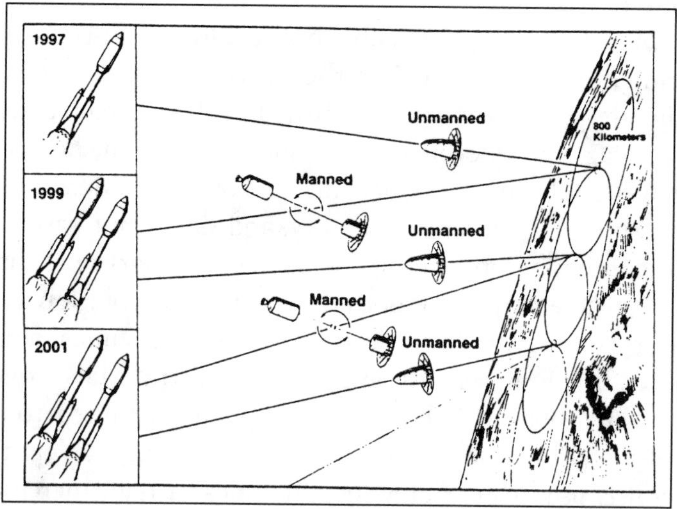

Figure 3.1. The Mars Direct mission sequence. Every 2 years two boosters are launched. One sends an unmanned Earth return vehicle (ERV) to fuel itself at a new site, the other sends a manned hab to rendezvous with an ERV at a previously prepared site.

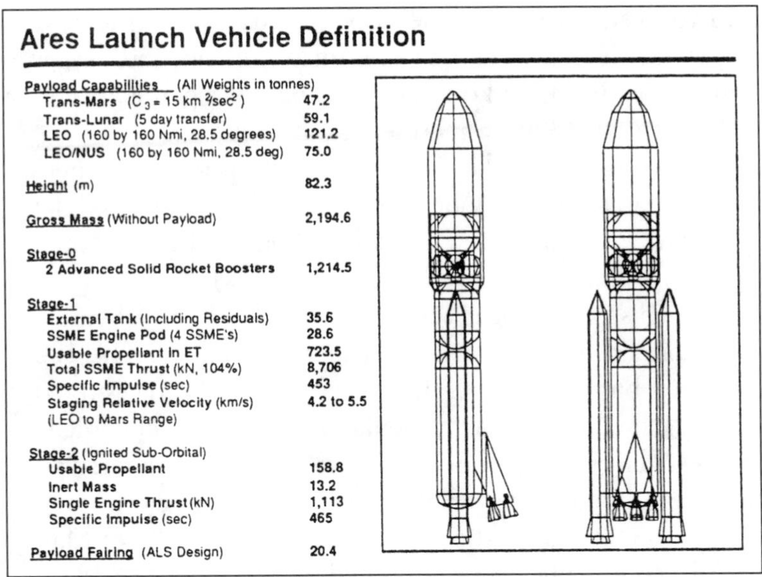

Ares Launch Vehicle Definition

Payload Capabilities (All Weights in tonnes)	
Trans-Mars (C_3 = 15 km^2/sec^2)	47.2
Trans-Lunar (5 day transfer)	59.1
LEO (160 by 160 Nmi, 28.5 degrees)	121.2
LEO/NUS (160 by 160 Nmi, 28.5 deg)	75.0
Height (m)	82.3
Gross Mass (Without Payload)	2,194.6
Stage-0	
2 Advanced Solid Rocket Boosters	1,214.5
Stage-1	
External Tank (Including Residuals)	35.6
SSME Engine Pod (4 SSME's)	28.6
Usable Propellant In ET	723.5
Total SSME Thrust (kN, 104%)	8,706
Specific Impulse (sec)	453
Staging Relative Velocity (km/s) (LEO to Mars Range)	4.2 to 5.5
Stage-2 (Ignited Sub-Orbital)	
Usable Propellant	158.8
Inert Mass	13.2
Single Engine Thrust (kN)	1,113
Specific Impulse (sec)	465
Payload Fairing (ALS Design)	20.4

Figure 3.2. The Ares launch vehicle can send 47 tonnes on direct trans-Mars injection, 59 tonnes to trans-Lunar injection, or 121 tonnes to LEO.

(1) an *unfueled* two-stage ascent and Earth return vehicle (ERV) employing methane/oxygen engines and including a life-support system and enough whole food for four people for 9 months, plus some dehydrated emergency rations; (2) 6 tons of liquid hydrogen; (3) 100-kilowatt-electric (kWe) nuclear reactor mounted within a small methane/oxygen internal combustion driven unpressurized utility truck; (4) a small set of compressors and automated chemical processing unit; and (5) two small robotic rovers.

As soon as the payload is landed, the 100-kWe reactor is driven a few hundred yards away from the landing site and lowered off the truck into either a natural depression in the terrain or one created by the robots with the aid of an explosive charge. Its radiators are then deployed and cable run back to the lander. Then, the reactor, which has not yet been used, is started up to provide 100 kW of electric power to the site facilities. The compressors are then run to acquire carbon dioxide out of the Martian atmosphere (which is 95% CO_2). With the help of a catalyst, this CO_2 can be made to react with the 6 tons of hydrogen cargo, transforming it in a few days into 39 tons of methane and water. This being accomplished, we no longer have to deal with the problem of storing cryogenic liquid hydrogen on the surface of Mars. Next, the chemical plant goes to work, electrolyzing the water into hydrogen and oxygen. The oxygen is stored as liquid oxygen, and the hydrogen is reacted with more CO_2 to create more methane and water, and so forth. Additional oxygen is produced by directly decomposing atmospheric CO_2 into oxygen and carbon monoxide, storing the oxygen and dumping the CO. In the course of 10 months, about 108 tons of methane/oxygen propellant is produced.

While this may appear somewhat involved, the chemical processes employed are nineteenth-century technology. The 100-kWe reactor isn't, but practical nuclear reactors have been operated since 1954, and the SP-100 in particular is currently scheduled to be ground tested in 1995, so that with the help of an accelerated program it can certainly be made ready in time for this mission.

It took 8 months for the unmanned payload to fly to Mars, plus 10 months to manufacture the propellant, for a total of 18 months. Since Mars launch windows occur at 26-month intervals, there is thus plenty of time for flight controllers to assure themselves that an adequate supply of methane/oxygen bipropellant has been produced to support crew surface operations and Earth return. If it has, in 1999 two more Ares boosters will lift from the cape within a few weeks of each other. One of them is an unmanned payload identical to the one launched in 1997. The other is a manned spacecraft looking somewhat like a checker "king," 8.4 m in diameter and 4.9 m tall. Its two decks contain some 110.2 m^2 of floor space, allowing it to accommodate a crew of four. With a mass of 40 metric tons (including parachute, landing propellant, provisions, and a pressurized methane/oxygen internal combustion-driven ground car) it is light enough that the booster upper stage can project it directly onto a minimum energy ($C_3 = 15\ km^2/s^2$) transfer orbit to Mars without any Earth-orbit refueling or assembly.

Once on its way to Mars, the manned habitat pulls away from the expended booster upper stage that launched it, but they are still connected by a tether 1500 m long. With the help of this tether, the empty upper stage can be used as a counterweight, and the assembly is spun up at 1 rpm to provide a level of artificial gravity equal to the 3/8 gee found on the surface of Mars. When the manned craft arrives at Mars, the tether and upper stage are discarded, and the ship lands in the immediate vicinity of the now fully fueled ascent vehicle that has been waiting for it since 1997. The landing is safe because the robotic rovers sent out in the advance landing have identified and given extensive characterization of the best landing site in the vicinity, and photos of the site will have been used for astronaut training for the final touchdown. The ERV has a radio beacon much like an ILS transmitter at an airport, giving the crew exact position and velocity data during their approach and terminal landing.

In 1976, the United States sent two Viking probes to Mars, and landed them within 30 km of their designated target sites. With the help of the landing beacon, superior technology, advance meteorological data from the ground site, and the on-the-spot decision making capability of a human pilot, we can vastly exceed the degree of landing precision demonstrated by Viking and land within a few meters of our desired touchdown point.

But even if we missed by a considerable distance, the mission plan has built into it three layered fallback options, a defense in depth to assure the safe return of the crew. First, the manned spacecraft carries with it a methane/oxygen driven pressurized rover with a one-way range of 1000 km, so if worst came to worst, the crew could still drive over to their return vehicle. Second, if by some inconceivable mischance the crew misses its landing site by a distance greater than 1000 km, they can still direct the second unmanned payload (which has been following them out a few days behind) to land near them. It contains a propellant factory of its own and can thus act as an emergency backup. Finally, if all else fails, the crew has with them in their habitat enough supplies to last them until a relief expedition can be sent out 2 years later.

However, assuming that the manned landing has been carried out correctly at the prepared site, and the flight readiness of the 1997 ERV is verified, the 1999 unmanned lander will be directed to a second landing site 800 km away from the first. There it will begin manufacturing propellant for the second manned mission, which will be sent out in 2001.

Thus, each manned Mars mission requires just two Ares booster launches; one to deliver a ride home, and the other to create a new outpost or add to an existing base on Mars. This is a much more economical mission than a conventional plan in which all the propellant is brought from Earth, which typically requires four to seven

Saturn-V class booster launches each. The Mars Direct mission plan is superior to the conventional plan in another respect: Mars Direct brings all of the crew and their hardware to the surface where they can do their job of exploring Mars. The conventional plan requires leaving a mother ship in orbit around Mars, whose crew will accomplish little except to soak up cosmic rays. The crew on the surface is protected by Mars's atmosphere from most of the solar flare hazard, and with the help of some sandbags placed on top of their landed habitats, can be protected from cosmic rays as well. The vulnerability of the crew of the orbiting mother ship tends to create an incentive to limit the stay time of a conventional mission at Mars. This leads to very inefficient missions. After all, if it takes 1.5 years of round-trip flight time to travel to Mars, a stay at the destination of only 30 days seems rather unrewarding. A not too rough analogy to such a mission would be planning Christmas vacation in Hawaii but arranging the itinerary to include 9 days of transferring around airports going out and back, and half a day at the beach. Worse yet, in their rush to get back from Mars, the conventional mission planners are forced to take disadvantageous high-energy orbits, which drive up the propulsion requirements and thus the mass of the mission, as well as a swing-by of the planet Venus where the Sun's radiation is twice that at Earth. In the plan we offer, the crew will spend 500 days on the surface of Mars, coming back via the most efficient, "minimum energy" orbit possible.

During their 500-day stay on the surface of Mars, the crew will be able to accomplish a great deal of exploration. Using 12 of the 108 metric tons of methane/oxygen propellant to power their ground car, they will be able to travel over 20,000 land km at speeds of over 30 km/hr, ranging out from their base 500 km in any direction. If a condenser is added to capture for later recycling the water vapor in the ground car engine exhaust, the 20,000 land km available to the ground car can be increased several times over. Once the second lander's propellant production operation is well underway, they can even drive over to use it as a second base for forays. Thus, about 1.5 million km^2 of territory will be available for exploration for the first mission crew alone. With a crew of four, a large landed habitat/laboratory, and a substantial power source, a large variety of scientific investigations can be accomplished. In addition to searching for past or present life and clues to the planet's geologic history, one key item on the exploratory party's agenda will be to locate pockets of readily exploitable water ice. Once native water is available, it will no longer be necessary to ship hydrogen from Earth, and future missions and settlements can be made independent of Earth for their transportation and life support consumables. But even on this first mission, an inflatable greenhouse can be set up and extended experiments undertaken in growing food crops. If successful, the greenhouse can even be left in operation after the crew departs, allowing research to continue telerobotically from Earth, and perhaps providing future crews with both food and earthly fragrances.

An artist's conception of what the Mars Direct surface base would look like is depicted in Figure 3.3. At the conclusion of the 500 days on the surface, the crew will climb into the methane/oxygen ascent vehicle and rocket back directly to Earth, where they will aerobrake into orbit and either rendezvous with the space station or be picked

Figure 3.3. Mars Direct surface base. Shown is the two-deck disc-shaped hab module, the two-stage conical methane/oxygen-driven ERV, an inflatable greenhouse, and a pressurized ground rover. A 100-kWe nuclear reactor positioned in the crater in the background has long since completed its job of driving the production of the ERV's propellent supply and now provides a copious source of power to the base, with backup power available from solar panels. (Painting by Robert Murray.)

up by a shuttle. Quarters aboard the ascent vehicle will be somewhat cramped, but no more so than in the space shuttle. The return trip will be carried out under zero-gravity conditions, but it will only last about 6 months, and Mir cosmonauts have proven that zero-gravity exposure of such length can be tolerated by humans without excessive bodily harm.

Not too long after the mission 1 crew has departed Mars, the mission 2 crew will arrive and land their habitat near the unmanned ascent vehicle that had been sent out following the mission 1 crew in 1999. Accompanying them will be a third unmanned ascent vehicle/fuel factory payload which will be landed at a new site 800 km further along, to be used for return by the mission 3 crew, which will depart Earth in 2003. Thus, every 2 years a new base will be established and its vicinity explored, and before long a string of small bases will dot the map of Mars, separated by distances within the capability of available ground transportation. With just two boosters being launched every 2 years, the total launch requirement needed to sustain this program of exploration averages to only one launch per year!

The Mars Direct vehicle systems can also be used to accomplish lunar missions in the following way. First, an Ares booster launch is used to throw a 59-metric-ton payload consisting of a standard hab module plus a cryogenic lunar orbital capture and lunar descent (LOC/LD) stage onto trans-lunar injection. The LOC/LD stage is then used to land the hab on the Moon. After one or more such habs have been thus enplaced at a given site, the crew is flown out to the Moon within a Mars Direct ERV. The ERV in this case has its (Mars ascent) first stage deleted, but its second stage is fueled with methane/oxygen bipropellant, and this provides sufficient thrust and ΔV for an Earth return direct from the lunar surface. Landing on the Moon at the prepared site is accomplished with the aid of the same cryogenic LOC/LD module used to land habs and cargo. After landing, the crew exits the ERV and enters the prelanded hab(s) and proceeds to operate on the lunar surface for an extended period, after which they reenter the ERV and execute a direct return to low Earth orbit (LEO).

Prior to lunar liquid oxygen (LOX) becoming available, the mass of the fully fueled Mars Direct ERV exceeds the lunar delivery capability of a single Ares launch by 5 tonnes. This problem could be resolved by scaling down the lunar ERV by 20% compared to the Mars version. However, if hardware commonality with the Mars ERV is desired, a simple solution would be to preland a cargo flight of liquid oxygen at the chosen site. Since such a cargo flight could land about 21 tonnes of LOX, one such flight could support four manned missions to that destination (the ERVs would fly out fully fueled with methane and 2/3 fueled with LOX), plus any number of cargo flights. At the conclusion of these missions, lunar LOX production could be in place and lunar LOX available at the site, eliminating the need for any further LOX delivery flights.

This lunar mission architecture has many advantages. First of all, no lunar orbit rendezvous (LOR) is required. This is almost essential for a lunar base mission (as opposed to Apollo short-stay missions), as it would be unthinkable to have astronauts exposed to zero-gravity and cosmic radiation in a lunar orbiting craft while awaiting the return of a 6- to 12-month duration lunar excursion crew, and on the other hand landing the entire crew would leave the vital Earth-return mother ship in an unstable lunar orbit for an extended period with no one minding the store. If its condition were to deteriorate, only limited corrective action could be taken and the crew might be stranded; if a failure on board were to remain undetected until LOR, the returning crew would find itself in a very difficult situation. Second, the use of methane/oxygen for direct return from the Moon has advantages compared to either the hydrogen/oxygen or conventional storable bipropellant (NTO/MMH) alternatives. Compared to hydrogen, methane is almost indefinitely storable on the lunar surface, thus facilitating extended stays. Methane/oxygen has a higher specific impulse than NTO/MMH (373 s compared to 343 s); however, once lunar oxygen is introduced, this advantage becomes greatly multiplied and the effective Isp of the methane/oxygen system exceeds 1700 s. What this means is that using NTO/MMH, 25 tons must be landed on the Moon to return a 10-ton ERV to LEO, while using methane and lunar oxygen, only 13 tons need be landed. Thus, 12 additional tons of cargo can be flown to the lunar surface with every manned flight, which means that if one crew and one cargo flight are flown each year, the total cargo delivered has been increased 50%. Finally, the Lunar Direct architecture has the key advantage of being totally coherent with the Mars Direct architecture, using the same vehicles. Thus, experience with Mars systems can be obtained in near-Earth space on lunar missions, and overall Space Exploration Initiative (SEI) program costs can be greatly reduced through reduction in the number of elements of the total space transportation architecture.

The complete set of vehicles required for this combined Lunar/Mars Direct architecture is shown in Figure 3.4. While no detailed

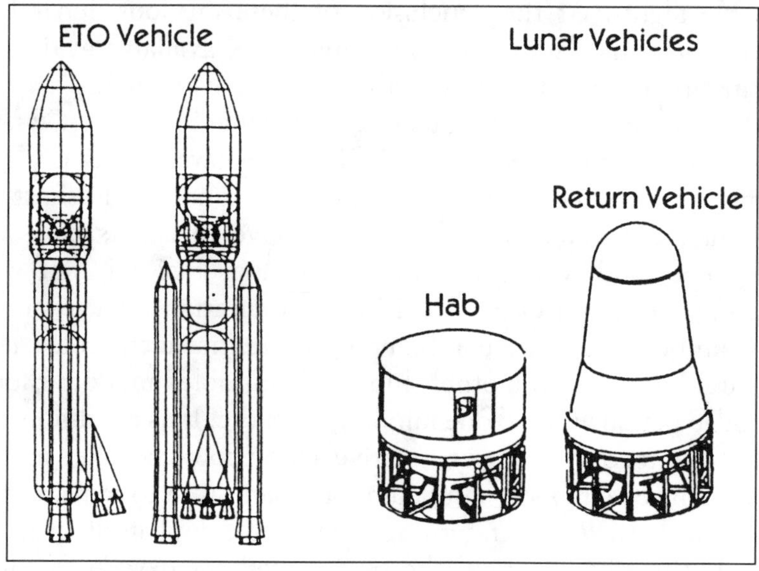

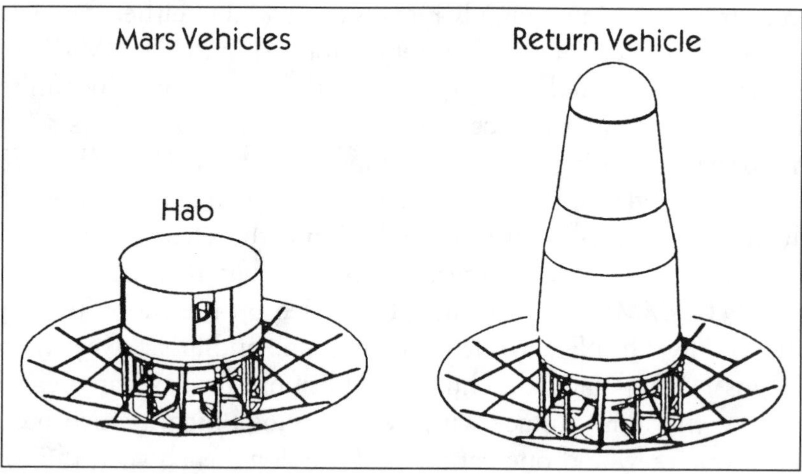

Figure 3.4. The complete space transportation system required to accomplish both the lunar and Mars objectives of SEI using the basic Mars Direct system architecture. The high degree of vehicle commonality can help keep SEI costs to a minimum.

costing of this architecture has been done, it is difficult to imagine how a SEI based on such a limited number of hardware elements could cost anything resembling the $400 billion price tag frequently cited for more conventional architectures, including as they do orbiting space stations, cryogenic depots, and a raft of specialized space transfer and lunar and Mars excursion vehicles.

MARS DIRECT: PHASE II

NTR for Increased Payload Delivery

At some point after the commencement of this program, a new technology, nuclear thermal rockets (NTR),[3] will come into use that will allow us to greatly increase the payload transferable to Mars with each launch. It is the advent of such technology, combined with a reorientation of mission strategy from simple exploration to exploration plus base building, that marks the transition of the Mars Direct plan from Phase I to Phase II.

In keeping with the overall approach of the Mars Direct architecture, namely the elimination of the need for orbital infrastructure, NTR technology is incorporated into the plan simply as a third stage to the Ares launch vehicle. Such a configuration is shown in Figure 3.5. The NTR stage has a specific impulse of 900 s, a power of 900 Megawatts-thermal (MWth), and a thrust of 45,000 lb. With the addition of this stage the Ares can throw 70 metric tons onto a minimum energy trans-Mars injection (TMI) trajectory (C3 = 15 km^2/s^2), an increase of about 50% over the 47-metric-ton TMI all-chemical Ares baseline.

The performance of the NTR augmented Ares is limited by the fact that the NTR must be fired from LEO, and the baseline 2-stage Ares vehicle is not optimized for LEO delivery, as with 250,000-lb thrust its second stage is underpowered. (The 250-klb thrust is optimized for direct trans-Mars injection). If the thrust of the second stage is increased, the LEO delivery capability can be increased, and the TMI throw also increased accordingly. Such results are shown in Table 3.1.

In this calculation, NTR thrust to weight ratio of 5 and tank fractions of 0.1 are assumed. Thus, if we augment the Ares upper stage to maximize its capability as a LEO delivery system, about 83

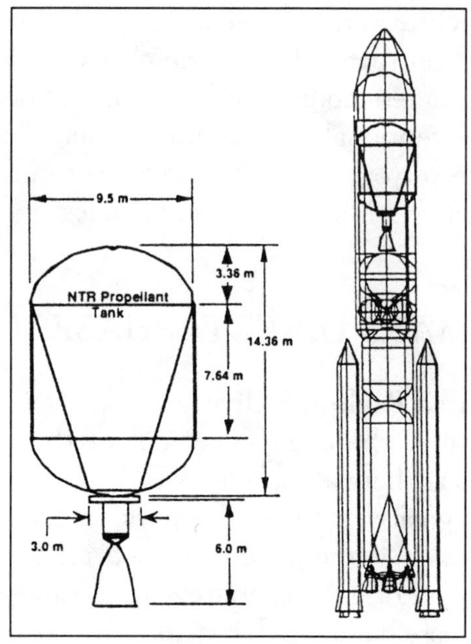

Figure 3.5. Ares with NTR third stage.

tonnes can be thrown to Mars with each launch (excluding the mass of the NTR stage, which is expended). This is about 77% higher than the Ares baseline, a TMI mass increase of 35 tonnes, which translates into an extra 20 tonnes of cargo delivered to the Martian surface with each launch.

If we stick with our early plan of two launches per mission, this will allow us to increase our crew complement of each flight to 12. Alternatively, if the size of the missions is kept the same, using NTR will allow us to launch each mission with a single booster, instead of a split between two.

As a third alternative, crew sizes can be kept at four for each two-launch mission, but large amounts of cargo landed with them,

Table 3.1. NTR augmented Ares TMI throw capability

Stage 2 Thrust (klb)	*LEO Payload (tonnes)*	*TMI Payload (tonnes)*
250	121	70
500	130	76
1000	144	83

allowing for the rapid buildup of a sizable base. Finally, if fast interplanetary transits are deemed important, the NTR stage can be used to throw a four-man Mars Direct hab onto a fast (80- to 120-day transit, $C_3 = 50\ km^2/s^2$) trajectory to Mars, while using its larger minimum energy TMI throw to deliver an ERV augmented with a third stage to the Martian surface. With the help of this third stage, the methane/oxygen-driven ERV is able to execute an equally fast Earth-return trip.

NIMF VEHICLES FOR GLOBAL MOBILITY

NTRs can also be designed to use Martian CO_2 as their propellant. Since this can be acquired at low-energy cost through direct compression out of the atmosphere, rocket vehicles so equipped will give Mars explorers complete global mobility, allowing them to hop around the planet in a craft that can refuel itself each time it lands. Such a vehicle concept, known as a NIMF[4,5,6] (Nuclear rocket using Indigenous Martian Fuel) is illustrated in Figures 3.6 and 3.7.

The NIMF vehicle shown in Figure 3.7 has a 2513-MWth engine that generates 436 klb of thrust at a specific impulse of 264 s by

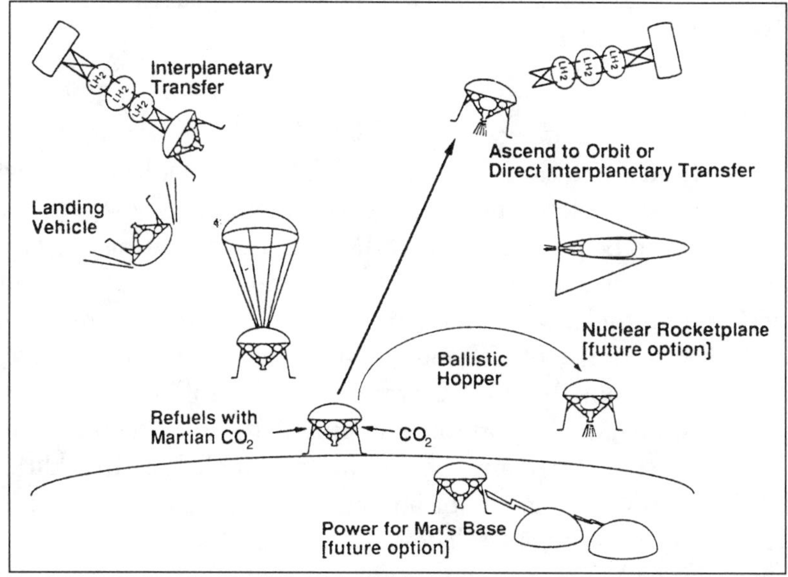

Figure 3.6. The NIMF concept in a variety of operational modes.

Figure 3.7. Ballistic NIMF vehicle on the Martian surface. From top to bottom we have the control deck, habitation deck, compressors, main propellant tank, and the NTR engine with coaxial tank wrapped around it for extra shielding on the surface. (Painting by Robert Murray.)

heating CO_2 to a temperature of 2800 K and exhausting it out a nozzle with an expansion ratio of 100. (The high molecular weight of CO_2, while very detrimental to specific impulse, allows for a much higher thrust to be generated by a NIMF engine operating at a given power level than a conventional hydrogen-fed NTR of the same power). The vehicle, which has a dry mass of 45 tonnes, can contain a total of 346 tonnes of CO_2 propellant, giving it the capability of attaining a 250-km by 33,000-km (250- by 1-sol) elliptical orbit about Mars, or more important, enabling it to hop from one point on the surface of Mars to any other point in a single hop. In addition, the NIMF can carry significant amounts of cargo over continental-scale distances, as shown in Table 3.2.

Because CO_2 becomes an oxidizing medium when heated to elevated temperatures, conventional NERVA[7] (Nuclear Engine for

Table 3.2. Cargo delivery capability of the ballistic NIMF

Cargo (tonnes)	*Mass Ratio*	ΔV *(km/s)*	*Range (km)*
10	7.03	5.047	Orbital
20	6.04	4.65	8500
30	5.23	4.28	6000
40	4.61	3.96	3920
50	4.13	3.67	3000
60	3.73	3.41	2280
70	3.41	3.17	1800
80	3.13	2.96	1450
90	2.90	2.75	1220
100	2.70	2.57	1000

Rocket Vehicle Applications, developed during the 1960s) type carbide fuel elements cannot be used in a NIMF engine. Instead either oxide or oxide-coated fuel pellets would have to be used. Uranium-thorium oxide has a melting point of about 3300 K, and such pellets coated with a layer of either zirconium or thorium oxide to retain fission products could well enable operation at 2800 K. Alternatively, preliminary data[8] indicates that "traditional" NERVA uranium carbide fuel elements coated with graphite can have their graphite coated with a further layer of thorium oxide, and that such thorium oxide outer coatings are resistant to both CO_2 and solid–solid reactions with the graphite at temperatures up to 3000 K.

Because the actual propellant temperature attainable in NIMF vehicles is unknown at this time, it is useful to parameterize NIMF performance as a function of propellant temperature. Such results are shown in Figure 3.8.

Since the NIMF vehicle shown in Figure 3.7 has a maximum mass ratio of about 8.7, we can see in Figure 3.8 that a propellant temperature of about 2600 K is required if the 250-km by 1-sol orbit is to be attained. If all that is required is to attain low Mars orbit, which would still give the NIMF complete global mobility, then a 2000 K propellant temperature is sufficient. Since this requirement is well below the expected range of performance, it seems clear that the development of NIMF vehicles capable of enabling full global

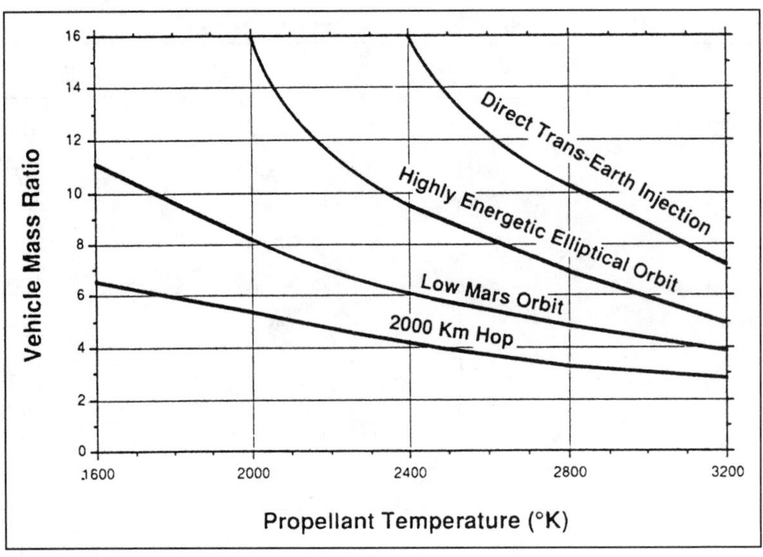

Figure 3.8. Performance of the NIMF as a function of temperature.

access on Mars is an objective attainable within the limits of conservative engineering practice.

CO_2 can be liquefied out of the Martian atmosphere by simple pump compression at an energy cost of about 84 kWe-hrs/tonne. What this means is that the NIMF, using a 25-kWe power source (either dynamic isotope power source [DIPS], deployable solar, or dual-mode NTR) can completely fuel itself in less than 50 days, without any dependence on surface infrastructure.

BUILDING A BASE ON MARS

Once NIMF vehicles have been developed and put into operation, there is no longer an incentive to land the Mars Direct hab modules in widely dispersed locations. Instead, landings can be concentrated at a single location chosen as a good site for a base during the Phase I period of surface exploration. Such a base will support the comparatively large population required to investigate and develop the industrial and agricultural processes needed to create a Martian civilization. While such research in extraterrestrial engineering and resource utilization is proceeding at the base, the field exploration of Mars can be continued at an accelerated pace by parties of scientists making long distance sorties in the NIMF.

In Figure 3.9, we see a depiction of a group of habs landed in the same area being moved together to form a large contiguous pressurized volume. The habs' landing gear can articulate both in the vertical and horizontal directions, allowing them to "walk" the short distances required for hook-up.

Let us examine how such a base might be built up on Mars using the Mars Direct space transportation infrastructure. We assume that a period of Phase I-type exploration has occurred, with minibases consisting of single four-man hab modules enplaced in a number of locations, and that one of these sites has now been selected for buildup into a major base. The results are shown in Table 3.3.

In Table 3.3, dates are given in months and years starting from the launching of the team that founds the base. (The "—" mission refers to the Phase I expedition that initially explored the chosen site.) Launches are given as "h," "e," or "c," for hab, ERV, or cargo launches, respectively, with lower case being used to describe a Phase I (chemical propulsion) type payload, and upper case for Phase II (Ares with NTR third stage). The cargo column is a record of the cumulative amount of useful cargo landed at the base site.

Figure 3.9. Mars Direct habs being mated together to form a large base. (Drawing by Carter Emmart.)

Table 3.3. Mars Direct base buildup plan

Date	*Crew*	*Launches*	*Habs*	*Decks*	*Vol./person* (m^3)	*Power* *(kWe)*	*Cargo* *(tonnes)*
—	4	1h,1e	1	1	32	100	15
1/1	8	2h,2e,1c	3	3	48	300	75
3/3	16	2h,2e,1c	5	7	56	500	135
5/5	16	2h,2e,1c	7	11	88	700	195
7/7	16	2h,2e,1c	9	15	120	900	255
9/9	20	2H,2E	11	21	134	1300	385
11/11	24	2H,2E	13	27	144	1700	515
1/14	28	2H,2E	15	33	151	3400	645
3/16	32	2H,2E	17	39	156	5100	775
5/18	36	2H,3E	19	45	160	10200	935
7/20	40	2H,3E	21	51	163	12750	1095
9/22	44	2H,3E	23	57	166	15300	1255
11/24	48	2H,3E	25	63	168	17850	1415

The base buildup strategy is as follows. First a Phase I mission consisting of one hab and one ERV characterizes the site, staying on the surface and exploring the surrounding region for 1.5 years before returning to Earth. The site having been thus selected for development on the basis of intimate knowledge of its characteristics, the 1/1 mission consisting of two standard Phase I habs (one hab deck, one cargo deck), plus two standard ERVs and one-way cargo launch is sent out. The eight-person crew of this mission will stay on the surface for 4 years, departing Mars on 8/5. Such long stays offer the advantage of increasing the total man days spent on the Martian surface at any given launch rate by a factor of two, as well as allowing each base crew to overlap its stay for 1.8 years with the team following on the next launch opportunity.

The second team departs Earth on 3/3, arriving at Mars on 10/3. This crew of 8 added to the 8 of the 1/1 team brings the base complement up to 16. Between the Phase I mission, the lower decks of the two habs of the 1/1 mission, and the two cargo launches (1/1 and 3/3), there are now five cargo decks/workshops at the base. This is quite sufficient for workshop space, and so the Phase I habs used on the 3/3, 5/5, and 7/7 missions are modified to accommodate habitation on both decks, thus giving the base a rapid expansion of living space per person, as shown in the volume/person column of Table 3.2.

Starting with the 9/9 mission, Phase II Ares launch vehicles with an NTR third stage are introduced, increasing the trans-Mars injection throw from 47 to 75 metric tonnes. This allows us to expand the hab to three decks, as well as ship about 25 extra tons of cargo with each hab or ERV launch. This eliminates the need for a separate cargo flight and enables the rapid buildup of enplaced base hardware, as can be seen in the landed cargo column of Table 3.2. While the three deck habs of Phase II can accommodate crews of 12, the 9/9 and 11/11 missions only fly with crews of 6 per hab, going to 8 in 1/14, 10 in 5/18, and 12 in 9/22, in order to increase the base crew size at a rate commensurate with the expansion of living space.

The 9/9 and 11/11 missions simply send out two 100-kWe reactors of the Phase I type with each ERV launch, but starting with the 1/14 mission, we assume that the reactor power system is switched from thermoelectrics to a Brayton cycle, increasing the power of each unit sent out to 850 kWe. One of these is sent with each ERV, leading to a very rapid buildup of base electric power capability. By the twenty-fifth year of the base, almost 18 MWe of power is in place, far, far, more than the 48-person installation needs for life support or propellant manufacture. Rather, this large amount of power will enable large-scale materials processing, to produce materials to construct vast volumes of pressurized agricultural, industrial, and living space. The highly productive, mechanized, energy-intensive industry and greenhouse agriculture that these will contain will create the large-scale economic base required to support the flood of immigrants destined for this Martian Plymouth.

THE COLONIZATION OF MARS

This proposition being made publike and coming to the scanning of all, it raised many variable opinions amongst men, and caused many fears & doubts amongst themselves. Some, from their reasons and hops conceived, laboured to stirr up & incourage the rest to undertake and prosecute the

> same; others, againe, out of their fears, objected against it & sought to diverte from it, aledging many things, and those neither unreasonable nor unprobable; as that it was a great designe, and subjecte to many unconceivable perils & dangers . . .
>
> It was answered that all great & honourable actions are accompanied with great difficulties, and must be both enterprised and overcome with answerable courages.
>
> Gov. William Bradford
> "*Of Plimoth Plantation*," 1621

By the twenty-fifth year of the Mars Direct base building effort, a large prebuilt town, complete with housing, an electric power grid, and manufacturing and agricultural industries can be in place on the Martian surface. The stage is now set for the colonization of Mars.

The difficulty of interplanetary travel may make Mars colonization seem visionary. However, colonization is, by definition, a one-way trip, and it is this fact which makes it possible to transport the large numbers of people that a colony in a new world needs to succeed.

In Figure 3.10 we see a twenty-first century reincarnation of the *Mayflower*, used to transport immigrants to Mars. An Ares variant with a 1000-klb thrust upper stage lifts 145 tonnes to low-Earth orbit, then a NTR stage hurls the two 40-tonne "habcraft" onto a 7-month trajectory to Mars. After separation from the NTR, the two habcraft separate, rendezvous, and tether off to each other to create Mars's normal artificial gravity at a spin rate of 1 rpm with the aid of a 700-meter long cable. Arriving at Mars, the tether is dropped, and the habcraft aerobrake, parachute, and land separately on their own sets of hydrogen/oxygen engines.

Each habcraft is 10 meters in diameter and includes two complete habitation decks, for a total living area of 157 m^2 (1700 ft^2), allowing it to comfortably house 12 people in space and on Mars. Expansion area is available in the third (uppermost) deck after the cargo it contains is unloaded upon arrival.

Thus, in a single booster launch, 24 people, complete with their housing, tools, and inflatable greenhouse, can be transported one way from Earth to Mars.

Now let us assume that starting in base year 25, or 2030 A.D., an average of four such boosters are launched every year from Earth

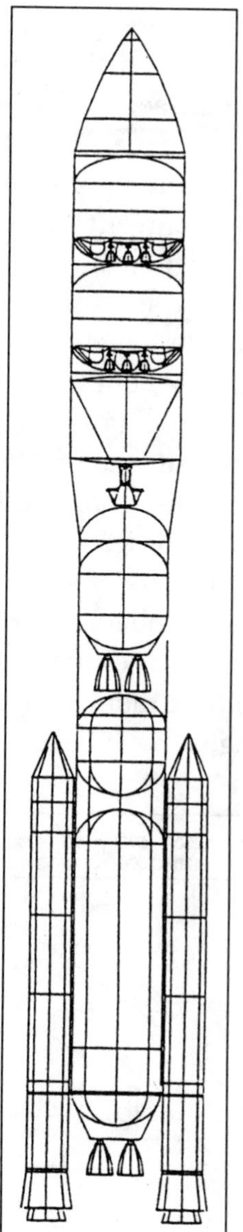

Figure 3.10. The Martian *Mayflower*, capable of transporting 24 colonists one way to the red planet.

(perhaps one from each of the four major spacefaring powers, although frankly an effort of this magnitude would be well within the resources of the United States alone). If we then make various reasonable demographic assumptions, the population curve for Mars can be computed. The results are shown in Figure 3.11. Examining the graph, we see that even with this minimal level of effort (and the technology frozen at ultraconservative late twentieth-century levels forever), the rate of human population growth of Mars in the twenty-first century closely approximates that experienced by colonial America in the seventeenth century.

This in itself is a very significant result. What it means is that the distance to Mars and the transportation challenge that it implies is not a major obstacle to the creation of a human civilization on the red planet. Rather, the key questions become those of resource utilization, growing food, building housing, and manufacturing all sorts of useful goods on the surface of Mars.

Can this be done? We believe so. Unlike the Moon, Mars is rich in carbon, nitrogen, and hydrogen, the key elements needed to support life. Bring a few packets of seeds, several breeding pairs of rabbits and goats, and some inflatable greenhouses to Mars, and a self-expanding agriculture can be established. Plastics, metals, glasses, brick, and concrete can all be manufactured out of native materials (many processes for doing so have been identified and presented in

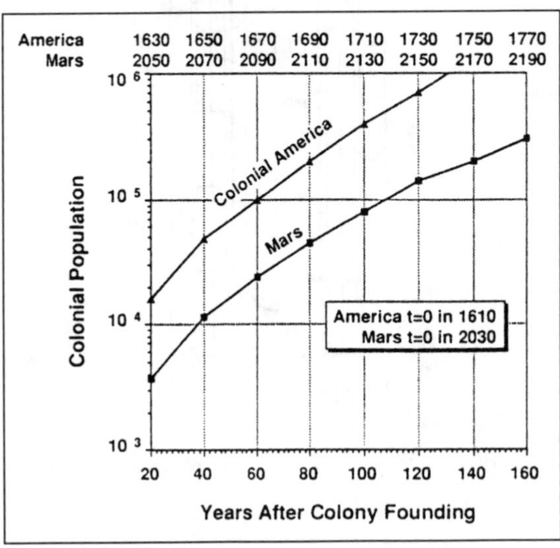

Figure 3.11. Colonization of Mars compared to North America. Analysis assumes 100 immigrants/year starting in 2030, increasing at 2% annual rate, 50/50 male/female. All immigrants are between ages 20 and 40. Average of 3.5 children to an ideal Martian family. Mortality rates are 0.1% per year between ages 0 and 59, 1% between ages 60 and 79, and 10% per year for those over 80.

the proceedings of the Case-for-Mars[9,10,11] conferences) and used to construct large-scale greenhouses, housing complexes, and even environmentally protected towns. As discussed previously, liquid fuels can be synthesized to propel high-powered ground vehicles and construction equipment. The required expanding consumer electric power grid can be provided by importing additional nuclear reactors at a rate of 1 850-kWe (dynamic cycle augmented) unit every 4 years, to start, with larger multiunits supplanting them later on in the program.

This latter requirement to import nuclear reactors brings up an important question. That is, while it is clear that a Mars colony could manufacture the large majority of its bulk requirements (consumables, propellants, housing materials), it seems equally clear that for a very long time there will remain a necessity to import a certain amount of high-tech manufactured goods from Earth. The question is, is there anything that a Mars colony could export to Earth to pay for such imports, or must Mars always be dependent upon terran charity?

One answer is that the Martians could export knowledge. Mars colony could be set up as a university town, with intensive research going on to produce patents which could be licensed for profit to Earthside industries. This may well suffice; however, it is interesting to inquire whether there are any material goods that can be exported from Mars for a profit.

At first glance this seems absurd. After all, how many times have we heard that if there were diamonds lying on the surface of the Moon, it wouldn't pay to go there and get them: how much worse must the situation be for distant Mars?

Actually, if there were diamonds lying on the surface of the Moon, it *would* pay to get them, not by flying individual Apollo-style missions, but by setting up a base with a catapult system and firing off the payloads to Earth. The situation on Mars, despite its long distance, is no worse, because at Mars we have indigenous propellant to work with.

Consider for example a large unmanned NIMF, a cargo NIMF if you will, capable of lifting 45 tonnes to Low Mars Orbit (LMO). If a methane/oxygen stage is used to fire the payload from LMO to Earth (where it aero-enters and is picked up on the ground after a parachute landing), about 40% of this payload in LMO, or 18 tonnes, can be useful cargo sent to Earth. Now the 45-tonne object in LMO weighs about 17 tonnes in Mars gravity, so for a desirable stage thrust/weight (T/W) ratio of 0.2 for trans-Earth injection we need about 3.4 tonnes, or 7.5 klb, of engine thrust. The typical T/W of a chemical engine is 40, so this means that for each 18 tonnes of useful cargo transported to Earth, an engine weighing 85 kg is required. Let's say that the tanks, and propellant and stage structure can all be manufactured on Mars, but that the engine must be imported, along with another 35 kg of spare parts to replace high-tech items expended in the course of producing the cargo or launching the NIMF. Thus, 18 tonnes of cargo can be transported to Earth at the cost of 120 kg of required imports. This mass transportation ratio, which we term M, is thus 18,000/120 = 150 for this example.

The balance of trade ratio, or B, which determines whether the Mars colony can produce any income, is then given by:

$$B = UMP \tag{1}$$

where P is the ratio of the price per kg of the Mars-produced cargo on Earth divided by the cost per kg (production plus transportation costs) of the Earth-produced items, and U is the fraction of total Martian imports that can be expended to support the export operation (the rest is used to support the colony).

To continue with the example, let's say that U = 0.1, and that the cost of terrestrial imports is $10,000/kg (which is about what it would be if a 121-tonne to LEO class Ares with an NTR third stage costs $500 million per launch). Then if the Martian-produced goods are worth $1000/kg on Earth, we find: B = UMP = (0.1)(150)(0.1) = 1.5, and the Mars colony is producing a 50% profit.

What could Mars produce that is worth $1000/kg on Earth? One possibility is minerals. Cordell[12] has shown that the history of the Mars, as we know it today, implies that ore-forming processes have occurred on Mars in the past, over an extended period of the planet's geologic history. Thus, while it must be said that such ores have yet to be discovered, geologic science indicates that Mars may be as richly endowed with mineral ores as was the natural Earth. However, unlike Earth, Mars has not had 4000 years of human civilization acting to scour up all the easiest-to-discover and richest ores, so that there is every reason to believe that Mars may possess an abundance of valuable ores far exceeding what is readily available on Earth today.

If this proves to be the case, then there are a large number of items that can potentially be extracted from Mars and exported to Earth for profit, as shown in Figure 3.12. Here we have stuck with our above example for the transportation ratio, assumed $10,000/kg costs for imports to Mars, current mineral prices, and examined a range of U values. It can be seen that, while there is considerable uncertainty in the analysis, if minerals at least as valuable as silver or germanium are available on Mars (and there are many such candidates), then a profitable Martian export operation can proceed.

It may be added that the introduction of advanced propulsion technology beyond NTR can improve this picture further. For example if a set of solar[13] or magnetic[14] sails were placed in operation cycling between LMO and a trans-Earth injection orbit, cargo delivery could be accomplished solely by operation of these craft in conjunction with the cargo NIMF. The need to export methane/oxygen engines in large numbers would thus be eliminated from our previous example, and the mass transportation ratio, M, would be increased from 150 to 514, with a very large benefit for the Martian economy.

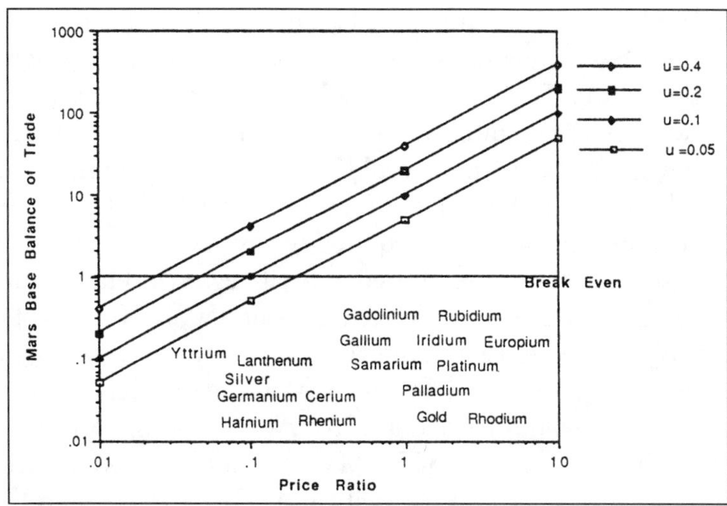

Figure 3.12. Mars base balance of trade. It can be seen that if valuable minerals do exist on Mars, their exploitation with large profit margins is possible.

TERRAFORMING MARS

One hundred years after the commencement of this colonization effort the population of Mars will reach 80,000 people, and a sufficient industrial base will have been established for serious terraforming operations to commence.

McKay[15] has offered two design points for a terraformed Mars. Basing himself on the near-conclusive evidence[16] that Mars was a warm wet planet for the first several billion years of its history (as shown by dry river channels and other water erosion features) he and his collaborators have proposed recreating the primeval greenhouse effect on Mars by reendowing the planet with the same 2 bar (1 bar = 14.7 pounds per square inch (psi) pressure) CO_2 atmosphere that it had in its childhood. The problem with this proposal is that while 2 bars of CO_2 are required to produce a Mars where the average equatorial temperatures are above the freezing point of water, only about 0.3 bar of volatile CO_2 is actually believed to be currently present on Mars (in the atmosphere, as south polar dry ice, and absorbed in the soil), the rest having become chemically bonded to form carbonates.

McKay's second proposal is to endow the planet with a 1 bar nitrogen/oxygen atmosphere. Since these gases are not major greenhouse effect contributors, in this scenario he proposes supplementing the atmosphere with a "mixed cocktail" of selected artificial CFC gases which have greenhouse potential several orders of magnitude higher than CO_2. The CFC gases, $CBrF_3$ (halon), C_2F_6, CF_3Cl, and CF_2Cl_2 would all be stable in the Martian atmosphere with half-lives of over 200 years, and would not be toxic to humans at the ppm levels required. A production rate of about 100,000 tonnes per year of this mixture would be required to sustain a greenhouse effect on Mars sufficient to raise the equatorial region's temperatures to Earth temperate zone levels (currently about 650,000 tonnes of these gases are produced per year on Earth). The estimated power required to support the steady state CFC manufacturing on Mars to maintain this greenhouse would be about 500 MWe, although a production of 1,000,000 tonnes/year (5000 MWe) would be required if the greenhouse is to be established within a 40-year time span. These requirements hardly seem excessive for a project of this value. The problem, however, is that while the CFC greenhouse appears technically feasible, the nitrogen/oxygen atmosphere does not, as chemically free nitrogen is not to be found in anything like the required quantities on Mars.

Given this situation, our proposal is for a compromise combining what is most feasible from the two McKay scenarios. That is, what we propose is to set up the CFC production on Mars and start to greenhouse the planet despite the fact that no nitrogen/oxygen atmosphere is to be had. The first thing that will happen as the planet starts to warm is that the CO_2 as dry ice in the south polar ice cap will vaporize, thickening the CO_2 atmosphere, and adding to the greenhouse effect of the CFCs. Within 40 years, nearly all of the volatile CO_2 can be made to outgas, forming an atmosphere of about 0.3 bar pressure (4.4 psi) on Mars. While this atmosphere would not be breathable by humans, it would eliminate the need to wear pressure suits. Rather, humans working on the outside on Mars would be able to wear street clothing, along with a kind of scuba gear breathing a mixture of 3 psi oxygen and 1.4 psi nitrogen out of a tank. As temperatures rise, the water frozen as permafrost into the Martian soil will begin to melt and flow again into the long dry river channels of Mars. Soon the rains would begin to fall, and it will become possible to grow plants in the open across large regions of the planet. Within 100 years of the commencement of the terraforming effort, desert areas such as Chryse Planitia may be covered with amber waves of genetically modified grain, while the lower slopes of the Olympus Mons are decorated with proud stands of ponderosa pine.

These plants will do more than produce food and look grand; they will transform Mars's atmosphere, just as their ancestors did for the Earth. The atmosphere they create will be nearly pure oxygen, at about the 3 psi level. As the experience of the Apollo and Skylab programs prove, humans can function quite well for extended periods of time in such an atmosphere. Thus, with the help of our biospheric allies, the day may come when humans standing on the surface of Mars doff their breathing gear and gratefully breathe in the cold crisp air of the Martian spring.

In 500 years, a space of time equal to that which separates the present age from that of Columbus, a civilization of over a billion people may live on a new Mars, a world not discovered, but created by the courage and enterprise of the human spirit.

Acknowledgments

The CAD drawings used in this article were done by Robert Spencer, while the paintings were done by Robert Murray. The sketch of the Mars base being assembled was done by Carter Emmart. Performance trajectory analysis on the Ares launch vehicle was done by Sid Early, while many useful engineering suggestions were made by Jim Greenwood. Dr. Chris McKay provided essential background in terraforming science. Dr. Ben Clark provided a valuable critique of the basic Mars Direct concept, and Al Schallenmuller has provided corporate support and assistance with the analysis of the methane/oxygen production process.

Chapter 4

Stephen L. Gillett

Inward Ho!

Mercury's the ugly duckling of the inner system; it's been pretty much ignored both in SF and in space development scenarios. "On to Mars!" "Out to the asteroids!" have been the slogans. "In to Mercury!" just doesn't have a lot of pizazz. Charles Pellegrino and James R. Powell have bucked this trend a little; in *Analog*,[1] they proposed covering Mercury with a solar-cell farm to collect the vast power required for interstellar flight. But there's more to Mercury than *that!* Don't cover over the planet itself; we need it for other things. Build the collector farm off-planet instead, as Robert L. Forward suggested in *Flight of the Dragonfly*.[2]

'Cause Mercury's got a lot of potential value, and not just because of the solar power there. So let me digress on a synergy between high-efficiency solar sails, Mercury, space development, and terraforming.

SOLAR SAILING AND MERCURY

Light boats sail swift . . .

Shakespeare
Troilus and Cressida, Act II[3]

As a solar sail gets real thin, it can support its own weight—and then some—while at rest with respect to the Sun. Obviously such an "ultrasail" is more efficient than a sail that can't support its weight. But its advantages run deeper than that. For one thing, as in the story "SunStat" by Oltion and Goodloe,[4] an ultrasail can hold a platform at rest with respect to the Sun (or another star, for that matter), which is convenient for many sorts of observations. But more than that, the closer to the star, the better the acceleration—despite being deeper in the gravity well! Explanations follow.

For a perfectly reflecting sail, the pressure of sunlight is given by:

$$P = 2S/c,$$

where P is the pressure, S the solar constant, and c the speed of light. The solar constant is the amount of energy that a given area receives from the Sun in a certain time, and has units of power per area (W/m^2, say). For a perfect absorber, the pressure is exactly half the above:

$$P = S/c.$$

At the distance of Earth, the value of solar constant is about 1340 W/m^2. Using $c = 300{,}000$ km/s, we get a pressure of 4.5×10^6 N/m^2, or 6.5×10^{10} psi, for a perfect reflector. Not a lot! (The *total* force, of course, will depend on the total area of the sail.)

Now, for various materials we can calculate the critical thickness at which a sail would be self-supporting at the distance of Earth. To do this, we need the density and reflectivity of the material, and the gravitational field of the Sun. Such data are in standard tables. For aluminum (*not* a perfect reflector), the critical thickness works out to be about 0.25 μm (i.e., microns—millionths of a meter), or about two-hundredth the thickness of a human hair. (The actual calculation is left as an exercise for the reader!) Obviously, a useful sail must be even thinner than this, to have any capacity to hold a payload.

Furthermore, even though I specified "at the distance of Earth," it turns out this thickness is independent of distance. For consider: If a sail is in balance, the *outward* force of the sunlight on the sail and its burden must equal the *inward* pull of gravity. Now mentally move this sail inward. The attractive force on it increases substantially, according to Newton's law of gravitation; it goes up as the inverse square of the distance. But the sunlight pressure also increases substantially. In fact, it increases in *exactly* the same inverse-square proportion, because light intensity drops off as the inverse square of the distance. Thus the effects exactly cancel. So if the sail hovers at the distance of Earth, it hovers anywhere.

Now consider a sail that can support *more* than its own weight plus payload. It cancels out gravity and then some, so there's a small net pressure left. Then what happens when we bring the sail sunward? Again, the Sun's gravity and sunlight intensity both increase according to the inverse-square law, so the closer you are, the more the sunlight pressure exceeds the gravitational pull. For example, say you were at a distance of 1 AU (astronomical unit—the average distance from Sun to Earth) and the light pressure on your ultrasail is 1.1 times its weight from gravity. Now move in to 1/2 AU. Gravity is now four times greater, but the light pressure is also four times greater. Now, 4×1 is 4, but 4×1.1 is 4.4, so the net force *outward* on the sail has also increased four times!

The upshot is that the excess pressure on the sail acts like an inverse-square *repulsion*. Obviously, then, the closer to the Sun, the stronger the force, and the better the acceleration. This has some bizarre consequences. For example, if you were going from Earth to Pluto with an ultrasail, it's far faster to drop in toward the Sun first. The extra acceleration near the Sun *much* more than compensates for the longer distance. (To calculate travel times from point A to point B in an inverse-square repulsive field, you can either integrate the inverse-square potential from first principles, or else look up the equation—which is much faster. I'm *not* going to give it here; it's given in reference 5. The equation is kind of messy, but that's what computers are for.)

So the closer to the Sun the better. Now, what's the closest planet to the Sun in the system? Right! Mercury is one dandy place to start ultrasails from.

MERCURY AND RESOURCES

Mercury—A Mini-Earth in Moon's Clothing?

Murray, Malin, and Greeley[6]

Mercury is probably one dandy place to *make* solar sails, too. Not only is it routinely the closest piece of matter to the Sun (and far and away the *biggest* piece, too), but it probably has an aluminum-rich crust. Why? I have to digress again, this time for a review of the state-of-the-art about Mercury.

As everyone knows, we found out in 1964 that the one thing we *knew* about Mercury wasn't true. It does not keep the same face to the Sun, but instead rotates with a 3/2 resonance (3 rotations in 2 revolutions). The error came about because the planet's very difficult to study from Earth. Although it's bright (I've seen Mercury, a sight Copernicus is said to have missed) it's always close to the horizon, visible only briefly after sunset or before sunrise, while the sky is still twilit. Now, with its true rotation, you see Mercury facing the same way every *other* orbit; but since it was very difficult to see Mercury at all, observers just saw Mercury facing the same way many times. They then naturally assumed it must always face the same way, and thus must be facing the Sun. The physicists have since shown that the 3/2 resonance is much more stable than the 1/1 resonance (Mercury always facing the Sun), and so we should have known beforehand there was a problem; but this sort of *post-hoc* analysis is not terribly impressive!

If from Earth you can't even be sure of the rotation period, you can figure that Earth-based telescopic studies are pretty useless. Thus, all detailed info on the planet comes from the Mariner 10 fly-by back in 1974. This mission was originally intended as a single fly-by, with the spacecraft then continuing on in an independent orbit around the Sun. Fortunately, someone thought to calculate where Mercury would be when the spacecraft crossed its orbit again, and sure enough, Mercury would be there again, too! So Mariner 10 made three separate passes by the planet and took pictures each time, before it ran out of attitude-control fuel. Unfortunately, due to Mercury's slow rotation and the details of orbital mechanics, the spacecraft saw the same view each pass, so one Mercurian hemisphere is still unknown. At this point, though, there's no reason to think it's spectacularly different from the side we've seen.

The first impression from the Mariner photos is that Mercury looks like the Moon. It's pocked with craters upon craters, very much like the lunar highlands. And also like the lunar highlands, it includes some very large craters indeed—"basins," as the planetary scientists now term them, hundreds to thousands of kilometers across. We know from dating Apollo samples that the "late heavy bombardment" recorded on the Moon had essentially ceased by 3.9 billion years ago. If the massive cratering on Mercury reflects the same bombardment, which seems reasonable, Mercury is a pretty inactive place. No other surface processes have modified that ancient crater-pocked crust, other than a little bit of "faulting" (i.e., fracturing), probably reflecting slight contraction of the Mercurian core, and some subsequent desultory cratering.

There's also no evidence of any ancient atmosphere; as Murray *et al.*[6] note, crater rays—bright streaks centered on the crater, consisting of a thin layer of powdered rock thrown out by impact—are not only common but preserved. It takes very little atmosphere to blow them away, or to keep them from being deposited in the first place.

So why is it like a "mini-Earth"? Mercury has no air, no water; it is inactive, unchurned by plate tectonics, unmarred by erupting volcanoes . . . it hardly seems Earthlike!

It is "Earthlike" in its density. Mercury has a density of 5.42 grams per cubic centimeter (g/cc), little less than Earth's 5.52 g/cc. (The Moon's average density, by comparison, is only 3.3 g/cc, not much more than ordinary rock.) The high density indicates that Mercury must contain a lot of dense material, material much denser than silicate rocks. A very *un*-Moonlike characteristic.

Earth's high mean density results from its iron-nickel core. And similarly for Mercury; it has a large core. (It even has a small magnetic field, also in contrast to the Moon.) In fact, Mercury's core makes up about 80% of the mass of the planet.

But the core's relevance for near-term resources is not clear. Even this big core is still pretty deep, buried under silicate rock—a crust and mantle—500–600 km thick. Digging that deep is going to take a while. (There's a little slop in these estimates, since we do not know exactly how dense the core is. Murray *et al.* note, though, that even with generous estimates of the thickness of the silicate crust and mantle. Mercury's core is bigger than Earth's Moon!)

So for the time being, resource-wise, we're going to have to settle for what's in the silicate mantle and crust atop that large core. As a working model, they probably are very similar to the Moon's.

Based on evidence from rocks collected by the Apollo missions, we now think the Moon was almost or completely molten after its formation—a notion picturesquely termed the "magma ocean." As the magma ocean cooled, minerals started to crystallize in it; most sank, but one in particular floated—plagioclase feldspar, a calcium-aluminum silicate. If things settled out undisturbed like a jar of salad dressing left in the fridge, you'd end up with a nicely layered planet; a plagioclase crust outside, and layers of denser, iron-magnesium-rich silicates inside. And to first order, that's a good description of the Moon. The top of that ancient plagioclase crust shows up as the lighter, densely cratered surface of the lunar highlands. (Of course, natural processes are *never* this simple. For one thing, the Moon's plagioclase crust is pervasively fractured by those mammoth craters, and bodies of iron-magnesium silicate rock squeezed into this fractured crust, like mud pushing up through a broken sidewalk. For another, some subsequent melting occurred as heat built up in the Moon from the decay of long-lived radioactive elements, and this led to some early volcanic activity—which caused the smooth dark lava plains, or "maria.")

So, if the silicate part of Mercury's like the Moon, there's bound to be a big variety of a lot of useful stuff right at the surface, all combined in silicates: oxygen, calcium, magnesium, iron, some sodium, and potassium. Rarer elements that have an affinity for oxygen and silicates are also likely to be concentrated locally; useful things like uranium, the rare-earth elements, zirconium, tungsten, niobium. . . .[7]

And in particular, aluminum—the raw material for solar sails—is probably one of the most abundant elements at the Mercurian surface, bound up in that feldspar crust.

By the same token, however, Mercury is probably essentially volatile-free, like the Moon. So you will have to bring all your water, carbon, and organics. As on the Moon, there are probably some volatiles, especially hydrogen, stuck in the regolith as a result of being implanted by the solar wind (the tenuous stream of atomic particles continually emitted by the Sun), and they'll help keep life-support stocks replenished, but that's probably all. (Oh, well. You can't have everything.)

Anyway, Mercury is also easy to get off. For all intents and purposes, there's no air, so mass drivers work fine. (If you want to quibble, there's a tenuous "atmosphere" consisting of a steady-state population of helium atoms detained awhile from the solar wind. It's interesting only to particle physicists.)

And although Mercury has over twice the escape velocity of the Moon, it's about twice as easy to *leave*, if you use mass drivers or some other electrically powered technology. Mercury has almost seven times the solar flux as the Moon (the exact amount varies due to the ellipticity of Mercury's orbit), and that more than compensates for the additional gravity. With just modest solar collectors you can get a lot of power. (To be sure, sunrise and sunset are a problem; solar cells don't work well at night. So you set up your fledgling operations near one of the poles; like the Moon, Mercury has little axial tilt, so there you can be in sunlight nearly year-round. And as a power grid spreads across the planet, the day/night cycle will become less and less a problem.)

And this echoes the point Pellegrino and Powell made: Mercury has *lots* of solar power. Its position is in stark contrast with the asteroids, which are a ballyhooed "obvious" destination for space development. Sure, there's lots of stuff out there in the Belt, volatiles and raw metal and whatnot, but there's *not* a lot of energy out there. From the old inverse-square law again, the ratio of solar flux at Mercury to that at a typical mainbelt asteroid—Ceres, say—is about 160; over two orders of magnitude. Thus, to yield the same energy, solar collectors of the same efficiency must be more than ten times as long on a side (because the square root of 156 is about 12.5). To get the same power, an acre of collector at Mercury blossoms to 160 acres—a quarter-section!—at Ceres. (All right, if you stick with near-Earth asteroids your solar power is more abundant. Near-Earth asteroids are a highly limited population, however, and we're going to be moving afield from there before too long.)

Ultimately, perhaps, we might even take Mercury apart. Reaching that gigantic nickel-iron core would be a big resource incentive. And, as a geologist myself, dismantling Mercury would have major scientific interest; dissection of a non-living planet would tell us *a lot* more about how planets work. (Of course, this would not happen for a long time.)

So why has Mercury's potential been so ignored? There's probably something emotionally disturbing about going in *closer* to the parent star. In part, maybe all that old SF about the hellish day side of Mercury has sunken into the collective subconscious, as a fundamentally irrational but very real fear. Or, maybe going *inward* goes against the psychological grain; we're going into space to get away from the confinements of Earth, to broaden our options, and so to move out "toward" other stars—however minutely—is more satisfying.

But any worry *is* psychological. Keeping a Mercury base cool will be no problem for twenty-first century technology, especially since all the actual mining and extraction operations will be robotic. For human habitation, just mound some regolith over the modules and it'll be just like the Moon. Mercury orbit is also an overlooked place for space colonies, if that's what you're into. And finally, two possible inner-system places, anticipated by George O. Smith in his classic "Venus Equilateral" stories, are the Venus L-4 and L-5 points. There may even be some asteroidal debris—"Venus Trojans"—accumulated there, to bootstrap the Mercury operations.

MERCURY: THE KEY TO VENUS?

> A curious shiny meteor eased into the planet's soupy atmosphere. As it plunged, atmospheric resistance heated it to glowing; then suddenly, as it slowed into the denser layers below, it ignited. Thick black smoke trailed the burning meteor as it fell through the thick CO_2 atmosphere. . . .

As *Analog* readers may remember, I discussed terraforming Venus in two previous articles (Dec. 1984 and Nov. 1985). At the Eighteenth Lunar and Planetary Science Conference—the "LPSC," held at the Johnson Space Center, Houston, in March, 1987—Jim Oberg put together an informal conference called Terraforming II, and invited interested people to come give talks. So I did. (Alas, although the LPSC lent us a room, Terraforming II was not part of its formal proceedings. Terraforming's still too far out. However, progress is being made. Back around 1976, another associated meeting, on "Lunar Utilization," also was not a formal part of the LPSC because it was too far out. In 1987, though, the LPSC had a *formal* session on "Space Utilization"!)

Anyway, at Terraforming II, I proposed a new notion for terraforming Venus, inspired by Freeman Dyson's Enceladus Project, a "thought experiment" for terraforming Mars.[8]

To briefly summarize Dyson's scenario: A robot package is sent to Enceladus, a large Saturnian moon assumed (for the sake of argument) to consist mostly of water ice. The package differentiates into several types of self-replicating robots, which eventually start launching packages of ice to Mars, guided by solar sails. As a steady stream of ice meteoroids warms the Martian atmosphere, water collects, rain falls, and *volià*—a habitable planet.

But what about Venus? As I reviewed in my December 1984 article, the overwhelming problem with terraforming Venus is getting rid of its massive CO_2 atmosphere—about 90 atm worth. All that air keeps the surface near red heat because of a powerful greenhouse effect; the atmosphere acts like a blanket, letting sunlight in but hindering the escape of heat.

And till the CO_2 is gotten rid of, sending a stream of Enceladus ice to Venus would just make things hotter. Water vapor itself is a dandy greenhouse gas. In fact, Venus probably arrived at its present sorry state through the so-called "runaway greenhouse"; if a planet's surface becomes too hot, enough water vapor evaporates so the greenhouse effect gets more efficient, so things get even hotter, so yet *more* water evaporates. . . . The oceans boil soon, and for a while you have an atmosphere of steam. (Quickly, as geologists measure time, the steam atmosphere is destroyed by solar ultraviolet, which breaks up water molecules so the hydrogen can escape to space.)

Earth has just as much CO_2 as Venus, but conveniently, it's virtually all locked away in carbonates in the crust, as limestone, mainly. Venus never had oceans (or lost them early on), so carbonates were never stable, so the CO_2 stayed in the air, so things got real hot. . . . And—if you were going to ask—we can't react Venus's air with its crust now; you'd have to garden the crust much too deeply, even if you could get quick and complete reaction. (And you'd get neither; the silicates making up rocks react too sluggishly.) In addition, things would need to cool for the rocks to react, but they can't cool till the CO_2's been removed! A classic Catch-22.

Seeding the Venus atmosphere with algae to break down the CO_2—Carl Sagan's venerable terraforming suggestion, back in the 1960s—won't work either, at least for the whole job. There's just too much air. Breaking up 90 atm of CO_2 gives you over 60 atm of oxygen, plus a layer of carbon over 100 m thick. They won't stay separated long; $C + O_2 = CO_2$. Boom! We need to get *rid* of the air.

Well, can we remove the CO_2 bodily? That's very hard. We could maybe seed the planet with self-rep robots to gather up the atmosphere (which involves compressing it, perhaps a kilo or so at a time) and shoot it off into space. But Venus is a big planet; you need a *lot* of ΔV to escape her, and because of her atmosphere, acceleration is difficult; catapults like mass drivers don't work because of air resistance.

What about precipitating out the CO_2 by reacting it with something from outside? Ah! Maybe here's the key.

The best reactant would be calcium or magnesium metal. Both will tend to reduce carbon dioxide to carbon, stripping out the oxygen:

$$2\,Mg + CO_2 = 2MgO + C$$

and

$$2\,Ca + CO_2 = 2CaO + C.$$

Magnesium actually burns in CO_2. It's a flashy lab demonstration; just poke a burning piece of magnesium ribbon into a bell jar full of CO_2 and watch the black smoke of carbon boiling off.

With both calcium and magnesium, moreover, the oxides further react with more CO_2 to make carbonate:

$$MgO + CO_2 = MgCO_3$$

and similarly for calcium. So, each atom of metal ends up removing a molecule and a half of CO_2. Not bad.

The problem? Not surprisingly, neither calcium nor magnesium occur uncombined in nature. They *are* reactive, after all. So the metal would have to be extracted, and that's hard; magnesium and calcium are both tightly bound into silicates and require a lot of energy to be broken out.

And, finally, a preposterous amount of metal is required, about 8×10^{20} kg calcium or 5×10^{20} kg magnesium. To give you a feel for *how* preposterous, this is approximately the mass of Ceres, the largest main-belt asteroid. If all this metal was formed into a sphere, it would be something over 1000 km in diameter.

It's absurd to think we could *ever* refine that much raw metal, especially for an economically marginal proposition like terraforming Venus. Just another silly science-fiction fantasy! Or is it?

Back to Mercury. (You thought I'd forgotten Mercury?) If its crust is really like the Moon's, it is fundamentally *made* of calcium-aluminum feldspar, abundantly invaded with magnesium-rich igneous rocks. So both calcium and magnesium are among the most abundant elements at its surface. Now, as I said, silicates are hard to break up, especially without a lab full of reagents. But it can be done. One simple (that's key!) way is to melt the rock. You can electrolyze it; stick electrodes into each side of your pool of molten rock, hook them up to a *big* battery, and watch. It's just like breaking water up into hydrogen and oxygen. Oxygen will bubble off the anode, and a mixture of metals will dribble off the cathode. And the melt's resistance to current provides the heating to *keep* it melted.

Well, of course it's not *that* simple. Silicate melts are *very* hot (over 1000°C, in this case), which makes them tricky to deal with. You're dealing with lava, after all. (It's easier in a vacuum, anyway, because they're easier to insulate.) They're corrosive; things like electrodes tend to dissolve. Preventing undesired side reactions at the cathode is another sticky issue: Only the least reactive metal tends to separate, since any more reactive metal tries to displace a less reactive metal from the melt instead. (The anode also tends to plate up with gunk for similar reasons.) And we've ignored the question of collecting the dirt and melting it in the first place.

But none of these problems is fundamental. (To quote a fatuous phrase, "they're just engineering!") And refining silicates in this way has *lots* of advantages: You don't need crushing or sorting; your feedstock is whatever random bunch of regolith you scoop up. You don't need *water*, with an expensive and complicated wet-chemical extraction facility; your working fluid is just molten rock. And finally, some work is already being done on such processes, to determine their feasibility for lunar smelting. The technology will be available when we need it.

So, let's extrapolate. From what's learned from the Enceladus Project and a couple generations of Moon-mining, the Venus Terraforming Project builds a package and sends it to Mercury, where it differentiates into several types of self-replicating robots. Some scoop up dirt, some set up solar-power collector and power distribution networks, some set up electrolysis vats, some build mass drivers. . . . And they start electrolyzing regolith into raw metal, and fashioning it into chunks, each with a little solar sail and a guidance chip telling it how to get to Venus.

Soon, the auto-assembled mass drivers start throwing the chunks off the planet, where their solar sails deploy. The guidance chip then steers the way to Venus, where the ingot smacks itself into her air, a rain of artificial meteors each munching up another kilogram or two of CO_2. Eventually the job is done.

Of course, once the atmosphere's thinned down quite a bit we'll need to add some water, but that's *trivial* by comparison; toward the end of the project, when there's no danger of retriggering a runaway greenhouse, the Enceladus project will send some ice cubes to Venus as well.

There's some curious economics here, hinted at by Dyson in his thought experiment. Each chunk of metal is nothing more than a self-guided ingot (self-guided with exquisite accuracy), and trillions of such lumps of metal, each with a tiny sophisticated guidance system, will be sacrificed utterly to atmospheric incineration. Bizarre! Not a way to treat precision machinery.

But the destruction of that exquisitely organized ingot does not matter; what matters is not organization *per se* but how cheaply it can be made. And the cost is virtually zero. It's analogous to products from living things on Earth. For example, consider a piece of firewood. Look at the exquisite pattern of this wondrous stick, the phenomenal organization of thousands of cells—each itself a marvel of complexity—that generated it. And you're going to casually burn it for *fuel?*

But of course. We think of wood as a "natural" product, easily made and casually destroyed, and so it is. Biological self-replicators produce it cheaply as a byproduct of their existence.

Or, consider an apple. It's just as marvelous as the firewood; but in addition, each one of those seeds, so thoughtlessly discarded, is a package that can build a whole new tree! But again, apples are made by the million; ironically, many fewer would be made if they *couldn't* be destroyed for food. Who's going to raise an orchard of fruitless trees?

Or consider a krill-eating whale, filtering tiny organisms out of seawater by the ton. Each one of those zillion planktonic lifeforms is a marvel of complexity unto itself, a whole independent life form, but each is doomed to be disaggregated and reformed into whale-stuff.

The degree of organization is not important. The important thing is how cheaply you can organize. Given self-rep robots, their products are no more valuable, and no less valuable, than the products of living things. That is, they are valuable for what they *are*, with no value added for the organization that went into them.

How long might terraforming take? The lower limit is set by how much solar energy it takes to make all that metal and send it to Venus. There are two main costs: (1) busting it out of the rocks, and (2) sending it out of Mercury's gravity well. For magnesium, the minimum extraction energy is going to be about 25 kilojoules per gram (kJ/g); for calcium, about 18 kJ/g. And then it takes about 9kJ/g to get something off Mercury. In both cases, the total energy we need adds up to about that in *all* the sunlight intercepted by Mercury in 4 years! And this assumes best-case extraction efficiencies; no energy lost, and completely pure silicate feedstock, so for real-world efficiencies the time goes up accordingly. (Of course, we could help things along by gathering additional solar power with off-planet collectors.)

And how much Mercury did we chew up to send to Venus? A *lot*. If we figure out how much rock we had to process to get that much metal, we arrive at something around 3 to 5% of the mass of Earth's Moon! This is not trivial; a great deal of Mercury's surface will be affected.

But this is not necessarily bad, either. By building extensive observational and recording capability into the self-rep robots, we could get unparalleled data on the internal constitution of Mercury as it was excavated. In fact, economics being what they are, probably much more scientific data could be gotten by piggy-backing onto such a project than could be obtained from a purely scientific investigation. (This also holds for the Enceladus project.)

And, if we're clever, at least one of the excavations could reach that iron-rich core, with all the scientific and resource potential *that* promises.

In fact, granting such a self-differentiating, self-replicating system, it turns out the big constraint is not how much metal you need but how much energy you're adding to the Venus atmosphere. If you're not careful, a tremendous amount of matter would be falling in from essentially infinity, and all that gravitational energy will show up as heat. My BOTE* calculations suggest the heat imparted in that case is about 100 times what's in the atmosphere already! (And, of course, one of the things we must do is *cool* Venus, not cook her.) To avoid this heat influx, you need some tricky guidance to decelerate *before* hitting the atmosphere. (And the deceleration can't involve atmospheric braking, because—after all!—that just dumps energy into the atmosphere.)

So. Would it work? I think so. Is it the best way? How should I know! And why terraform Venus anyway? That's a different question . . . but the reason *not* to terraform Venus is not "because it's impossible!"

(Dr. Bob Forward, well-known to *Analog* readers, also attended the Terraforming II conference. He gave the talk after mine. After I had finished, he said he thought *he* was supposed to give the science-fiction scenarios. I took it as a compliment!)

* Back-of-the-envelope

Chapter 5

Robert M. Zubrin

Colonizing the Outer Solar System

Currently, the outer solar system is largely a curiosity. Despite its immensity, its four spectacular giant planets, its mysterious minor planet, six moons of planetary size, and scores of smaller moons, as well as several known and probable myriads of unknown asteroidal and cometary objects of every description imaginable, the distance separating us from this vast domain appears to relegate it to merely academic interest. Such appearances are deceptive. It is safe to say that within a century, a mere blink of an eye in human history, it will be evident that these outer worlds contain the keys to continued human survival and progress, to war and peace, and to humanity's hopes for the stars. Let's see why.

SOURCES OF POWER

To get a glimpse of the probable nature of humans in the late twenty-first century, it is first necessary to look at the trends of the past. The history of the technological advance of the human species can be written as a history of increasing utilization of energy. Consider the energy consumed not only in daily life, but also in transportation and the production of industrial and agricultural goods. Americans in the electrified 1990s use approximately three times as much energy per capita as their predecessors of the steam and gaslight 1890s, who in turn had nearly triple the per capita energy consumption of the pre-industrial 1790s. Some people see this trend as a direct threat to the world's resources, but such rising levels of energy consumption historically have correlated directly with rising living standards. If we compare living standards and per capita energy consumption of the advanced sector nations with those of the impoverished Third World, we see that they are still directly correlated. This relationship between energy consumption and the wealth of nations will place extreme demands on humanity's present set of available resources. First, to raise the entire *present* world population to *current* American living standards (and in a world of global communications, it is doubtful that any other arrangement will be acceptable in the long run) would require increasing the global energy consumption at least a factor of ten. However, world population is increasing, and while global industrialization will slow this trend, it is probable that population levels will at least triple before they stabilize. Second, current American living standards and technology utilization are hardly likely to be the ultimate (even in late twentieth-century America, there is still an abundance of poverty) and will be no more acceptable to our descendants a century hence than those of a century ago are to us today. All in all, it is clear that the exponential rise in human energy utilization will continue. In 1992 humanity consumed about 12 TW (TW = terawatt = 1 million MW) of power; at the current 2.6% growth rate, we will be using nearly 200 TW by the year 2100. The total anticipated power utilization and the cumulative resources used (beginning with 1992) are given in Table 5.1.

For comparison, the total known or estimated energy resources are given in Table 5.2.

In Table 5.2, the amount of He3 listed for each of the giant planets is that present in their atmospheres down to a depth where the pressure is ten times that of sea level on Earth. If one extracted at a depth where the pressure is greater than this, the total available He3 would increase proportionally. If we compare the energy needs for a growing human civilization with the availability of resources, it is clear that, even if the environmental problems associated with

Table 5.1. Projected human use of energy resources

Year	*Power (TW)*	*Energy Used after 1992 (TW-years)*
2000	15	107
2025	28	623
2050	53	1600
2075	101	3460
2100	192	7000
2125	365	13700
2150	693	26400
2175	1320	50600
2200	2500	96500

burning fossil fuels and nuclear fission are completely ignored, within a few centuries the energy resources of the Earth and Moon will be effectively exhausted. Large-scale use of solar power can alter this picture somewhat, but eventually the enormous energy reserves in the atmospheres of these giant planets must and will be brought into play.

Thermonuclear fusion reactors work by using magnetic fields to confine a plasma consisting of ultra-hot charged particles within a vacuum chamber where they can collide and react. Because high-energy particles can gradually fight their way out of the magnetic

Table 5.2. Solar system energy resources

Resource	*Amount (TW-years)*
Known terrestrial fossil fuels	3000
Estimated unknown terrestrial fossil fuels	7000
Nuclear fission without breeder reactors	300
Nuclear fission with breeder reactors	22,000
Fusion using lunar He3	10,000
Fusion using Jupiter He3	5,600,000,000
Fusion using Saturn He3	3,040,000,000
Fusion using Uranus He3	3,160,000,000
Fusion using Neptune He3	2,100,000,000

trap, the reactor chamber must be of a certain minimum size to delay the particles' escape long enough for a reaction to occur. This minimum size requirement generally makes fusion power plants unattractive for low-power applications, but in the future, where human energy needs will be on a scale tens or hundreds of times greater than today, fusion will be far and away the cheapest game in town.

In the twenty-first century, nuclear fusion using the clean-burning (no radioactive waste) deuterium–helium-3 reaction will be one of humanity's two primary sources of energy, and the outer planets will be the Persian Gulf of the solar system.

THE PERSIAN GULF OF THE SOLAR SYSTEM

Today, Earth's economy thirsts for oil, which is transported across oceans from the Persian Gulf and Alaska's North Slope by fleets of oil-powered tankers, for use in industrial sectors. In the future, the inhabitants of the inner solar system will have fuel for their fusion reactors delivered from the outer worlds by fleets of spacecraft driven by the same thermonuclear power source. Although the ballistic interplanetary trajectories made possible by chemical or nuclear thermal propulsion are adequate for human exploration of the inner solar system and unmanned probes beyond, something much faster will be needed to sustain interplanetary commerce encompassing the gas giants.

Fusion reactors powered by D–He3 are a good candidate for a very advanced spacecraft propulsion system because the fuel has the highest energy-to-mass ratio of any substance found in nature, and also because in space the vacuum in which the reaction must run can be had for free in any desired size. A rocket engine based on controlled fusion could work by allowing the plasma to leak out of one end of the magnetic trap, adding ordinary hydrogen to the leaked plasma, and then directing the exhaust mixture away from the ship with a magnetic nozzle. The more hydrogen added, the higher the thrust, but the lower the exhaust velocity. For travel to the outer solar system, the exhaust would contain more than 95% ordinary hydrogen, and the exhaust velocity would be over 250 km/s (which compares quite well with the exhaust velocities of chemical or nuclear thermal rockets of 4.5 and 9 km/s, respectively). Large nuclear-electric propulsion (NEP) systems using fission reactors and ion engines, a more near-term possibility than fusion, could also achieve an exhaust velocity of 250 km/s. However, because of the complex electric conversion systems required, such NEP engines would weigh about eight times as much as fusion systems, and the trips would take twice as long. If no hydrogen is added, a fusion configuration could theoretically yield exhaust velocities as high as 15,000 km/s, or one-twentieth the speed of light! Although the thrust level of such a pure D–He3 rocket would be too low for in-system travel, the terrific exhaust velocity would enable voyages to nearby stars with flight times of less than a century.

Extracting the He3 from the atmospheres of the giant planets will be difficult, but not impossible. A winged transatmospheric vehicle is required that can use the planet's atmosphere for propellant, heating it in a nuclear reactor to produce thrust. I call such a craft a NIFT (Nuclear Indigenous Fueled Transatmospheric vehicle). After leaving its base on one of the planet's moons, a NIFT would either cruise the atmosphere of a gas giant, separating out the He3, or rendezvous in the atmosphere with an aerostat station that had already produced a shipment. In either case, after acquiring its cargo, the NIFT would then fuel itself with liquid hydrogen and then rocket out of the atmosphere to deliver the He3 shipment to an orbiting fusion-powered tanker bound for the inner solar system.

In Table 5.3 we show the basic facts that will govern the commerce of He3 from the outer solar system. The flight times listed are one-way from Earth to the planet, with the ballistic flight times being those for minimum-energy orbit transfers. Although these can be shortened somewhat at the expense of propellant (gravity assists

Table 5.3. Getting around the outer solar system

		One-Way Flight Time				
Planet	*Distance from Sun (Au)*	*Ballistic (yrs)*	*NEP (yrs)*	*Fusion (yrs)*	*Velocity to Orbit (km/s)*	*NIFT Vehicle Mass Ratio*
Jupiter	5.2	2.7	2.2	1.1	29.5	23.7
Saturn	9.5	6.0	3.0	1.5	14.8	4.6
Uranus	19.2	16.0	5.0	2.5	12.6	3.6
Neptune	30.1	30.7	6.6	3.3	14.2	4.3

can help as well, but are available too infrequently to support regular commerce), they are too long for commercial traffic to Saturn and beyond (even if the vessels are fully automated, time is money). The NEP and fusion trip times shown assume that 40% of the ship's initial mass in Earth orbit is payload, 36% is propellant (for one-way travel; the ships refuel with local hydrogen at the outer planet), and 24% is engine. Jupiter is much closer than the other giants, but its gravity is so strong that even with the help of its very high equatorial rotational velocity, the velocity required to achieve orbit is an enormous 29.5 km/s. A NIFT is basically a nuclear thermal rocket with an exhaust velocity of approximately 9 km/s, and so even assuming a "running start" air speed of 1 km/s, the mass ratio (mass ratio is the mass of the rocket with fuel divided by the mass of it with its tanks empty) it would need to achieve such an ascent is more than 20. This means that Jupiter is off limits for He3 mining, because it's probably impossible to build a hydrogen-fueled rocket with a mass ratio greater than 6 or 7. In contrast, with the help of lower gravity and still large equatorial rotational velocities, NIFTs with buildable mass ratios of about 4 would be able to achieve orbit around Saturn, Uranus, and Neptune.

CREATING A NEW MARS

The control of nature that late twenty-first-century human civilization will possess will enable engineering works on a massive scale, with the most profound being the terraforming of Mars.

The first steps required in the terraforming of Mars can be accomplished with surprisingly modest means. The Martian soil contains enough carbon dioxide (CO_2) gas to give the planet an atmosphere with about a third the pressure of Earth's at sea level; if the planet were warmed slightly, this material would begin to outgas. Such a warming (about 6C) can be achieved by placing on the planet's surface factories that manufacture about 300 tonnes of super-greenhouse-effect halocarbon (CFC) gases per hour, an output rate that would demand a mere 1500 MW (0.0015 TW) of power. As the CO_2 emerged from the soil, it would add its own potent greenhousing capability to the atmosphere, accelerating the warming process like an avalanche until temperatures in the Martian tropics during the summer approached the freezing point of water. Such a Mars could allow some plant life to exist in the open in the tropical regions, and humans could walk abroad without spacesuits (needing only warm clothes and oxygen masks). However, the atmospheric levels of oxygen and nitrogen would be too low for many plants, and if left in this condition the planet would remain relatively dry, as the warmer temperatures took centuries to melt Mars' ice and deeply buried permafrost. It is during this second phase of terraforming Mars, in which the hydrosphere is activated, the atmosphere is made breathable for advanced plants and primitive animals, and the temperature is increased further, that human activity in the outer solar system assumes an important role.

Activating the Martian hydrosphere in a timely fashion will require doing some violence to the planet, and one of the best ways this can be done is with targeted asteroidal impacts. Why go to the outer solar system then? The reason, strange as it may seem, is that it is easier to move an asteroid from the outer solar system to Mars than it is to do so from the Main Belt or any other inner solar system orbit. This odd result follows from the laws of orbital mechanics, which cause an object farther away from the Sun to orbit it more slowly than one that is closer in. Because an object in the outer solar system moves slower, it requires a smaller velocity change (or ΔV) to change its orbit from a circular to an elliptical shape. Furthermore, the orbit need not be so elliptical that it stretches from Mars to the outer solar system; it is sufficient to distort the object's orbit so that it intersects the path of a major planet, after which a gravity assist can do the rest. If these tricks are used, the required ΔV needed to move an outer solar system asteroid onto a trajectory where it will hit Mars can be as little as 300 m/s. Moreover, because an outer solar system asteroid is likely to be made of ice, ammonia, and other frozen gases, these materials provide a ready-made source of propellant to move them. When heated to high-temperature vapor in a nuclear thermal rocket engine, such materials can generate gas streams with exhaust velocities of about 4000 m/s. This means that less than 10% of the asteroid's mass would be sacrificed as propellant in order to send the rest of it on its way.

Consider an asteroid made of frozen ammonia with a mass of 10 billion tonnes orbiting the Sun at 12 AU, slightly beyond Saturn. Four 5000-MW nuclear thermal rocket engines could move it

300 m/s with 10 years of steady thrusting. This would be enough to cause it to swing by Saturn, after which it would coast for about 20 years until its impact. When the object finally hit Mars, the energy released would be about 10 TW-years, enough to melt 1 trillion tonnes of soil and release enough ammonia to raise the planet's temperature by about 3 C, incidentally forming a shield that would effectively mask the planet's surface from ultraviolet radiation at the same time. If one such mission were launched every year, in about half a century most of Mars would have a temperate climate, and enough water would have been melted to fill a sea 1 million km^2 in area 50 m deep.

Only the potential energy of outer solar system objects can do such work. In comparison, the explosive power of thermonuclear weapons is puny; it would take 70,000 1-megaton hydrogen bombs to deliver the same punch as one of the small asteroids discussed previously. Even if so many thermonuclear explosives could be manufactured, their use would cause the planet to become unacceptably radioactive.

HIGH GROUND

If swords can be beaten into plowshares, the reverse is also true. The vastly superior firepower offered by the use of outer solar system objects over thermonuclear weapons will not escape the attention of military planners. It is a historic axiom of military science that he who controls the high ground controls the battlefield; in the relationship between the outer solar system and the inner planets, this axiom is doubly true since in this case the high ground comes fully equipped with an artillery battery that would outgun Zeus. It therefore follows that not only economic, but military security from the mid-twenty-first century onward will be impossible without control of the outer solar system. If the future should see humanity divided into various nations, then the outer solar system a century hence will see their bases, fortresses, and fleets. Warships of every major power will patrol the outer darkness to protect commerce and prevent any unauthorized attempts to move celestial objects. Addressing the needs of these outposts will create another form of interplanetary commerce, with high-technology products shipped out from the inner solar system, and settlements of civilians springing up to produce the consumables and other goods that can be made locally.

COLONIES IN THE COLD

Just as in the old west towns spring up in the vicinity of mining camps, cavalry forts, and trading posts, so in the outer solar system true colonies will develop around the He3 mining operations, the military bases and their supporting shipping businesses. However, as elsewhere in the past, within a generation or two after their founding, such settlements will tend to take upon a life of their own. To those born on Titan or Miranda, the moons of Saturn or Uranus will be home, and few will have any greater desire to move to Earth than most terrestrials today have to live on Venus. It is not just a matter of sentiment; those raised in low-gravity environments, such as the moons of the outer planets, will be ill-adapted to live on Earth. Why be squashed to the ground on a crowded planet where even the native humans must travel by foot or vehicle, when you can live on the wide open spaces of Titan and soar like a bird? Furthermore, why live in a place where people must pay to have energy shipped to them from across the solar system, when you can live near the energy source and enjoy virtually unlimited power and all the advantages that come with it practically for free? Finally, why live on a planet whose social laws and possibilities are defined by generations long dead, when you can be a pioneer and help to shape a new world according to reason as you see it?

ROAD TO THE STARS

No, humans will go to the outer solar system not merely to work, but to live, to love, to build, and to stay. But the irony of the life of pioneers is that if they are successful, they conquer the frontier which is their only true home, and a frontier conquered is a frontier destroyed. For the best of humanity then, the move must be ever outward. In the early twenty-first century, humans will settle Mars using ballistic transportation systems that will be, at best, marginal for the job. The growth of Martian settlements will force the development of fusion rocketry that will make the red planet commonplace, but give the pioneers the outer solar system in return. However, it won't end here; each step demands another. The farther we go, the farther we will become able to go. Ultimately, the outer solar system will simply be a way station toward the vaster universe beyond. For, although the stars may be distant, human creativity is infinite.

Chapter 6

Richard P. Terra

Islands in the Sky
Human Exploration and Settlement of the Oort Cloud

After spreading throughout the warm, compact inner core of the solar system, the human race will face the daunting challenge of crossing the deep ocean of space that lies between Sol and even the nearest neighboring stars. But just off shore, at the outer fringe of Sol's gravitational reach, countless small icy islands are scattered in a vast spherical archipelago reaching almost halfway to the Sun's nearest neighbors—the myriad comet nuclei of the Oort Cloud.

Human exploration and settlement of the Oort Cloud will create a new environment for a diverse array of social, economic, and biological experimentation, and that diversity may indicate the future course of the evolution of our species. The Oort Cloud will also be the proving ground for the technology of interstellar travel: these tiny, scattered islands on the periphery of the solar system may be our first stepping stones to the stars.

Although the notion of human settlement on comet nuclei dates back to the eighteenth century, it was not until the latter part of this century that the concept began to receive serious attention. In 1972, physicist Freeman Dyson offered this challenging vision:

> It is generally considered that beyond the Sun's family of planets there is absolute emptiness extending for light-years until you come to another star. In fact it is likely that the space around the Solar System is populated by huge numbers of comets, small worlds a few miles in diameter, rich in water and other chemicals essential to life . . . comets, not planets, are the major potential habitat of life in space.[1]

More recently, astronomers, biologists, sociologists, historians, and design engineers have begun to subject the idea to rigorous—if somewhat speculative—scientific and engineering analysis. They have begun to explore the very real possibility of establishing human settlements in the distant reaches of the Oort Cloud, and what life might be like there.

The Oort Cloud is thought to form a vast, spherical collection of small icy bodies orbiting at enormous distances from the Sun. Although direct observational evidence is sketchy, there are sound theoretical reasons for postulating its existence.

It is generally believed that the comet nuclei in the Oort Cloud formed along with the inner solar system about 4.6 billion years ago. In the most widely accepted theories, the solar system originated in the gravitational collapse of an immense cloud of interstellar gas and dust. As it collapsed the cloud flattened out into the classic solar nebula, a broad, fairly thin disk of material slowly rotating about the infant sun.

Within the nebula, the gas and dust particles began to condense and clump together into small aggregates that grew slowly into larger and larger bodies, forming planets, moons, asteroids—and comets.

Most comets are thought to have formed on the outer fringe of the solar nebula, at about the same distance from Sol as Uranus and Neptune (roughly 20 to 30 astronomical units [AU]). The bulk composition of these two planets is close to what would be expected if a similar mass of comet nuclei were collected together into a single, planet-sized body.

In another line of evidence, most comets seem to be significantly depleted in carbon relative to the average cosmic abundance of that element. This can be interpreted as an indication that comets formed in a region of the nebula warm enough to evaporate much of the methane (CH_4) present and prevent it from condensing with the remaining gasses and dust. As expected, comets are also badly depleted in hydrogen, as are all the other bodies in the solar system except for Jupiter, Saturn, and the Sun.

Most of these small bodies would be swept up into the growing planets, but the orbits of many others would be perturbed and altered by close encounters. An encounter with Jupiter or Saturn would most likely result in complete ejection from the solar system into interstellar space. In the vicinity of less massive Uranus and Neptune, comet nuclei would also be perturbed into orbits far from the Sun—but not entirely beyond its gravitational reach.

Initially, the comets would orbit more or less in the same plane as the inner system, but over time the faint tug from passing stars would randomize their orbital inclinations, creating a vast, dispersed, spherical cloud of small icy bodies—the Oort Cloud, named for Dutch astronomer Jan Oort, who first postulated its existence and structure in the 1950s.

Estimates of the total number of comet nuclei in the Oort Cloud range from about 100 billion to several trillion—more than the total number of stars in the entire galaxy. Their total mass is difficult to estimate with any precision, but is probably at least equal to the mass of Earth, and may be much greater. It is thought that the original population of the Oort Cloud was about 2 trillion comets with a mass about 30 times that of Earth, but has since been depleted by escape into interstellar space and perturbation into orbits closer to the Sun, where the icy bodies evaporate after a time.

The majority of the comet nuclei in the Oort Cloud are probably distributed throughout a broad spherical shell between 40,000 and 60,000 AU from the Sun (although some astronomers place the density peak a bit closer, at around 25,000 AU). This is just shy of one light-year (64,000 AU). It is possible that a substantial number orbit much closer to the Sun, between 100 and 10,000 AU, forming an inner Oort Cloud. Within about 10,000 AU of the Sun, the orbits of the comets would lie more or less in the plane of the ecliptic. Beyond that distance, the influence of passing stars is strong enough to produce the random spherical distribution of the outer Cloud. The outer periphery of the main Cloud is probably at about 100,000 AU—close to 2 light-years. The maximum dynamic limit is about 200,000 AU, where the gravitational pull of the galactic core begins to overcome that of the Sun (see Figure 6.1).

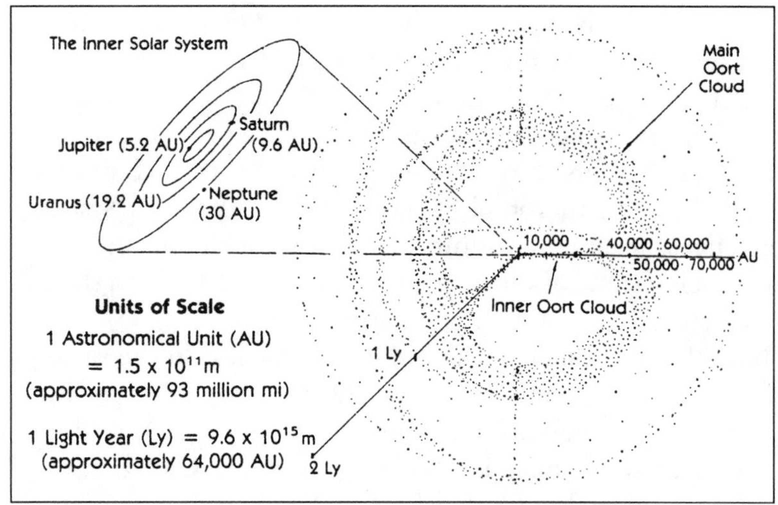

Figure 6.1. A schematic representation of the Oort Cloud.

The typical separation between comet nuclei in the Oort Cloud is probably about 20 AU: very widely spaced indeed. In the main Cloud the orbital periods would range from one to ten million years.

Since the close encounters of Halley's Comet by Soviet and European spacecraft in 1986, a clearer picture of the nature of comet nuclei has begun to emerge. They are estimated to range in size from 0.1 to 10 km in diameter and in mass from 10^{13} to 10^{19} g—between 10 million and 10 trillion metric tons. Though small in comparison to the planets, comet nuclei still contain huge amounts of material.

Comets are thought to be made up of an extremely light, porous aggregation of the ices of various volatile elements and compounds, with a scattering of embedded dust and complex organic molecules. The ratio of dust to gas is estimated to range from 0.7 to 0.85 by mass.

The volatile component is thought to consist chiefly of water ice but also includes CO, CO_2, methane (CH_4), ammonia (NH_3), and a variety of other compounds containing oxygen, sulfur, and nitrogen. The ices are thought to include a high proportion of clathrates, in which other molecules are trapped inside the lattices of the frozen gases. The grains of dust and organic material may be remnants of the interstellar cloud or the condensing solar nebula. A breakdown of the estimated abundances of the chief elemental and chemical constituents of a typical comet is presented in Table 6.1.

Table 6.1. Composition of comet nuclei: estimated abundances and distributions

Elemental Abundances[a]			*Mass & Volume Distribution*[b] *of Principal Components*		
Element	Number (%)	Mass (%)	Component	Mass (%)	Volume (%)
H	43.9	4.2	Silicates	21	8.6
C	6.7	7.7	Carbon (graphite)	6	3.4
N	2.7	3.8	Very Complex	19	21.0
O	40.2	62.5	Organics		
S	1.0	3.1	H_2O	19	27.0
Mg	1.9	4.5	CO	10	13.0
Si	1.8	4.9	Other	25	27.0
Fe	1.6	8.8	Other Volatiles: CO_2, CH_4, N_2, NH_3,		
Ni + Cr	0.1	0.6	HCN, etc.		
Al	—	0.4			

[a] After Delsemme, in Wilkening (ed): *Comets*, p 122.
[b] After Greenberg, in Wilkening, p 157.

The average density of cometary material is estimated to be about 1 to 1.5 g/cm^3—close to that of water (1.0 g/cm^3). This material is thought to be a porous matrix of solid grains and larger particles, with the gaps between them filled with ice. Comet nuclei are likely to be irregular in shape, uncompacted and undifferentiated: For a body under about 10 km in diameter, the force of gravity is simply too weak to affect shape or structure to any significant degree. The aggregate would have a light, very fragile structure resembling that of windblown snow. Both structure and composition are expected to be fairly homogenous throughout, although the surface layers (to a depth of perhaps 10 m) may undergo some alteration due to sublimation of ices, irradiation by cosmic rays and other radiation, and occasional sandblasting from interstellar gas and dust.

This light fragile structure means that the resources present in the comet nuclei will be readily accessible to any human settlers. The porous mixture of dust and ice would offer little mechanical resistance, and the two components could easily be separated by the application of heat. Volatiles could be further refined through fractional distillation while the dust, which has a high content of iron and other ferrous metals, could easily be manipulated with magnetic fields. Little additional crushing or other mechanical processing of the dust would be necessary, and its fine, loose-grained structure would make it ideal for subsequent chemical processing and refining. Comet nuclei thus represent a vast reservoir of easily accessible materials; water, carbon dioxide, ammonia, methane, and a variety of metals and complex organics.

Although comets offer a huge reserve of easily accessible resources for any would-be settlers, they will be useless without a readily available supply of energy. Conditions at those distances from the Sun will be bleak: the Sun will not even be the brightest star in the deep black sky, and the temperature is a bare 10 K. Making the cold, barren ice islands of the comet nuclei habitable will be a formidable task, and energy consumption is likely to be very great. Yet energy will be the scarcest resource in the Oort Cloud.

The size of any comet-based communities will be closely constrained by two factors: the availability of energy sources and the rate of energy consumption. Access to a dependable, long-term energy source will be crucial to the establishment of a viable, self-sufficient settlement. Energy consumption levels will affect both the size and complexity of the economy, the standard of living, and longevity of the community as a whole.

What are some of the potential energy sources likely to be available? Nuclear power—fission—is unlikely. Heavy elements such as uranium will be present in only miniscule amounts, certainly not enough to form the basis for a comfortable, long-term settlement. In addition, fission processes are "dirty" in the sense that they generate a relatively high flux of radioactivity that may be undesirable.

Another potential energy source is the controlled combustion of hydrogen and oxygen, which both occur in abundance in the vast amounts of water ice that makes up about one-fifth of each comet's mass. The catch, of course, is that water must first be hydrolyzed, an energy-consuming process. Settlements closer to the Sun, say within 1000 AU, or those with sufficient surplus energy from other sources, may employ H_2/O_2 reaction cells for some purposes. Hydrogen combustion will probably serve as the major propellant for long-distance travel, but is unsuitable for basic power generation.

There is an alternate means of using hydrogen as an energy source—fusion. It seems reasonable to assume that the technology for fusion employing deuterium, a heavy isotope of hydrogen that fuses relatively easily, will be available by the time settlement of the Oort Cloud begins. Estimates of the ratio of deuterium to simple hydrogen in interstellar gases vary from about 1 in 10,000 to 1 in 100,000. Although rare, for an average-size comet this represents about 50,000 to 100,000 metric tons of deuterium.

This enormous store represents enough energy to support a population of millions for several centuries—but when the supply is gone, those millions will perish. It seems much more likely that Oort Cloud communities will choose to support much smaller populations for much greater lengths of time, husbanding their precious supply of deuterium for perhaps thousands or tens of thousands of years. They may also employ a more efficient alternative fusion pathway involving a mixture of deuterium, tritium (another hydrogen isotope), and helium to extend the lifetime of the available supply.

At some point humans may also learn how to initiate proton fusion and thereby assure a virtually unlimited supply of energy employing simple hydrogen, the most common element in the cosmos. But as yet, only the stars themselves have accomplished this on a large scale.

Finally, there is one alternative renewable source of energy available: starlight. The concept of harvesting starlight to support comet-based communities was first put forward by astrophysicist Eric Jones and anthropologist Ben Finney[2,3]:

> In principle all one needs is a giant mirror to concentrate the thin photon stream. The mirrors would be truly gigantic. . . . At half a parsec [about 1 1/2 light-years] from a Sun-like star the mirror would have to be about 1500 kilometers radius to collect a megawatt (roughly the size of the continental U.S.). Practicality and common sense might well dictate a larger number of much smaller collectors.

Jones and Finney estimate a typical medium-sized comet could supply enough aluminum for mirror surfaces to collect about 300 megawatts (MW) from starlight. If additional metals were used, this capacity could be enhanced somewhat. Jones and Finney estimated per capita power consumption at 0.6 MW, about 30 times the current U.S. rate of 20 to 25 KW per capita; thus the typical population of a comet-based community would be about 500.

The amount of aluminum and other reflective metals in a given comet will set a definite upper limit on the area of mirror surface that can be created, and thus on the population that can be supported by collecting starlight. Comet-based communities closer to the Sun in the inner Oort Cloud will therefore enjoy a higher photon flux and will have more energy available to them, and will be able to support larger populations.

Although the energy supply will be the most important limiting factor for any comet-based settlements, there are a host of other factors that will influence the nature of their economies.

Most of these communities are likely to be small and isolated, with populations of only a few hundred. Such small economic systems are sure to face many limitations and constraints. Many types of tools, specialized pieces of equipment and expert skilled labor will all be in short supply. The economy will essentially be a closed system, especially for the more distant and isolated settlements. For many items and commodities, supply will not be related in any way to need or demand.

The members of these communities will of necessity be very dependent upon one another and are also likely to develop a strong conservation ethic; they will recycle as much as possible. Their relative isolation will encourage self-reliance and cooperation, as well as the pooling of skills, labor, and resources. Small, isolated, tightly closed economies are thus likely to be more communal in their outlook, particularly in regard to resources, power consumption, and the allocation of labor. Larger communities will probably have a wider variety of economic patterns.

Because populations are likely to be small, each individual will be of immense value to the community, representing a pool of knowledge, skills, and experiences, as well as a heavy investment in training and education. It will be necessary for the settlers to become generalists: A small community will simply not have enough people to support a specialized expert in every field. Each person will have to develop a sound working knowledge in many overlapping fields, and consequently will have less time to devote to becoming expert in any one of them. Some specialties may have to be eliminated altogether in very small communities.

Many of these limitations and constraints can likely be alleviated or even eliminated with the aid of sophisticated technology.

The exploration and settlement of the Oort Cloud, the establishment of viable communities in the cold deeps of space, will demand heavy reliance on many different forms of high-technology equipment. A combination of the right tools and skills to use them will be vital.

It seems unlikely that a small band of pioneers will be able to create a secure, comfortable niche in the Oort Cloud without the use of automated systems and artificial intelligence (AI). Such systems will eliminate the need for human intervention at many basic but routine levels of activity, freeing people to apply their skills where they are needed most. Computers and automated systems are skilled tools which can enhance and multiply human capabilities manyfold.

The human residents of the Oort Cloud will control and monitor the operation of a complex array of self-directed systems. Most of the basic comet-mining and materials-processing operations will probably be automated. They will produce stockpiles of refined materials and, at the highest level of complexity, produce many types of finished products.

Artificially intelligent systems will also be essential to the viability of the communities, particularly for small settlements. They will rely heavily on expert systems—sophisticated computer programs that combine an extensive store of information with a powerful decision-making capability for interpreting complex data. They will operate at the level of a human expert that perhaps the community cannot support.

The human members of the community, with their generalized skills and experiences, will be capable of handling all the normal operations and events; the expert systems would serve to supplement and complete the basic suite of skills and abilities required to keep the community healthy.

Because of their dependence on AI systems, residents of the Oort communities will also need to be skilled in the manipulation and application of information. They will have access to the vast sum of human knowledge, but it will be useless to them without sophisticated information processing systems. They will have to become adept at working in cooperation with their AI systems to manage the masses of data available, to sift through it to extract what they need. The use of sophisticated computer-based systems will be a basic skill in every Oort Cloud community, and it seems likely that education will be based in large part on AI systems.

All these factors will have a number of important effects on the shape of the settlement's economy. The distribution of activity will be very different for any Earth-bound economic system.

The primary sector of the economy—the exploitation of natural resources—is likely to be small and almost completely automated. Human involvement will be minimal. The primary sector will consist of two basic activities: energy production and the harvesting of cometary resources. Once the appropriate systems are established, both will be relatively simple activities.

The secondary sector—the transformation of the natural resources—will include refining and processing the raw cometary feedstock, manufacturing, construction and assembly operations, agriculture and food production, and recycling. Again, many of these activities will be highly automated, but closer human supervision will be necessary to tailor these activities to the current needs of the community.

It is the tertiary sector of the economy, support services, that will engage the majority of human skill and attention. It will include operation of the utility and life support systems, maintenance and repair operations, transportation, health care, information processing, storage and retrieval, education and administration, business and commerce.

The settlers will have to choose between many different possible paths for development. Will they allow the community to grow, or should they impose controls on themselves to maintain a small population? Will they want their community to last many years at a low rate of consumption, or will they want to trade communal longevity for a higher rate of resource consumption? The outcome of these decisions will depend primarily on two factors: the available supply of resources and the standard of living that the community desires and will defend.

The average standard of living is likely to be quite comfortable, within the limits of the communities' capabilities. Because of its extreme fragility, the surface of the comet itself will be unsuitable for permanent dwellings; the habitats will probably be free-flying. Physically, they may resemble the Bernal Spheres and O'Neill Cylinders already envisioned for space-based communities in the inner solar system. The most significant difference will be the lack of large window surfaces, since there will be no need to admit sunlight for illumination, which will allow for an increase in the usable surface area inside the habitats.

Communities lacking a large supply of deuterium or those choosing to conserve their supply would locate their habitats at the center of huge arrays of mirrors for the collection of starlight. A variety of social and economic factors suggest the members of such a community, which would number about 500, would be dispersed throughout the array in bands of about 25 persons—a dozen adult men and women and their children.

Each band would tend a mirror farm stretching across perhaps 30,000 km of space, overseeing a complex network of robots and other automated systems responsible for the routine operation and maintenance of the mirror farm. In the event of an emergency requiring human intervention, the settlers would need to be able to reach even the edge of the array quickly, and so will gather the mirrors in tightly packed arrangements.

The individual mirror farms of the separate bands would then be clustered into a vast array supporting the community's entire population, spread out over 150,000 to 200,000 km of space: an immense surface area of ultra-thin metal film centered around the invisible point of the comet nucleus, gathering the faint light of the stars (see Figure 6.2). Communication between bands within the community could easily be maintained by radio and laser.

Despite the limitations of the environment, Oort Cloud communities that choose to grow and develop large economies will have many options. One of the most obvious ways to enhance their resource base will be to create clusters of comet nuclei. Clustering would require the commitment of significant amounts of time, energy and resources, but the potential rewards will ensure that some communities will begin to move additional comets into more convenient orbits.

Given the average separations and relative orbital velocities of comet nuclei in the Cloud, it would take between 5 and 10 years to bring a new comet into a cluster. The energy required represents only about 3 to 5% of the available deuterium supply; clustering

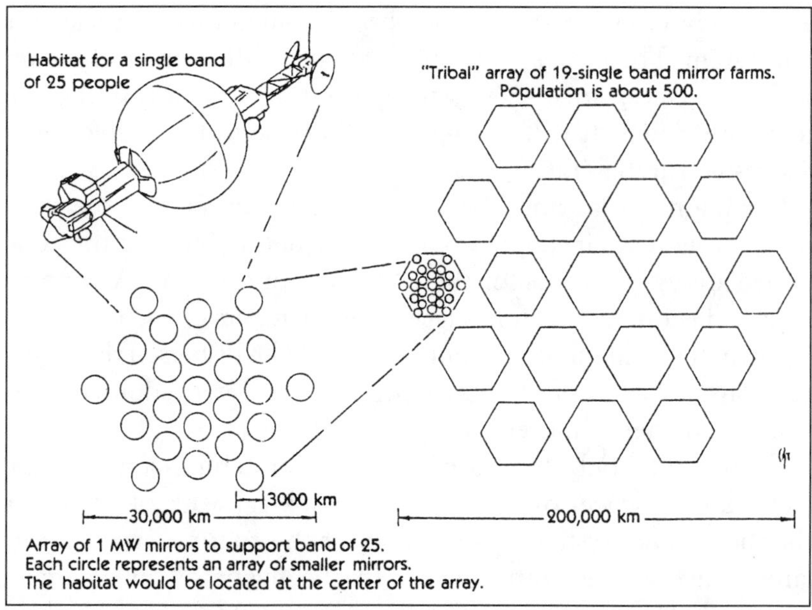

Figure 6.2. Schematic representation of "mirror farm" arrays for harvesting starlight. (Illustration after Ref. 3.)

will be relatively economical once the necessary resources are committed to the project. Clustering will probably be common, if only because large comets will be rare.

Clustering would allow relatively large populations to exist, especially in the inner Oort Cloud, where the photon flux from the Sun will be fairly high and consequent energy production levels will be capable of supporting much larger communities. Jones and Finney have estimated that the largest practical population for a cluster will be about 100,000, when the energy consumed in transport between the dispersed habitats of the cluster begins to strain the reserves of the community. Social factors may also limit the size of large cluster-based communities.

In addition to clustering, there will be other means by which the settlements can enhance their economies. Their isolation in the depths of space will be a relative thing; they will be in constant communication with neighboring communities. The average separation between comets in the Cloud is thought to be a few light-hours; between settlements it will be perhaps a light-day. News, messages, and other information will flow back and forth across the empty space between them.

Some settlements, particularly the larger ones, may engage in some sort of trade, both with the inner system and among themselves. Initially, many communities will need to import those items that they cannot make for themselves. As they develop, they may consider more complex forms of trade; it is certain the decision to expend the time, energy, and resources in long-distance commerce will be a complex cost/benefit calculation.

Items for trade might include specialized technology, bioengineered species specifically tailored for conditions in the Oort Cloud, computer and AI programs, and information itself. Perhaps some communities will specialize within a larger dispersed cluster or bloc of trading communities.

Because of the constraints and limitation imposed by the environment, one primary social concern of the Oort Cloud communities will be the careful regulation of the health and size of their populations.

Until the settlement has developed the skills and resource base to support growth, some form of control will be necessary to limit the size of the population. In very small, isolated populations, even the timing of reproduction may need to be regulated, in order to maintain an appropriate distribution of age and sex.

Unless communities adopt fairly stringent measures, the population will inevitably grow. The members of the settlement will then have to choose between a higher rate of resource consumption, making a commitment to enhancing their resource base, or assisting their excess population in establishing daughter settlements around other comet nuclei.

Both static and growing communities will also need to be concerned with the genetic health of their populations. Within the small, relatively isolated gene pools of the Oort Cloud settlements, population genetics will become a factor that will affect both everyday life and the long-term viability of the community.

Very early on, when a new community is being planned or established, a major concern will be the "founder effect"—the skewing of the genetic composition of a population because its founding members are very few. The danger exists that the founding members of a community may share too high a proportion of deleterious genes that will soon become reinforced in subsequent interbreeding. This problem could be largely eliminated by careful screening during the planning and recruitment stages for a new settlement. New colonists would in part be chosen to maximize genetic variation in the new population, providing a sound base for healthy future growth.

Founding populations can be very low—perhaps as low as 10 or 20 individuals—if the original breeders are genetically diverse and share few common deleterious genes. The negative effects of early inbreeding can also be avoided by social customs or other regulations that prevent bad crosses, particularly among close relatives.

The potential negative effects of inbreeding will remain, however, as the settlement's population grows and becomes more uniform, but will be of major concern only to very small, isolated groups. Both natural and artificial selection will come into play before inbreeding could cause serious damage to the health of the community. In nature, inbreeding often results in a high level of spontaneous abortions and early deaths; natural selection operates to remove the bad crosses from the breeding population. In healthy communities, matings would be structured either by intent or by social custom to minimize the negative effects of inbreeding. It is also important to remember that genetic uniformity need not be a problem provided that any deleterious genes are eliminated from the founding population and that any new negative traits arising by mutation are culled or otherwise prevented from breeding. Genetic engineering techniques may also be employed to maintain a healthy gene pool.

The human consequences of such requirements for the maintenance of the community's genetic health will be great. The social tensions generated by the practice of eugenics and genetic engineering may also be difficult to manage. However, there are other options for communities that wish to avoid negative inbreeding, including outbreeding with other settlements.

Outbreeding has the obvious positive effect of increasing genetic variability. But its practice also serves as a mechanism for complex social interaction as well.

Prior to the terrestrial agricultural revolution, people tended to live within small hunting and gathering bands of about 20 to 30 men, women, and children. It has been noted by various social anthropologists that groups of this size still seem to be the most congenial to humans worldwide in both their private and professional lives. This preference is no doubt part of our physical and social evolutionary heritage.

But humans also tended to form larger social units, gathering into clans or tribes numbering about 500 or so. Normally dispersed as individual bands, the tribes maintained social cohesion through intermarriage. Indeed, the size of such groups is just about the minimum number needed to maintain a healthy diversity within the common gene pool and to avoid inbreeding.

It is possible to anticipate, then, that the dispersed communities of the Oort Cloud may form similar social links. A single community tending an extensive mirror farm as described earlier could form a viable, self-contained breeding population by marriage exchanges between bands. In addition to preserving the genetic health of the community, such exchanges would serve to link the bands into a large, cohesive social unit. Just as dispersed tribes on Earth gathered periodically for important social and religious observances, so too might the dispersed bands of a comet-based settlement gather their entire population on occasion.

Outbreeding would also allow individuals whose reproduction might otherwise be restricted or forbidden to find an alternative, providing an outlet for any tensions that might arise. And if such a place could not be found within the tribe, there is also the possibility of exchanges with other communities around other nearby comets. Such exchanges would be more expensive in terms of time and energy, but would serve to cement social ties between settlements.

The necessity for monitoring gene flow within a given population, along with all the other shaping influences of the deep space environment, will have profound social consequences for the Oort Cloud communities.

Habitat residents will be able to set temperature, humidity, day length, the weather, atmospheric pressure, even the level of gravity according to their collective preference and the limitations of human physiology. They may even choose to live in zero gravity. Lifestyle and social values, the entire "world view" of the Oort Cloud settlers will be very different from those of any terrestrial culture.

Without diurnal or seasonal variations, their sense of time will differ. Their perceptions and use of space may also differ, and the ways in which private and public volumes are used and arranged thereby altered. In a tightly closed artificial environment, attitudes toward clothing and nudity are likely to change radically, as is the concept of privacy.

In personal relationships, love, sex, and mating will all be quite separate. Family structures are likely to be very different when marriage or cohabitation preferences may differ from permissible genetic crosses. Breeding will be much more of a social decision than it is on Earth. Given a basic band-and-tribe social structure, extended families are likely to be common. Communal or collective family arrangements may also be common.

Social, political, and administrative systems will also change, and new ones will arise. They will be shaped not only by the age-old needs and limitations of human social interaction, but also by wholly new factors unique to the deep space environment. Settlers in the Oort Cloud will face the exciting challenge of creating workable societies from whole cloth.

As always, the basic social conflict within these communities will be between the needs and constraints of society as a whole and the personal freedom of individuals. Members of these small, isolated communities will be faced with a variety of constraints.

Restrictions on breeding practices may be imposed by the community in order to maintain a balanced, genetically healthy population. In very small settlements, even the timing of births may be regulated in order to preserve a balanced distribution of male and female, young, middle-aged, and elderly. Communities aiming for a low or static population growth rate may impose strict absolute limits on breeding until the resource base has been developed to support larger numbers.

Similarly, young people born and raised in an Oort Cloud settlement may face fairly tight constraints in their choice of career or vocation. As in all economies, the needs or demands of the community will determine the types of work available; career choices may often be a matter of timing and happenstance. In small communities, where age and gender distributions may have to be carefully controlled, career choices will be limited for the limited number of youths available for apprenticeship: They will be pressured to take the positions that need to be filled as they come of age.

New settlements with undeveloped capabilities, and smaller settlements with few resources or a limited energy supply may also impose some restraints; small, isolated communities will probably be conservative in approving unnecessary expenditures of scarce resources, thus limiting the range of possible private and professional activity.

Social values are likely to have an enormous shaping influence on the types of social systems that develop in the distant Oort Cloud communities. These settlements, perhaps comprised of highly interrelated clans, are likely to place a high value on cooperation, consensus decision making, and compromise. In the hostile and unrelenting deep space environment, where cooperation and mutual interdependence will be crucial to survival, they will feel a strong need to maintain social harmony.

Members of such tightly knit communities will face a variety of social pressures: They will be part of a symbiotic network of duties and obligations. There will be ties to family and to tribe or clan, in addition to the community as a whole. Complex interrelationships will arise when emotional and sexual relations must be separated from breeding, as well as when family and friends emigrate to other habitats and communities. As in Earthbound societies, education, in addition to training each person for the complex task of deep space survival, will probably also serve as a primary means of inculcating the community's social values.

But there are other factors to counterbalance these pressures and constraints, to allow for the preservation of individual freedoms. In a community where every individual represents a heavy investment in education and training, and a valuable pool of badly needed skills and experience, rigid social controls such as ostracism, imprisonment, or capital punishment seem unlikely; a large range of social behavior will have to be tolerated. Coercion would be difficult at best, especially in very small communities with few resources or personnel to spare for "police actions"; nonconformists and dissidents must be allowed to find or to create an acceptable niche within the community. Larger settlements, in which any one individual plays a less vital role, may develop more rigid social structures.

The Oort Cloud communities will need to develop social and political mechanisms to ensure the freedom to express diversity and individual choice, to avoid oppressive measures aimed at enforcing unnecessary conformity to arbitrary community standards, and to eliminate or at least alleviate the negative consequences of community decisions.

It is likely that a wide variety of social systems will develop among the Oort Cloud settlements. In some, social pressures may win out, and a rigid, authoritarian social structure created. But the need for consensus and close cooperation among community residents may help prevent the development of oppressive, highly stratified societies, at least among the smaller settlements. Similarly, the necessities of cooperation and mutual dependence will temper any tendency toward extreme individualism. Individuals will be expected to take responsibility for their actions and their role in the community; both wild individualism and blind obedience to social convention would be frowned upon.

In such a social context, within a culture that values diversity, mutualism, and social harmony, current Western-style democracy may be considered inappropriate. Despite constitutional guarantees, majority rule often enforces homogeneity and suppresses minority viewpoints. Democratic systems, in which individuals are expected to "vote in their own interests," might also foster a divisiveness that small, isolated communities could ill afford.

The smaller band-and-tribe settlement may favor consensus decision making, in which minority and dissident viewpoints can be more easily accommodated. But such systems also have a drawback: Because everyone must agree to the joint decision to reach a consensus, community members may feel pressured to "go along with the group." If the pressures became strong enough, they might foster a dangerous and oppressive homogeneity.

Another communal decision-making system that often appears among communities of closely-related, tribal people is the "hardship-on-no-one" arrangement. In such a system, the emphasis is not so much on the final decision reached as on the consequences of each option. Decisions are often based on finding the option that places the least burden on the least number of individuals, and working to alleviate even those negative results of communal decisions. For example, youths guided toward a career specialty the community deems important might be allowed to pursue secondary specialties of their own choosing.

A drawback to this system as well as for consensus decision-making systems is that they are often very time-consuming processes.

As on Earth, the Oort Cloud communities may choose to deal with some social pressures by displacing them spatially. Nonconformists and dissidents in one band may find a comfortable and rewarding social niche in another habitat within their native tribe. Although a single clustered community would have a pool of shared communal values, each habitat within the settlement might have its own individual system, offering enough diversity to accommodate and alleviate most social frictions. As a last resort, migration between settlements would provide a social safety valve.

It thus seems likely that a variety of social systems would arise among the Cloud settlements. They will have to respond to numerous needs and demands, seeking to find a balance between maintaining a stable, functional society and personal freedom for individuals.

The size of the community will be an important factor in its social development. The larger Oort Cloud settlements will probably offer a wider range of social forms. They may be able to accommodate more competition and divisiveness. Large communities, however, are also difficult to administer by consensus, and may employ a form of electronic democracy. Clustering, trade, and the development of the settlement's resource base and capabilities would create opportunities for the creation of more diverse and complex societies. A mosaic of many different social forms, distributed throughout the settlement, seems possible.

But even the largest of the Oort Cloud communities will be quite small in comparison to the societies of billions that will develop in the inner solar system. As the relatively compact inner core of the system is developed, it will become more tightly integrated socially and economically, more centralized, and its culture more homogeneous. Although it may take some centuries, it is likely that mass cultures with populations of billions will eventually develop.

The small, dispersed communities of the Oort Cloud will remain largely independent of the inner core government and societies. Their potential for diversity may offer a refuge for dissident groups seeking to leave the mass societies of the inner solar system.

Just as the relative isolation of the Oort Cloud settlements from the inner system and from each other will foster social divergence and cultural diversity, so, too, will it create the conditions necessary for biological divergence and evolutionary change. As we know from terrestrial experience, reproductive isolation fosters such change—as Charles Darwin observed when he visited the Galapagos Islands as a young man. Diversity also fosters adaptive radiation—the opening and exploitation of new niches in the environment.

Many factors are likely to encourage human evolutionary diversity in the Oort Cloud. Despite all efforts, the founder effect and random drift will cause some changes in the small isolated gene pools. Fortuitous beneficial mutations may be retained and encouraged to spread, and perhaps enhanced by artificial means. Eugenics and genetic engineering are likely to be well integrated into the social and economic life of the settlements, both as a means of maintaining a healthy gene pool and in the production of goods and trade items. Bioengineered products may be common.

Social values will also be very different, and the distant Oort Cloud communities will feel much less keenly the social, cultural and governmental pressures that might prevent biological experimentation among the inner system cultures. Their environment and lives will be very different; they may choose to remake themselves in their own image, to adapt themselves to the needs of living in deep space.

Estimates of the time required for natural selection to produce a new species of human being range upward toward a million years. However, in the small, isolated gene pools of the Oort Cloud settlements, perhaps encouraged by directed breeding practices and human genetic engineering, it would not take long for any chances to become widespread. Minor changes might take a few generations—perhaps a century—to become entrenched. Major structural or biochemical alterations would probably be attempted more slowly, on a scale of many hundreds or thousands of years. But it is clear that a new species of genus *Homo* could appear within about 10,000 years.

The exploration and settlement of the far reaches of the Oort Cloud will also have a profound effect on the course of human migration to other star systems. Simply reaching the Oort Cloud and establishing viable, long-term settlements there will spur the development of the technology required for interstellar flight. Although the propulsion systems needed for journeys of tens of hundreds of light-years will differ from those used to travel only 1 or 2, the opening of the Oort Cloud will serve as the proving ground for such systems, as well as the development of closed artificial ecosystems. The social experiments of the Cloud communities may also play an important role in starship design.

Though many interstellar missions may be launched by the large and wealthy inner solar system cultures, others may depart from construction sites or launch points in the far reaches of Sol's Oort Cloud, which stretches out to perhaps 2 light-years—a significant head start. Such ships may travel directly across the deep oceans of space to reach other stars, but others may visit way stations during their journey: comets drifting in interstellar space.[4]

Estimates of the total amount of material ejected from the solar system during its formation and subsequent evolution range from as low as 5 to 25 times the mass of the Earth up to 100 or even 1000 Earth masses. Presumably, other stars would produce roughly similar numbers of rogue comets. Interstellar space should be strewn with small, isolated islands.

Distances between these drifting islands are difficult to estimate. They may be no more widely spaced than the comets of the Oort Cloud—about 20 AU. Other estimates range up to hundreds of thousands of AU between these wandering interstellar comets.

Some of these interlopers are bound to be found within Sol's own Oort Cloud, working their way free of the Sun's grip, at perhaps one in every several thousand. Relative velocities between solar and interstellar comets will be low, and it will be tempting for Oort Cloud residents to hitch a ride outward—perhaps farther out into the permanent Cloud, perhaps out into interstellar space. Drifting outward at about 10 km/s or about 2 AU per year, they will make slow progress indeed. In 50,000 years they will be halfway to the nearest stars. But by then they will be wholly adapted to life in interstellar space and will perhaps not be too concerned with visiting other star systems.

One could imagine the human species slowly spreading throughout the galaxy in this way, but it seems more likely humanity will move from star to star by fast ship, followed by slowly expanding waves of comet-based settlements meeting and overlapping in the voids between the settled stars.

Other, more daring Oort Cloud communities may choose to take their home comet with them. If the slow outward drift seems too slow to them, and fast ships too expensive, they may attempt to launch themselves out of the solar system via a gravity-assist maneuver close to the Sun.[5]

Large rocket engines burning hydrogen and oxygen, or perhaps a mass driver, could be used to dissipate the comet's orbital velocity using only a fraction of the comet's resources. During the long fall toward the Sun, the adventurers could use the rapidly increasing flux of solar energy to produce huge stores of hydrogen, to be consumed in fuel cells to provide power during the long interstellar cruise. The mirror farms or other solar power collectors would also serve to shield the comet nucleus from the Sun.

After curving around Sol, the comet would leave the system with a velocity of 100 to 150 km/s, or about 1 light-year every 2000 years. Travel times between star systems would be on the order of 10,000 years—far shorter than that of drifting "wild" comets. During the interstellar journey the settlers would live as they had in the Oort Cloud, relying on their comet's stock of deuterium or on hydrogen produced when close to the sun. In the target system, a small band of colonists would be dropped off aboard habitats constructed during the long cruise, before rounding the new star and heading off toward a new destination.

It thus seems likely that human expansion into the comet archipelago of the distant reaches of the Oort Cloud will only be the first step toward expansion to other star systems. Comet-based settlements will be humanity's stepping stones to the stars, across the far-flung islands in the deep ocean of interstellar space.

Chapter 7

Dr. Robert L. Forward

Alien Life Between Here and the Stars

Life is ubiquitous. We find it in every nook and cranny Earth possesses. One goal of space exploration is to find life on some body other than Earth. Using our robot proxies, we have explored some of the more likely places for life in the solar system, but presently, it appears as though there is no alien life in the solar system. If this is found to be true, then the usual conclusion is that the nearest alien life will be found on an Earth-like planet around some distant star. It is possible, however, that alien life exists *between* here and the stars.

Beyond the planets lie the comets. Some of them are so large that even though they have ice-covered surfaces like comets, they have rocky cores like asteroids. They can be considered "cometoids"—half comet and half asteroid. In 1992, a large cometoid was found in the Kuiper Belt with an orbit at 42 AU, far beyond Neptune, which orbits at 30 AU. Since then many more cometoids have been observed. The Kuiper Comet Belt merges into the Oort Comet Cloud, a spherical collection of ice-covered bodies loosely bound to the Sun, extending to the nearest stars.

In the previous chapter on human exploration and settlement of the Oort Cloud, Richard P. Terra discusses the difficulty of living in a region of space far from any source of light. What could be a viable source of energy out in those cold depths? One answer is to convert the metals in a cometoid into large thin-film mirrors to collect starlight. Terra doesn't believe that nuclear fission energy is viable, but the most common nuclear fuel, uranium 235, is relatively abundant and is found in nearly all rocks. In comet ice, where most of the volatiles have evaporated away, the mass abundance of uranium 235 is about one part per billion. That means, in a comet 1000 meters in diameter, with a mass of a billion tons, there is a *ton* of uranium 235!

There are other sources of energy in comet ice. The ice is continually bombarded by high speed cosmic rays that create ionized atoms known as free radicals. On Earth, where the average temperature is near 290° above absolute zero, these free radicals quickly recombine, releasing their energy as heat. In the Oort Cloud, where the average temperature is 20° above absolute zero, the free radicals remain frozen in the ice, ready to release their energy. Also, the grains of dirt embedded in the ice contain many radioisotopes that emit charged particles called alpha and beta particles. These also create free radicals within the ice. The problem with these Oort Cloud energy sources is that, like starlight, the energy is spread out over a large volume, making it difficult to collect. The method for collecting starlight is obvious—produce large mirrors. The methods for collecting uranium 235, radioisotopes, and free radicals are not as obvious.

It is unrealistic to expect human beings to power an Oort Cloud civilization by collecting these alternate sources of energy, but the right species of alien could thrive and reproduce on these energy sources. For my novel[1] *Camelot 30K*, I created an alien species called the keracks—intelligent, civilized creatures the size and shape of a crawfish—living on a cometoid they call Ice (of course!).

Because the cometoid has a near vacuum for its atmosphere and a surface temperature of 30 K, or 30° above absolute zero, I raised the internal pressure of the keracks to five atmospheres and their body temperature to 70 K. To hold the pressure differential, I designed them with strong boron carbide carapaces. For their blood I chose F_2O—difluorine oxide—a yellow-brown liquid that melts at 49 K and boils at 128 K, so it is liquid at kerack body temperature. This fluid is explosive when heated, which is put to good use in the story.

Next, I needed a scientifically plausible method of extracting and concentrating the dilute energy sources. I designed the kerack "cities" along the lines of an ant colony. Like ants, the keracks are merely specialized "units" of the "city organism." The keracks are the motiles that direct and tend the other units, and also collect and shape the materials that are gathered into the city. There are other specialized units; including a fungus that spreads through the ice, obtaining energy from the free radicals and extracting and concentrating such nutrients as radioisotopes and metals. There are iceworms that eat this fungus, further concentrating the nutrients and elements, which they can separate by isotopic mass. These iceworms are the primary "meat" source for the keracks. There are multiberry plants which concentrate metals and inorganic compounds, again separated into different isotopes. There are large beasts of burden, called heullers, that perform the major excavations and also supply meat. Then there is the Queen, whose task it is to lay eggs. The alien equivalent of DNA in these eggs contains the prescription for each different unit. What the larvae become when they hatch depends on what they are fed. Almost all the heavy elements that pass through the "belly-button" mouths of the keracks are excreted, except for one—which is gathered into a metal ball in their midsection, called the "soul." The soul of each kerack consists of pure uranium 235. The major energy source of each "city" is the slow nuclear fission of the uranium in each kerack soul. The "city" is a living nuclear reactor! The boron in the kerack shells is pure boron 10. When boron 10 captures a neutron, it fissions into an alpha particle and a lithium-7 nucleus, releasing energy. Thus, it converts nuclear energy in the form of free neutrons into heat to keep the kerack body warm.

At the time of "fruition" of the city organism, the keracks produce the gamete units needed for reproduction of the species, sexually cross-combine them, and transform them into spores, which are then scattered into space so that the species can find new cometoids on which to grow. For small cometoids, the high pressure inside the kerack bodies squirts the spores to escape velocity. For larger cometoids, the explosive power of the kerack blood drives the spores into space. For extremely large cometoids, an even more powerful explosive force is available. . . .

If I, a mere human, can, in a few months, design an alien life form that could live and reproduce in the Kuiper Comet Belt, then Nature, given billions of years, can certainly create even better examples. Hence, when we venture out to explore the comets, we should be prepared to be surprised.

The comets lie at one end of the mass spectrum. Astronomers now have a good idea of the mass distribution of objects in deep space. There are many small objects such as comets and a few large objects such as galactic black holes. From these statistics, astronomers estimate that there are moderate numbers of medium-sized objects like cometoids, planetoids, gas giants, and those unlit substars called "brown dwarfs."

A brown dwarf is a massive body that is bigger than Jupiter and smaller than a star. It has been estimated[2] that there should be *dozens* of brown dwarfs between here and the stars. All are potential targets for precursor interstellar probes, for there may be life forms on them. The outer cloud layer of a brown dwarf is cold; the central core is hot. Somewhere between the cold surface and the hot center lies a region where water is a liquid. On Jupiter and Saturn, this region is down in the third cloud deck, at a pressure of 5 to 10 atm, where the clouds are composed of water drops.

Carl Sagan has written many papers[3] in which he not only describes, but also actually "designs" various life forms that could reproduce in the darkness under the cloud decks of the gas giant planets in the solar system. He has designed "sinkers" that are carried upward by convection currents when they are young and small in diameter, but then begin to sink as they mature and grow larger. As long as they have time to reproduce new small young before they fall down to depths where the temperatures are so hot that they are "pyrolized" (fried to a carbon crisp), then they are a viable life form.

Sagan also describes "floaters" that are large enough to use hydrogen-filled gas bladders that allow them to float in the slightly more dense atmosphere of 94% hydrogen and 6% helium. The floaters feed off the sinkers. Sagan also describes "hunters" that feed off of both the floaters and sinkers. The hunters could be huge "air whales" the size of an Earth whale, perhaps even as large as a city or state. (This sounds interesting; I think I'll write a book about an intelligent air whale on Saturn that is as big as Central Park.) As the source of energy for his air creatures, Sagan mostly assumed that some photocatalytic process was used, either chemical photosynthesis inside a sinker or photoproduction of energetic molecules within the atmosphere. He also designed life forms that don't need sunlight and which could live off of energetic molecules welling up from the depths of the planet. Ethane, for example, has an excess of free energy compared to methane, which is the most common carbon molecule at equilibrium within the atmosphere. The giant red spot on Jupiter is evidence that there are giant upwellings of exotically colored unknown compounds on large gas giants.

We know of life forms here on Earth that don't require sunlight to thrive and reproduce. These are found in the hydrothermal volcanic vent fields along the Mid-Ocean Ridge. In those vent fields are mineral-rich springs of super-hot water supporting cases of life: long tube worms, miniature crabs, and blizzards of bacteria, all surviving, not on sunlight, but the chemical energy in the hot minerals and energetic chemical compounds, such as hydrogen sulfide, gushing from the vent springs.

The tube worms are the most alien lifeform that dwell near the hydrothermal vents under Earth's oceans. They have no mouths or digestive tracts. Instead, they have a symbiotic relationship with sulfur-eating bacteria living inside a sac within the interior of their bodies. These worms have gill-like plumes on the portion of their bodies that extends from their protective shells. Specialized blood in these plumes extracts hydrogen sulfide and carbon dioxide from the spring water, and carries them to the sac containing the symbiotic bacteria. The bacteria oxidize the hydrogen sulfide with the carbon dioxide to produce organic carbon, which the tube worm then uses to build the hydrocarbon molecules it needs.

If these alien creatures can exist and grow in the dark hydrothermal vent fields in the ocean of Earth, then similar alien creatures could exist and grow in the dark hydrothermal vent fields in oceans on brown planetoids between here and the stars.

We know the stars exist—we can see them. They are calling to us. But they are far, far away, and the journey to the planetoids they harbor and nurture with their light is a long one. One day we will go there and search for alien life.

We do not know if there are suitable abodes for alien life *between* here and the stars, since we haven't been able to see any planetoids or brown dwarf substars *yet*. But, as we take our first baby steps on that long journey to Alpha Centauri, perhaps we can stop along the way at one of these potential abodes for alien life, and paddle around in the clouds and oceans to see if we can scare up something interesting to talk to.

Part Three

Creating New Worlds

Chapter 8

Robert M. Zubrin and Christopher P. McKay

Terraforming Mars

Not so long ago, the subject of human voyages to the Moon was the domain of science fiction. Today, lunar expeditions are a subject for historians, and manned Mars exploration the province of hard-headed engineers. A great many people now accept the idea that, in the not too distant future, humanity will have a permanently staffed base on Mars, or even a number of large settlements. However, the prospect of drastically changing the planet's temperature and atmosphere toward more Earth-like conditions, in other words "terraforming" Mars, still seems to the large majority to be either sheer fantasy or at best a technological challenge for the far distant future.

But is this pessimistic point of view correct? Despite the fact that Mars today is a cold, dry, and probably lifeless planet, it has all the elements required to support life: water, carbon and oxygen (as carbon dioxide), and nitrogen. The physical aspects of Mars—its gravity, rotation rate, and axial tilt—are close enough to those of Earth to be acceptable and it is not too far from the Sun to be made inhabitable.

In fact, recent computational studies utilizing climate models suggest that it could be possible to make Mars habitable with foreseeable technology. The essence of the situation is that while Mars' CO_2 atmosphere has only about 1% the pressure of the Earth's at sea level, it is believed that there are reserves of CO_2 frozen in the south polar cap and adsorbed within the soil sufficient to thicken the atmosphere to the point where its pressure would be about 30% that of Earth. The way to get this gas to emerge is to heat the planet. In fact, the warming and cooling of Mars that occurs each Martian year as the planet cycles between its nearest and furthest positions from the Sun, in its slightly elliptical orbit, cause the atmospheric pressure on Mars to vary by plus or minus 25% compared to its average value on a seasonal basis.

We cannot, of course, move Mars to a warmer orbit. However, we do know another way to heat a planet, through an artificially induced greenhouse effect that traps the Sun's heat within the atmosphere. Such an atmospheric greenhouse could be created on Mars in at least three different ways. One way would be to set up factories on Mars to produce very powerful artificial greenhouse gasses such as halocarbons (CFCs) and release them into the atmosphere. Another way would be to use orbital mirrors or other large-scale power sources to warm selected areas of the planet, such as the south polar cap, to release large reservoirs of the native greenhouse gas, CO_2, which may be trapped there in frozen or adsorbed form. Finally natural greenhouse gasses more powerful than CO_2 (but much less so than halocarbons) such as ammonia or methane could be imported to Mars in large quantities if asteroidal objects rich with such volatiles in frozen form should prove to exist in the outer solar system.

Each of these methods of planetary warming would be enhanced by large amounts of CO_2 from the polar cap and from the soil that would be released as a result of the induced temperature rise. This CO_2 would add massively to the greenhouse effect being created directly, speeding and multiplying the warming process.

The Mars atmosphere/regolith greenhouse effect system is thus one with a built-in positive feedback. The warmer it gets, the thicker the atmosphere becomes; and the thicker the atmosphere becomes the warmer it gets. In the following sections, we'll show how this system can be modeled, and present the results of our calculations using such a model. Our results give very strong support to the belief that humans will be able to effect radical improvements in the habitability of the Martian environment in the course of the twenty-first century.

EQUATIONS FOR MODELING THE MARTIAN SYSTEM

An equation for estimating the mean temperature on the surface of Mars as a function of the CO_2 atmospheric pressure and the solar constant is given by McKay and Davis[1] as:

$$T_{mean} = 213.5(S^{0.25}) + 20(1 + S)P^{0.5} \quad (1)$$

where T_{mean} is the mean planetary temperature in Kelvin, S is the amount of solar output, where that of the present day Sun = 1, and P is the atmospheric pressure at Mars's mean surface elevation, given in bars. (One bar is what flatlanders believe is normal atmospheric pressure, 14.7 psi. Since people living in the fetid swamps near such major capitals as Washington, London, and Paris are influential in such things, this bizarre unit has become a standard.)

Since the atmosphere is an effective means of heat transport from the equator to the pole, we estimate:

$$T_{pole} = T_{mean} - 75(S^{0.25})/(1 + 5P) \quad (2)$$

We further assume, based upon a rough approximation to observed data, that:

$$T_{max} = T_{equator} = 1.1T_{mean} \quad (3)$$

and that the global temperature distribution is given by:

$$T(\Theta) = T_{max} = (T_{max} - T_{pole})\sin^{1.5}\Theta \quad (4)$$

where Θ is the latitude (north or south).

Equations (1) through (4) give the temperature on Mars as a function of CO_2 pressure. However, as mentioned above, the CO_2 pressure on Mars is itself a function of the temperature. There are three reservoirs of CO_2 on Mars: the atmosphere, dry ice in the polar caps, and gas adsorbed in the soil. The interaction of the polar cap reservoirs with the atmosphere is well understood and is given simply by the relationship between the vapor pressure of CO_2 and the temperature at the poles. This is given by the vapor pressure curve for CO_2, which is approximated by:

$$P = 1.23 \times 10^7\{\exp(-3170/T_{pole})\} \qquad (5)$$

So long as there is CO_2 in both the atmosphere and the cap, equation (5) gives an exact answer to what the CO_2 atmospheric pressure will be as a function of polar temperature. However, if the polar temperature should rise to a point where the vapor pressure is much greater than that which can be produced by the mass in the cap reservoir (between 50 and 100 mb), then the cap will disappear and the atmosphere will be regulated by the soil reservoir.

The relationship between the soil reservoir, the atmosphere, and the temperature is not known with precision. An educated guess is given in parametric form in reference 1 as:

$$P = \{CM_a\exp(T/T_d)\}^{3.64} \qquad (6)$$

where M_a is the amount of gas (in bars) adsorbed in the soil, C is a constant set so that equation (6) will reflect known Martian conditions, and T_d is the characteristic energy required for release of gas from the soil (the "desorption temperature"). Equation (6) is essentially a variation of a well-known law for the change in chemical equilibrium with temperature, and so there is fair confidence that its general form is correct. However, the value of T_d is unknown and probably will remain so until after human exploration of Mars. While we don't know what the right value for T_d is, we can bracket the problem by varying T_d from 15 to 40 K (the lower the value of T_d the easier things are for prospective terraformers). Then we use the global temperature distribution given by equation (4) to integrate equation (6) over the surface of the planet to give us a global "soil pressure." This gives a reasonably accurate quasi 2-dimensional view of the atmosphere/regolith equilibrium problem in which most of the adsorbed CO_2 is distributed to the planet's colder regions. Thus, in our model, regional (in the sense of latitude) temperature changes, especially in the near-polar regions, can have as important a bearing on the atmosphere/regolith interaction as changes in the planet's mean temperature.

RESULTS OF CALCULATIONS

In Figure 8.1 we see the results of our model when applied to the situation at Mars' south polar cap, where it is believed that enough CO_2 may be held frozen as dry ice to give Mars an atmosphere on the order of 50 to 100 mbar. We have plotted the polar temperature as a function of the pressure, in accord with equations (1) and (2), and the vapor pressure as a function of the polar temperature, in accord with equation (5). There are two equilibrium points, labeled A and B, where the values of P and T are mutually consistent. However, A is a stable equilibrium, while B is unstable. This can be seen by examining the dynamics of the system wherever the two curves do not coincide. Whenever the temperature curve lies above the vapor pressure curve, the system will move to the right, that is, toward increased temperature and pressure; this would represent a runaway greenhouse effect. Whenever the pressure curve lies above the temperature curve, the system will move to the left, that is, temperatures and pressure will both drop in a runaway icebox effect. Mars today is at point A, with 6 mbar of pressure and a temperature of about 147 K at the pole.

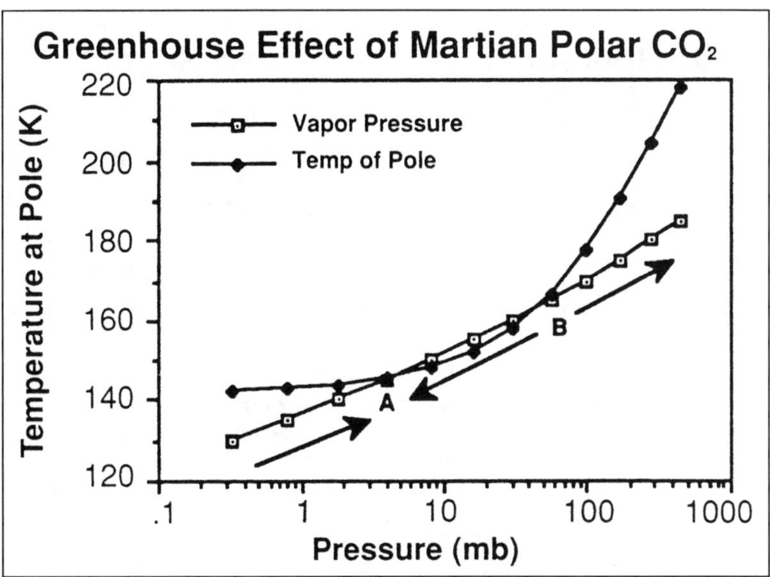

Figure 8.1. Mars polar cap/atmosphere dynamics. Current equilibrium is at point A. Raising polar temperatures by 4 K would drive equilibria A and B together, causing runaway heating that would lead to the elimination of the cap.

Now consider what would happen if someone artificially increased the temperature of the Martian pole by several degrees K. As the temperature is increased, points A and B would move toward each other until they met. If the temperature increase were 4 K, the temperature curve would be moved upward on the graph sufficiently so that it would lie above the vapor pressure curve everywhere. The result would be a runaway greenhouse effect that would cause the entire pole to evaporate, perhaps in less than a decade. Once the pressure and temperature have moved past the current location point B, Mars will be in a runaway greenhouse condition even without artificial heating, so if later the heating activity were discontinued the atmosphere would remain in place.

As the polar cap evaporates, the dynamics of the greenhouse effect caused by the reserves of CO_2 held in the Martian soil come into play. These reserves exist primarily in the high-latitude regions, and by themselves are estimated to be enough to give Mars a 400-mbar atmosphere. We can't get them all out, however, because as they are forced out of the ground by warming, the soil becomes an increasingly effective "dry sponge" acting to hold them back. The dynamics of this system are shown in Figure 8.2, in which we

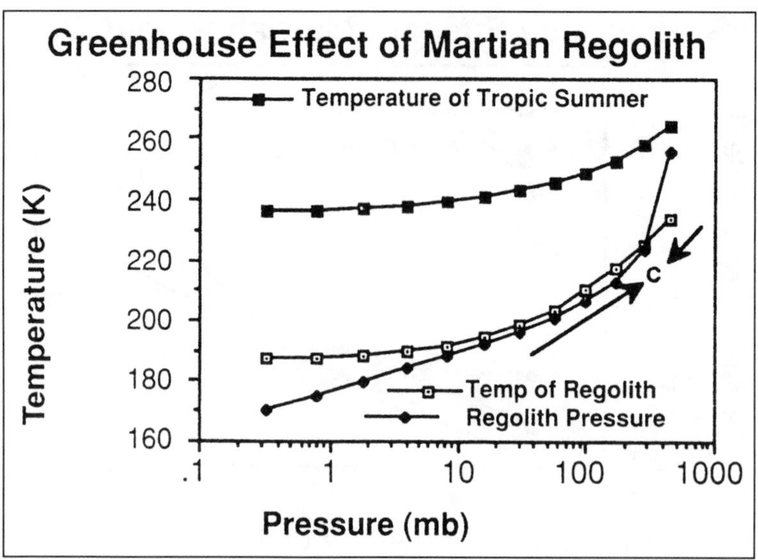

Figure 8.2. Mars regolith/atmosphere dynamics under conditions of T_d = 20 with a volatile inventory of 500 mb of CO_2.

assume $T_d = 20$, current polar reserves of 100 mb, and regolith reserves of 394 mb, and graph the pressure on the planet as a function of the regolith temperature, T_{reg}, where T_{reg} is the average of the planet's temperature with different regions weighted in accordance with how much adsorbed gas they can hold at their own local temperature.

Since T_{reg} is a function of the temperature distribution and T_{mean}, it is ultimately just a function of the pressure, and thus $T_{reg}(P)$ can also be graphed. The result is a set of T(P) curves and P(T) curves, whose crossing points reflect stable or unstable equilibrium, just as in the case of the polar cap analysis.

It can be seen in Figure 8.2 that the atmosphere soil system under the chosen assumption of $T_d = 20$ K has only 1 equilibrium point, which is stable, and which will be overrun by the pressure generated by the vaporized polar cap. Thus, by the time the process is brought to a halt, an atmosphere with a total pressure of about 300 mbar, or 4.4 psi, can be brought into being. Also shown in Figure 8.2 is the day-night average temperature that will result in Mars's tropical regions (T_{max}) during summertime. It can be seen that the 273 K freezing point of water will be approached. With the addition of modest ongoing artificial greenhouse efforts, it can be exceeded.

The assumption of $T_d = 20$ is optimistic, however, and the location of the equilibrium convergence point (point C in Figure 8.2) is very sensitive to the value chosen for T_d. In Figure 8.3 we show what happens if values of $T_d = 25$ and $T_d = 30$ are assumed. In these cases, the convergence point moves from 300 mb at $T_d = 20$ to 31 and 16 mb for $T_d = 25$ and $T_d = 30$, respectively. (The value of the T_{reg} curve in Figure 8.3 was calculated under the assumption of $T_d = 25$; it varies from this value by a degree or two for $T_d = 20$ or 30.) Such extraordinary sensitivity of the final condition to the unknown value of T_d may appear at first glance to put the entire viability of the terraforming concept at risk. However, in Figure 8.3 we also show (dotted line) the situation if artificial greenhouse methods are employed to maintain T_{reg} at a temperature 10 K above those produced by the CO_2 outgassing itself. It can be seen that drastic improvements in the final T and P values are effected for the $T_d = 25$ and 30 cases, with all three cases converging upon final

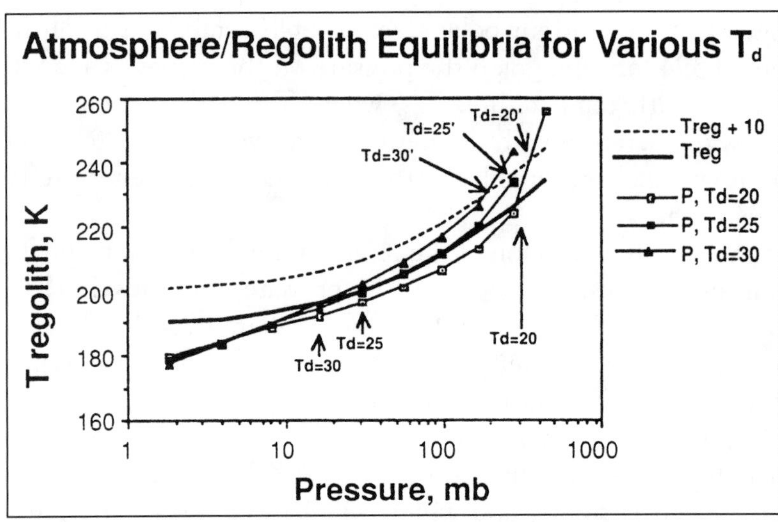

Figure 8.3. An induced 10 K rise in regolith temperature can counter the effect of T_d variations. Data shown assumes a planetary volatile inventory of 500 mb CO_2.

states with Mars possessing atmospheres with several hundred mb of pressure.

In Figures 8.4–8.7 we show the convergence condition pressure and maximum seasonal average temperature in the Martian tropics

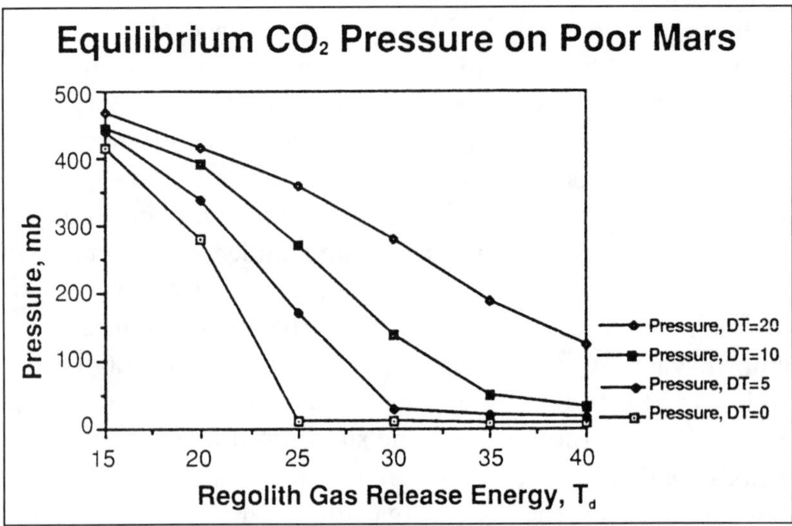

Figure 8.4. Equilibrium pressure reached on Mars with a planetary volatile inventory of 500 mb CO_2 after 50 mb polar cap has been evaporated. DT (ΔT in text) is artificially imposed sustained temperature rise.

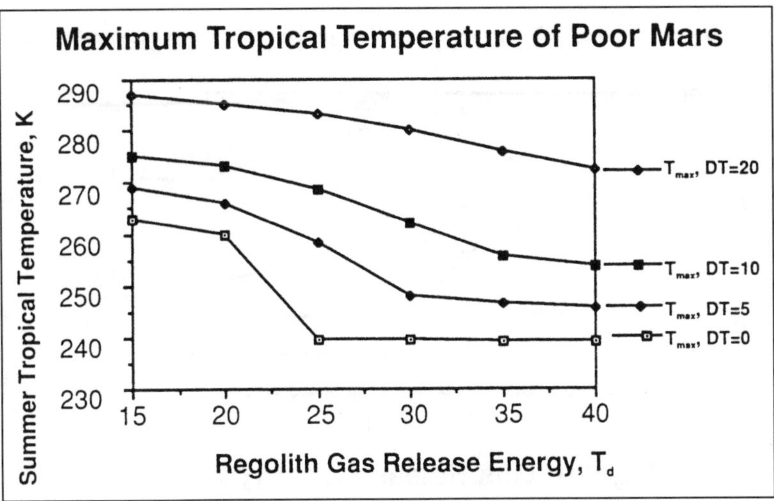

Figure 8.5. Equilibrium maximum seasonal (diurnal average) temperature reached on Mars with a planetary volatile inventory of 500 mb CO_2 after 50 mb polar cap has been evaporated.

resulting in either a "poor" Mars, possessing a total supply of 500 mb of CO_2 (50 mb of CO_2 in the polar cap and 444 mb in the regolith), or a "rich" Mars possessing 1000 mb of CO_2 (100 mb in the polar cap and 894 mb in the regolith). Different

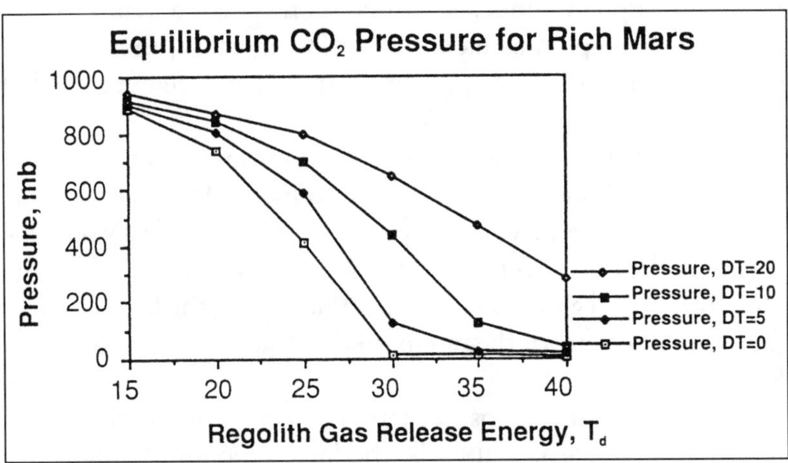

Figure 8.6. Equilibrium pressure reached on Mars with a planetary volatile inventory of 1000 mb CO_2 after 100 mb polar cap has been evaporated.

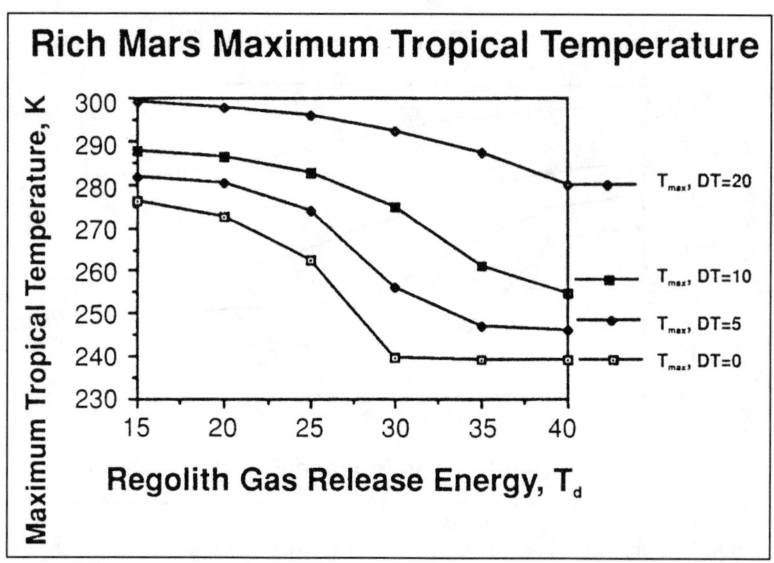

Figure 8.7. Equilibrium maximum seasonal temperature (diurnal average) reached on Mars with a planetary volatile inventory of 1000 mb CO_2 after 100 mb polar cap has been evaporated.

curves are shown under the assumptions that either no sustained greenhouse effort is mounted after the initial polar cap release, or that continued efforts are employed to maintain the planet's mean temperature at a ΔT of 5, 10, or 20° above the value produced by the CO_2 atmosphere alone. It can be seen that if a sustained effort is mounted to keep an artificial ΔT of 20° in place, then a tangible atmosphere and acceptable pressures can be produced even if T_d has a pessimistic value of 40 K.

The important conclusion to be drawn from this analysis is that while the final conditions on a terraformed Mars may be highly sensitive to the currently unknown value of the regolith's outgassing energy, T_d, they are even more sensitive to the level of sustained artificially induced greenhousing, ΔT. Put simply, the final conditions of the atmosphere/regolith system on a terraformed Mars are *controllable*.

Once significant regions of Mars rise above the freezing point of water on at least a seasonal basis, the large amounts of water frozen into the soil as permafrost would begin to melt, and eventually flow out into the dry riverbeds of Mars. Water vapor is also a very effective greenhouse gas, and since the vapor pressure of water on Mars would rise enormously under such circumstances, the reappearance of liquid water on the Martian surface would add to the avalanche of self-accelerating effects all contributing to the rapid warming of Mars. The seasonal availability of liquid water is also the key factor in allowing the establishment of natural ecosystems on the surface of Mars.

The dynamics of the regolith gas-release process are only approximately understood, and the total available reserves of CO_2 won't be known until human explorers journey to Mars to make a detailed assessment, so these results must be regarded as approximate and uncertain. Nevertheless, it is clear that the positive feedback generated by the Martian CO_2 greenhouse system greatly reduces the amount of engineering effort that would otherwise be required to transform the red planet. In fact, since the amount of a greenhouse gas needed to heat a planet is roughly proportional to the square of the temperature change required, driving Mars into a runaway greenhouse with an artificial 5 K temperature rise only requires about 1% the engineering effort that would be needed if the entire 50 K rise had to be engineered by brute force. The question we now examine is how such a 5 K global temperature rise could be induced.

METHODS OF ACCOMPLISHING GLOBAL WARMING ON MARS

The three most promising options for inducing the required temperature rise to produce a runaway greenhouse on Mars appear to be the use of orbital mirrors to change the heat balance of the south polar cap (thereby causing its CO_2 reservoir to vaporize), the importation of ammonia-rich objects from the outer solar system, and the production of artificial halocarbon (CFC) gases on the Martian surface. We'll look at each of these in turn. It may be, however, that synergistic[2] combination of several such methods may yield better results than any one of them used alone.

ORBITING MIRRORS

While the production of a space-based sunlight-reflecting device capable of warming the entire surface of Mars to terrestrial temperatures is theoretically possible,[3] the engineering challenges involved in such a task place such a project well outside the technological horizon of this article. A much more practical idea would be to construct a more modest mirror capable of warming a limited area of Mars by a few degrees. As shown by the data in Figure 8.1, a 5°-K temperature rise imposed at the pole should be sufficient to cause the evaporation of the CO_2 reservoir in the south polar cap. Based on the total amount of solar energy required to raise the black-body temperature of a given area a certain number of degrees above the polar value of 150 K, it turns out that a space-based mirror with a radius of 125 km could reflect enough sunlight to raise the entire area south of 70° south latitude by 5 K. If made of solar sail-type aluminized Mylar material with a density of 4 tonnes/km^2, such a sail would have a mass of 200,000 tonnes. Many ships of this size are currently sailing the Earth's oceans. Thus, while this is too large to consider launching from Earth, if space-based manufacturing techniques are available its construction in space out of asteroidal or Martian moon material is a serious option. The total amount of energy required to process the materials for such a reflector would be about 120 MWe-years, which could be readily provided by a set of 5-MWe nuclear reactors such as are now being considered for use in piloted nuclear electric spacecraft. Interestingly, if stationed near Mars, such a device would not have to orbit the planet. Rather, solar light pressure could be made to balance the planet's gravity, allowing it to hover as a "statite"[4] with its power output trained constantly at the polar region. For the sail density assumed, the required operating altitude would be 214,000 km. The statite reflector concept and the required mirror size to produce a given polar temperature rise is shown in Figures 8.8 and 8.9.

If the value of T_d is lower than 20 K, then the release of the polar CO_2 reserves by themselves could be enough to trigger the

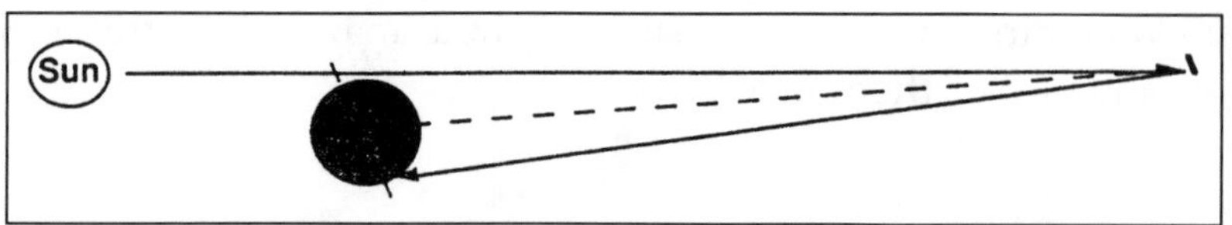

Figure 8.8. Solar sails of 4 tonnes/km^2 density can be held stationary above Mars by light pressure at an altitude of 214,000 km. Wasting a small amount of light allows shadowing to be avoided.

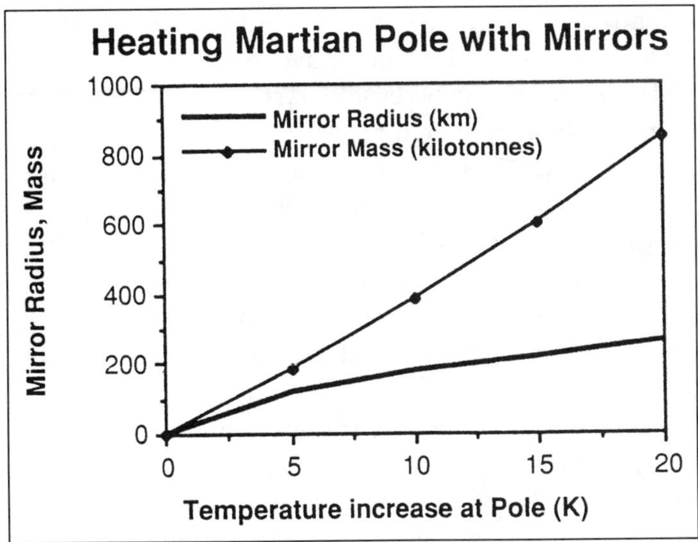

Figure 8.9. Solar sail mirrors with radii on the order of 100 km and masses of 200,000 tonnes can produce the 5 K temperature rise required to vaporize the CO_2 in Mars' south polar cap. It may be possible to construct such mirrors in space.

release of the regolith's reserves in a runaway greenhouse effect. If however, as seems probable, T_d is greater than 20 K, then either the importation or production of strong greenhouse gases will be required to force a global temperature rise sufficient to create a tangible atmospheric pressure on Mars.

MOVING AMMONIA ASTEROIDS

Ammonia is a powerful greenhouse gas, and it is possible that nature has stockpiled large amounts of it in frozen form on asteroidal-sized objects orbiting in the outer solar system. If moving material from such objects to Mars is envisioned, then such orbits would be quite convenient, because strange as it may seem, it is easier to move an asteroid from the outer solar system to Mars than it is to do so from the Main Belt or any other inner solar system orbit. This odd result follows from the laws of orbital mechanics, which cause an object farther away from the Sun to orbit it slower than one that is closer in. Because an object in the outer solar system moves slower, it takes a smaller ΔV to change its orbit from a circular to an ellipse. Furthermore, the orbit does not have to be so elliptical that it stretches from Mars to the outer solar system; it is sufficient to distort the object's orbit so that it intersects the path of a major planet, after which a gravity assist can do the rest. The results are shown in Figure 8.10. It can be seen that moving an asteroid positioned in a circular orbit at 25 AU, by way of a Uranus gravity assist to Mars, requires a ΔV of only 0.3 km/s, compared to a 3.0 km/s ΔV to move an asteroid directly to Mars from a 2.7 AU position in the Main Belt. The time of flight required for such transfers is shown in Figure 8.11.

Now we don't know for sure if there are numerous asteroid-size objects in the outer solar system, but there is no reason to believe that there aren't. As of this writing, only one is known, but that one, Chiron, orbiting between Saturn and Uranus, is rather large (180 km diameter), and it may be expected that a lot of small objects can be found for every big one. In all probability, the outer solar system contains thousands of asteroids that we have yet to discover because they shine so dimly compared to those in the Main Belt (the brightness of an asteroid as seen from Earth is inversely propor-

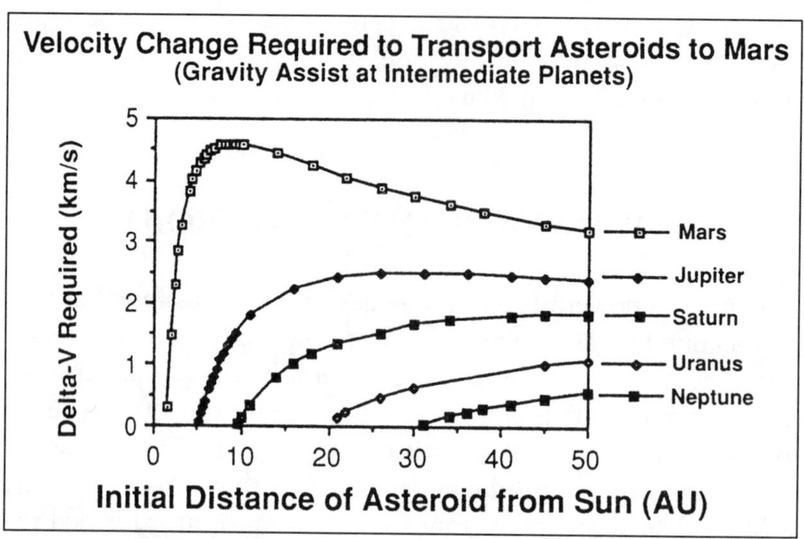

Figure 8.10. Using gravity assists, the ΔV required to propel an outer solar system asteroid onto a collision course with Mars can be less than 0.5 km/s. Such "falling" objects can release much more energy upon impact than is required to set them in motion.

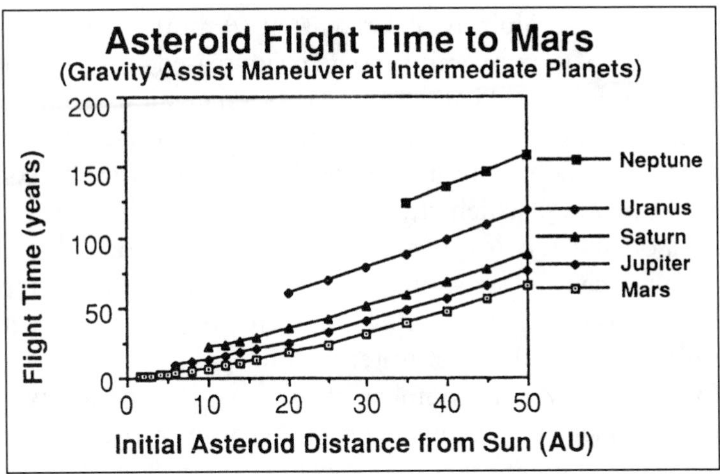

Figure 8.11. Ballistic flight times from the outer solar system to Mars are typically between 25 and 50 years.

tional to the fourth power of its distance from the Sun). Furthermore, because water, ammonia, and other volatiles freeze so completely in the outer solar system, it is likely that the asteroids to be found beyond Saturn are largely composed of frozen gases (such appears to be the case for Chiron). This makes it possible for us to move them.

Consider an asteroid made of frozen ammonia with a mass of 10 billion tonnes orbiting the Sun at a distance of 12 AU. Such an object, if spherical, would have a diameter of about 2.6 km, and changing its orbit to intersect Saturn's (where it could get a trans-Mars gravity assist) would require a ΔV of 0.3 km/s. If a quartet of 5000-MW nuclear thermal rocket (NTR) engines powered by either fission or fusion were used to heat some of its ammonia up to 2,200 K (5000 MW fission NTRs operating at 2500 K were tested in the 1960s), they would produce an exhaust velocity of 4 km/s, which would allow them to move the asteroid onto its required course using only 8% of its material as propellant. Ten years of steady thrusting would be required, followed by about a 20-year coast to impact. When the object hits Mars, the energy released would be about 10 TW-years, enough to melt 1 trillion tonnes of water (a lake 140 km on a side and 50 meters deep). In addition, the ammonia released by a single such object would raise the planet's temperature by about 3 K and form a shield that would effectively mask the planet's surface from ultraviolet radiation. As further missions proceeded, the planet's temperature could be increased globally in accord with the data shown in Figure 8.12. Forty such missions would double the nitrogen content of Mars' atmosphere by direct importation, and could produce much more if some of the asteroids were targeted to hit beds of nitrates, which they would volatilize into nitrogen and oxygen upon impact. If one such mission were launched per year, within half a century or so most of Mars would have a temperate climate, and enough water would have been melted to cover a quarter of the planet with a layer of water 1 m deep.

While attractive in a number of respects, the feasibility of the asteroidal impact concept is uncertain because of the lack of data on outer solar system ammonia objects. Moreover, if T_d is greater than 20 K, a sustained greenhousing effort will be required. As the characteristic lifetime of an ammonia molecule on Mars is likely to be less than a century, this means that even after the temperature is raised, ammonia objects would need to continue to be imported to Mars, albeit at a reduced rate. As each object will hit Mars with an energy yield of about 70,000 1-megaton hydrogen bombs, the continuation of such a program may be incompatible with the objective of making Mars suitable for human settlement.

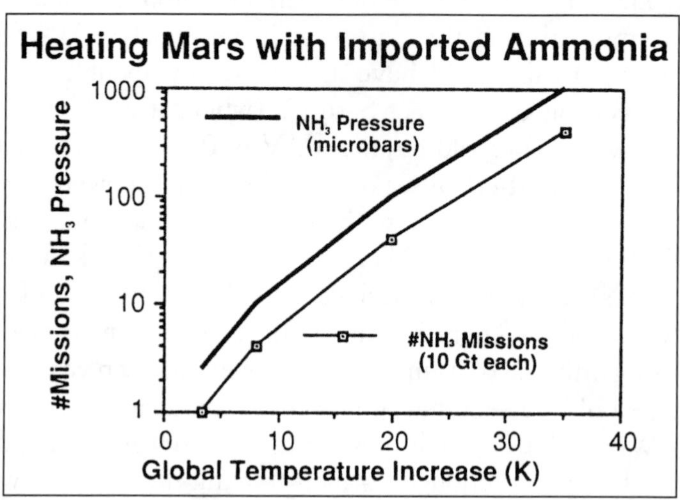

Figure 8.12. Importing four 10-billion-tonne ammonia asteroids to Mars would impose an 8 K temperature rise, which after amplification by CO_2 feedback could create drastic changes in global conditions.

A possible improvement to the ammonia impact method is suggested by ideas given in reference 5, where it is pointed out that bacteria exist which can metabolize nitrogen and water to produce ammonia. If an initial greenhouse condition were to be created by ammonia object importation, it may be possible that a bacterial ecology could be set up on the planet's surface that would recycle the nitrogen resulting from ammonia photolysis back into the atmosphere as ammonia, thereby maintaining the system without the need for further impacts. Similar schemes might also be feasible for recycling methane, another short-lived natural greenhouse gas which might be imported to the planet.

PRODUCING HALOCARBONS ON MARS

In Table 8.1 we show the amount of halocarbon gases (CFCs) needed in Mars' atmosphere to create a given temperature rise, and the power that would be needed on the Martian surface to produce the required CFCs over a period of 20 years. If the gases have an atmospheric lifetime of 100 years, then approximately one-fifth the power levels shown in the table will be needed to maintain the CFC concentration after it has been built up. For purposes of comparison, a typical nuclear power plant used on Earth today has a power output of about 1000 MW_e and provides enough energy for a medium-sized (Denver) American city. The industrial effort associated with such a power level would be substantial, producing about a trainload of refined material every day and requiring the support of a work crew of several thousand people on the Martian surface. A total project

Table 8.1. Greenhousing Mars with CFCs

Induced Heating (K)	*CFC Pressure (micro-bar)*	*CFC Production (tonnes/hour)*	*Power Required (MWe)*
5	0.012	263	1315
10	0.04	878	4490
20	0.11	2414	12070
30	0.22	4829	24145
40	0.80	17569	87845

budget of several hundred billion dollars might well be required. Nevertheless, all things considered, such an operation is hardly likely to be beyond the capabilities of the mid-twenty-first century.

Using such an approach, Mars could be transformed from its current dry and frozen state into a warm and slightly moist planet capable of supporting life for several decades. Humans could not breathe the air of the thus transformed Mars, but they would no longer require space suits and instead could travel freely in the open wearing ordinary clothes and simple SCUBA-type breathing gear. However, because the outside atmospheric pressure will have been raised to human-tolerable levels, it will be possible to have large habitable areas for humans under huge domelike inflatable tents containing breathable air. In contrast, simple hardy plants could thrive in the CO_2-rich outside environment, and spread rapidly across the planet's surface. In the course of centuries, these plants would introduce oxygen into Mars' atmosphere in increasingly breathable quantities, opening up the surface to advanced plants and increasing numbers of animal types. As this occurred, the CO_2 content of the atmosphere would be reduced, which would cause the planet to cool unless artificial greenhouse gases were introduced capable of blocking off those sections of the infrared spectrum previously protected by CO_2. The halocarbon gases employed would also have to be varieties lacking in chlorine, if an ultraviolet shielding ozone layer is to be built up. One good candidate for such a gas would be perfluoromethane, CF_4, which also has the desirable feature of being very long-lived (about 10,000 years) in an upper atmosphere. Providing these matters are attended to, however, the day would eventually come when the domed tents would no longer be necessary.

ACTIVATING THE HYDROSPHERE

The first steps required in the terraforming of Mars, warming the planet and thickening its atmosphere, can be accomplished with surprisingly modest means using *in situ* production of halocarbon gases. However, the oxygen and nitrogen levels in the atmosphere would be too low for many plants, and if left in this condition the planet would remain relatively dry, as the warmer temperatures took centuries to melt Mars' ice and deeply buried permafrost. It is in this, the second phase of terraforming Mars, during which the hydrosphere is activated, the atmosphere made breathable for advanced plants and primitive animals, and the temperature increased further, that either space-based manufacturing of large solar concentrators or human activity in the outer solar system is likely to assume an important role.

Activating the Martian hydrosphere in a timely fashion will require doing some violence to the planet, and, as discussed previously, one way this can be done is with targeted asteroidal impacts. Each such impact releases the energy equivalent of 10 TW-yrs. If Plowshare methods of shock treatment for Mars are desired, then the use of such projectiles is certainly to be preferred to the alternative option[3] of detonation of hundreds of thousands of thermonuclear explosives. After all, even if so much explosive could be manufactured, its use would leave the planet unacceptably radioactive.

The use of orbiting mirrors provides an alternative method for hydrosphere activation. For example, if the 125-km radius reflector discussed earlier for use in vaporizing the pole were to concentrate its power on a smaller region, 27 TW would be available to melt lakes or volatilize nitrate beds. This is triple the power available from the impact of a 10-billion tonne asteroid every year, and in all probability would be far more controllable. A single such mirror could drive vast amounts of water out of the permafrost and into the nascent Martian ecosystem very quickly. Thus, while the engineering of such mirrors may be somewhat grandiose, the benefits to terraforming, of being able to wield tens of TW of power in a controllable way can hardly be overstated.

OXYGENATING THE PLANET

The most technologically challenging aspect of terraforming Mars will be the creation of sufficient oxygen in the planet's atmosphere to support animal life. While primitive plants can survive in an atmosphere without oxygen, advanced plants require about 1 mb and humans need 120 mb. While Mars may have super-oxides in its soil or nitrates that can be pyrolysed to release oxygen (and nitrogen) gas, the problem is the amount of energy needed: about 2200 TW-yrs for every mb produced. Similar amounts of energy are required for plants to release oxygen from CO_2. Plants, however, offer the advantage that once established they can propagate themselves. The production of an oxygen atmosphere on Mars thus breaks down into two phases. In the first phase, brute force engineering techniques are employed to produce sufficient oxygen (about 1 mb) to allow advanced plants to propagate across Mars. Assuming there are three 125-km radius space mirrors active in supporting such a program and sufficient supplies of suitable target material on the ground, such a goal could be achieved in about 25 years. At that point, with a temperate climate, a thickened CO_2 atmosphere to supply pressure and greatly reduce the space radiation dose, and a good deal of water in circulation, plants that have been genetically engineered to tolerate Martian soils and to perform photosynthesis at high efficiency could be released together with their bacterial symbiotes. Assuming that global coverage could be achieved in a few decades and that such plants could be engineered to be 1% efficient (rather high, but not unheard of among terrestrial plants), then they would represent an equivalent oxygen-producing power source of about 200 TW. By combining the efforts of such biological systems with perhaps 90 TW of space-based reflectors and 10 TW of installed power on the surface (terrestrial civilization today uses about 12 TW), the required 120 mb of oxygen needed to support humans and other advanced animals in the open could be produced in about 900 years. If more powerful artificial energy sources or still more efficient plants were engineered, then this schedule could be accelerated accordingly, a fact which may well prove a driver in bringing such technologies into being. It may be noted that thermonuclear fusion power on the scale required for the acceleration of terraforming also represents the key technology for enabling piloted interstellar flight. If terraforming Mars were to produce such a spinoff, then the ultimate result of the project will be to confer upon humanity not only one new world for habitation, but myriads.

CONCLUSION

What we have shown in this article is that within broad tolerances of uncertainty of Martian conditions, that drastic improvements in the life-sustaining characteristics of the environment of the red planet may be effected by humans using early to mid-twenty-first century technologies. While our immediate descendants cannot expect to use such near-term methods to "terraform" the planet in the full sense of the word, it at least should be possible to rejuvenate Mars, making it again as receptive to life as it once was. Moreover, in the process of modifying Mars, they are certain to learn much more about how planets really function and evolve, enough perhaps to assure wise management of our native planet.

Beyond such near-term milestones, the tasks associated with full terraforming become more daunting and the technologies required more speculative. Yet, who can doubt that if the first steps are taken, that the developments required to complete the job will not follow, for what is ultimately at stake is an infinite universe of habitable worlds.

Seen in such light the task facing our generation—that of exploring Mars and learning enough about the planet and the methods of utilizing its resources to begin to transform it into a habitable planet—could not be more urgent, or more noble.

Chapter 9

Martyn J. Fogg

A Planet Dweller's Dreams

Many of you reading this article would like to believe that the stars are our ultimate destination. One day, a branch of our species, taking with it other life forms from Earth, may embark upon the grandest odyssey of all: a million-year galactic diaspora, traveling from star to star, exploring, discovering, and learning, gradually dispersing throughout the spiral arms and disc of the Milky Way. It is possible to imagine an almost infinite variety of settings within which our space-faring descendants might choose to settle. However, what will the overall picture be like, where will our homes of the future be?

If the imaginations of science fiction authors are to be a reliable guide, the answer is *other planets about other stars*. Extra-solar planets remain a major theme within SF. The majority of future histories, whether composed of one novel or many, see planets as being the fundamental building blocks of interstellar empires.

Yet, this has not been taken for granted by a large fraction of space scientists who speculate over interstellar colonization. Especially from the mid-1970s onward, after Gerard O'Neill's pioneering work on space colonies, the emphasis of many has switched to the *colonization of space itself*. By this I mean the construction of large, free-floating, artificial habitats, enclosing an environment comfortable for human beings. One can think of these space colonies as being extraterrestrial city-states or daughter biospheres of the Earth—miniaturized maybe, but still large enough to support a population of thousands of people.

O'Neill's cohorts coined the term "planetary chauvinism" to attack what they saw as an outdated view that planets are the natural goal of any future space colonization effort. Their reasoning is quite persuasive: Space is rich in solar energy, which is free; space is rich in easily accessible raw materials, asteroids, comets, and the like, which are also free; and planets share an unfortunate property called a gravity well which makes travel to and fro much more expensive. An additional ingredient, when looking at the interstellar perspective, is that theoretical studies of the likely abundance of Earth-like planets about other stars indicate that they may be very rare.

The most optimistic study to date was that of Stephen Dole of the Rand Corporation, who published a report in 1964 which estimated that about 1 in 200 stars possess a habitable planet. This means that we would have to search, on average, about 25 light-years of space to locate such a world. In contrast to this, William Pollard of the ORAU Institute for Energy Analysis estimated that only 1 in 100,000 to 1 in 10,000,000 stars may be encircled by an Earth-like planet, requiring a search for a needle in a haystack 200 to 1,000 light-years in radius! Thus, argued the space colony enthusiasts, planet dwelling as a life-style will be outgrown by the human species. Instead, large colony-starships known as "world-ships," such as Arthur C. Clarke's *Rama*, will travel the space lanes setting up shop in any convenient star system (for almost all are likely to possess asteroidal material) where a new, entirely space-based civilization can be established.

As I said, their reasoning is very persuasive, but as many SF authors have implicitly recognized—and they *do* have to entertain us—it is rather boring! Personally I'd rather live long-term on the outer skin of a large ball of rock than on the inside of a smaller metal can. I confess therefore to being a reactionary planetary chauvinist with an interest in re-engineering those planets that don't suit into a condition where they do, a process called *terraforming*. Having conducted and published terraforming-related research for several years, I decided to look at the potential effect of terraforming processes on interstellar colonization. Now obviously, a starship is not going to have the capability to terraform any terrestrial planet it finds and so, for the dreary logic of the space colony brigade to be overcome, there must exist a large extra-solar population of near-Earth-like worlds, planets that would be easy to terraform.

Is this possible, or even likely? The study I completed and published in the *Journal of the British Interplanetary Society*[1] suggests the answer might be *yes*.

DEFINITIONS

A problem with comparing past estimates of the prevalence of habitable planets is that the relevant studies on which they are based all adopt a different meaning of the word "habitable." So, before we go on any further, I'd better define what I mean.

We're going to speak of three different types of terrestrial planet.

1. *Habitable Planet* (HP): A world with an environment sufficiently similar to the Earth as to allow comfortable and free human habitation.
2. *Biocompatible Planet* (BP): A planet possessing the necessary physical parameters for life to flourish on its surface. If initially lifeless, then such a world could host a biosphere of considerable complexity without the need for terraforming.
3. *Easily Terraformable Planet* (ETP): A planet that might be rendered biocompatible, or possibly habitable, and maintained so by modest planetary engineering techniques and with the limited resources of a starship or robot precursor mission.

Now, it is plain that these three planetary categories are nested: (1) being a subset of (2), being a subset of (3). Clearly the solar system at the present time contains just *one* ETP, which also happens to be a habitable planet, the Earth. However, this was not always so. The history of our solar system as revealed by planetary scientists suggests that early on, two other planets could have been included within the groupings defined previously. With a sample of more than one, our ability to extrapolate to the likely situation about other stars is much improved. The best way to approach this problem is by studying and understanding the history of the Sun's *ecosphere* and the planets within it.

THE ECOSPHERE AND BIOCOMPATIBLE PLANETS

One can define the ecosphere as that zone surrounding a star within which conditions are thermally compatible with life. It is a finite volume with inner and outer boundaries: too close to a star and a planet's water exists as vapor, too far away and it is permanently frozen. Since we assume a crucial requirement of life is the presence of stable liquid water on a planetary surface, then the ecosphere is the place where we might expect to find biocompatible planets.

The boundaries of the ecosphere are obviously controlled primarily by the amount of radiation received from the central star. (The Earth receives about 1370 W/m^2 of solar energy, an illuminance known as the solar constant, which I shall denote by the letter S.) However, the luminosity of the star itself is not constant over long time scales but gradually increases throughout its main sequence lifetime. Our Sun was only about 70% as bright 4.6 billion years ago, when newly born, than it is now, and so the ecosphere is not a static volume but one which expands gradually outward. Planets can thus move in or out of the ecosphere as the central star evolves; moreover there are processes of planetary evolution which can result in a planet losing its liquid water so that, even though it may remain in the ecosphere, it ceases to be biocompatible. Therefore, the dimension of time, as well as distance, is of importance in our discussion.

One problem is that we don't actually know the true extent of the Sun's ecosphere. As astronomical theory has advanced, estimates of the width of this biocompatible zone have fluctuated. Before the space age, it was thought that Mars and Venus might be biocompatible, implying that the ecosphere extended to their orbits and maybe beyond. By the mid-1970s, modeling of terrestrial evolution was suggesting that the ecosphere was wafer thin and the Earth only situated within it by the merest of flukes. The most modern research, however, has swung the other way; it now seems that the ecosphere may extend farther from the Sun than hitherto thought.

One of the conundrums that has dogged planetary scientists is the so-called "Faint Young Sun Paradox." As far back as we can look in the Earth's geological record, we find evidence for the presence of liquid water. This implies a global average surface temperature maintained consistently above freezing, despite the changing luminosity of the Sun. Yet, the young Earth, illuminated by sunlight with only 70% its present brightness (0.7 S), should have been frozen and should have stayed frozen up until comparatively recently. The fact that this didn't happen indicates that there must have been some mechanism at work capable of keeping the Earth's surface warm even though the planet was receiving less energy; a self-regulatory mechanism rather akin to that of a warm-blooded animal, which can automatically keep its body temperature constant whether the day is sunny or cool.

In 1981 James Walker and coworkers at the University of Michigan proposed just such a mechanism, the *Carbonate-Silicate Cycle*, which is capable of linking the amount of sunlight received by a terrestrial planet with the greenhouse effect of its atmosphere. It hinges on the fact that carbon dioxide in the atmosphere of a planet with liquid water on its surface is not stable—it weathers silicate rocks, reacting with them chemically to produce carbonate minerals, such as calcite, the main constituent of limestone. Why then does the Earth's atmosphere contain CO_2? This is because carbonate minerals are not stable either, under conditions of high temperature and pressure. Since the Earth's crust is tectonically active (it moves about, overturning parts of itself over time scales of millions of years), then carbonate rocks can be deeply buried where they become heated and squeezed. This drives the carbon dioxide out of the mineral phase whereupon it escapes back into the atmosphere via volcanoes. The clever bit is that the weathering rate at the surface is sensitive to temperature. If the planet cools then the weathering rate falls. However, the rate of volcanic outgassing of CO_2 stays the same because of the delays inherent in the cycle and so the amount of CO_2 in the atmosphere increases. This strengthens the atmosphere's greenhouse effect, producing a warming trend to counteract the original cooling. Conversely, if the planet warms up for any reason, surface weathering increases, CO_2 is drawn down out of the atmosphere, reducing the greenhouse effect and producing a cooling. What we in fact have is a planetary engine that operates automatically to maintain temperatures a few tens of degrees above the freezing point of water—conditions ideally suited for life!

The Faint Young Sun Paradox for the Earth may thus be explained. Surface temperatures have been maintained constant over our planet's history by a controlled decline of the atmospheric partial pressure of CO_2 from an initial value of about 1 bar to the 0.0003 bar of today—a change that would have kept pace with the brightening of the Sun.

However, this is not all of the explanatory power of the carbonate-silicate cycle; it also enables us to explain the history of Mars and to estimate the position of the outer edge of the ecosphere. Mars was not always the frozen desert it is today. Images returned by space probes have revealed areas of the planet cut by what look like dried-up river beds; there are desiccated lake beds too, and some even claim to be able to point out the fossil shore lines of an empty ocean. These structures mostly occur on the most ancient of Martian terrain, that dating from the first billion years of the planet's history. Thus, it seems that Mars experienced an early warm and wet epoch, a time when water ran and pooled on its surface, a time when Mars was a biocompatible planet, irrespective of whether life actually evolved there. How can we reconcile a faint young Sun with a warm Mars? Well, if early Mars had an atmosphere of about 5 bars of carbon dioxide, with maybe other greenhouse gases too, then surface temperatures could have been at or a little above freezing. It is thought that this atmosphere could have been maintained by an active carbonate-silicate cycle, CO_2 being resupplied by intense volcanism powered by the internal heat of a young, recently formed, world. Why then is Mars still not like this? Why instead did the atmosphere dwindle, the seas dry up, and the planet's temperature plummet to −60 C? After all, the Sun is now hotter than it once was.

The answer is that Mars is *small*, smaller and less massive than Earth and therefore has a larger surface-to-volume ratio. The little world lost its internal heat much more rapidly. Its crust thickened until it could no longer bury and decompose its carbonates. The carbonate-silicate cycle was cut. From that point on, biocompatible Mars was doomed. Its air reacted permanently with the surface; even after all of Mars' water froze, this process continued gradually to leave the planet with the tenuous atmospheric remnant we see today. Mars died, *even though it was situated within the ecosphere*. Yes! The fact that Mars was once biocompatible suggests that the outer boundary extends beyond the Martian orbit. A planet at about 1.8 AU from the present-day Sun receives about as much radiation as a young Mars, about 0.3 S, and so we can speculate that any terrestrial planet with *active volcanism and tectonics*, capable of sustaining an *active carbonate-silicate cycle*, could remain biocompatible out to this distance or a little farther.

Now let's look closer to the Sun for the inner edge of the ecosphere. Computer models of the Earth's climate suggest that were our planet's illuminance to be increased to 1.1 S, the oceans would start to evaporate. Large quantities of water vapor would start to accumulate in the atmosphere, a sufficient mass to keep a lid on a sort of planetary pressure cooker which would keep the oceans from disappearing entirely. Although water vapor is a powerful greenhouse gas, the increase in atmospheric pressure would prevent the boiling point of water, which itself increases with pressure, from being overtaken by rising surface temperatures. The Earth would be in a climatic regime known as the *wet greenhouse* with a 2-bar atmosphere of half nitrogen and half water vapor overlying scalding oceans at about 100 C. Increasing our planet's illuminance to 1.4 S would cause the pressure cooker to blow; the oceans would evaporate entirely, and the surface would dry out, reducing the ease with which volcanically produced carbon dioxide could weather back into the surface. Here we have a situation called the *runaway greenhouse*, a state in which we currently find the planet Venus. However, the Venusian atmosphere is now very dry. If, as seems likely, Venus once had a similar amount of water to the Earth, then where has it all gone? Both greenhouse states initially result in an atmosphere which is so wet that, unlike on Earth, large quantities of water vapor can rise to the edge of space. Here, ultraviolet radiation in sunlight can dissociate water molecules into hydrogen and oxygen. Hydrogen being a very light gas escapes to space; some of the oxygen does too, while the rest reacts with surface rocks. It has been calculated that an amount of water equivalent to an entire terrestrial ocean can be lost in this way in about 500 million years.

If these conclusions are correct, then at about 1.1 S, equivalent to a distance from the Sun of 0.95 AU, the wet greenhouse becomes established—a state incompatible with life of almost any sort. We have reached the inner edge of the ecosphere.

Since the Sun was significantly less luminous when it was young, might Venus have once been within the ecosphere? The answer is no: the minimum illuminance Venus might have received was about 1.38 S, so that it was gripped by a greenhouse climate from the start. However, it may have started off in the wet greenhouse before evolving a few hundred million years later to a full runaway. Thus, during the earliest history of the solar system, there may have been *three* terrestrial planets with oceans, *two* of which were within the ecosphere and at least one of which gave rise to life.

EASILY TERRAFORMABLE AND HABITABLE PLANETS

To complete our discussion of the three categories of planets we are interested in, we must briefly talk about ETPs and HPs. The former may be approached by asking the question, "Will it be easy to terraform Mars and Venus?" (Remember that the word "easy" in this context is defined as being within the wherewithal of a space colony/starship, the size of a city-state or small nation.) Well, the answer is a fairly firm *no* and if you have taken in the discussion in the last section it should be clear why.

Mars has lost its ability to recycle CO_2, with the result that its ancient atmosphere has become literally petrified into the rocks of its surface. Recreating an atmosphere thick enough to make Mars biocompatible again would be a huge undertaking. It could be done, but not as previously thought by simply warming the planet with orbiting mirrors. The gases would need to be shocked out of the crust by buried explosions or impacts—replacing the internal heat that the planet has lost—or even imported from elsewhere in the solar system (see my article in the January 1991 *Analog*). This could perhaps be achieved by a mature civilization but not by the inhabitants of one ship lately arrived from a long interstellar journey.

For Venus we will have to replace an ocean's worth of water, and the large mass of its CO_2 atmosphere must be eliminated. The old idea that all of this could be achieved by dumping a few photosynthetic algae into the planet's cloud deck, waiting a few years and then "*bingo!* We have a habitable planet" is, of course, bunkum. Any realistic proposal for terraforming Venus (see the reference list) inevitably requires a massive project well beyond the capabilities of a few hundred thousand interstellar travelers.

However, as we have seen, conditions on these two worlds may have been much less hostile during the first billion years of their respective histories. *In fact, both planets at that time would have been much easier to terraform than at present*. Mars was already biocompatible and could have been made more so by raising its illuminance. This would have increased the weathering rate at its surface, reducing the mass of carbon dioxide in the atmosphere. This process could have been speeded further by implanting photosynthetic life on Mars capable of using solar energy to use still more CO_2 to increase its own biomass, releasing oxygen in the process. While Venus was in the wet greenhouse stage, a reduction in its illuminance to below 1.1 S would have caused most of the water in the atmosphere to rain out, resulting in a relatively rapid transition from greenhouse to more Earth-like conditions.

Now the modification of a planet's illuminance is likely to be one of the simplest and cheapest planetary engineering techniques. Construction of large orbiting sunshades or mirrors from hyperthin aluminum solar sail material would not be too difficult, especially to a civilization used to obtaining and processing space resources. This is the sort of terraforming that one can imagine interstellar travelers getting to grips with straight away. Thus, in the context of the model of the ecosphere discussed previously, we can define *the set of easily terraformable planets to consist of all biocompatible planets, plus planets in the wet greenhouse state that have retained a substantial fraction of their water*.

Now we just have to put the icing on our definition of a habitable planet. Of course, the fact that the Earth is habitable is the one data point we are certain of; however, this has not always been the case. In fact, for most of the history of our planet, you or I could not have survived exposure to the environment unprotected. We would have suffocated, gasping for the 21% oxygen we are used to from air that contained less than 1%. It is thought that oxygen levels in the atmosphere only approached present levels about 600 million years ago at the beginning of the Cambrian period, when the Earth experienced a rapid and dramatic proliferation of complex lifeforms—the so-called "Cambrian Explosion." Before that stretches the long eons of the Precambrian age, the age of anaerobic life—bacteria, algae, and so forth—floating in the photic zones of the seas or living in the slime on the ocean floor. The Earth in the Precambrian age was not therefore a habitable planet, but was of course biocompatible. Such a world would be even easier to terraform than a young Mars or Venus.

Since our model of the ecosphere is based on the carbonate-silicate cycle, which links the level of planetary illuminance with the chemical makeup of its atmosphere, we can take a leap of faith and choose the illuminance of the Earth at the beginning of the Cambrian age (0.94 S) as the threshold at which a planet with Earth-like parameters can be considered habitable. Thus, *the set of habitable planets is assumed to be those biocompatible planets with an illuminance of* > 0.94 S.

WE NEED TO SUMMARIZE!

If you don't know much about planetology, then some of you may be feeling a little punch-drunk by now. A summary of the model just described is definitely needed, something preferably which sums up the whole picture in one diagram. Have a look at Figure 9.1. On the vertical axis we have a scale of illuminance. All biocompatible planets are contained within the ecosphere that lies between 0.25 S and 1.1 S and is divided into three zones: *Juvenile Martian*, where planets could be similar to the early Mars; *Juvenile Terran*, where planets would be similar to the Precambrian Earth, and the *Habitable*, which we have already defined. The horizontal axis is a scale of planetary volcanic/tectonic activity which you needn't worry about other than to note that the central dividing line where the scale reads zero is the point at which planets cool to the extent that they cannot sustain a closed carbonate-silicate cycle. Since both solar luminosity and volcanic activity vary with time, the position of a planet on the diagram changes, tracing out an evolutionary track. Such tracks are shown on the diagram for the Earth, Mars, and Venus, each one being marked at intervals of 1 billion years.

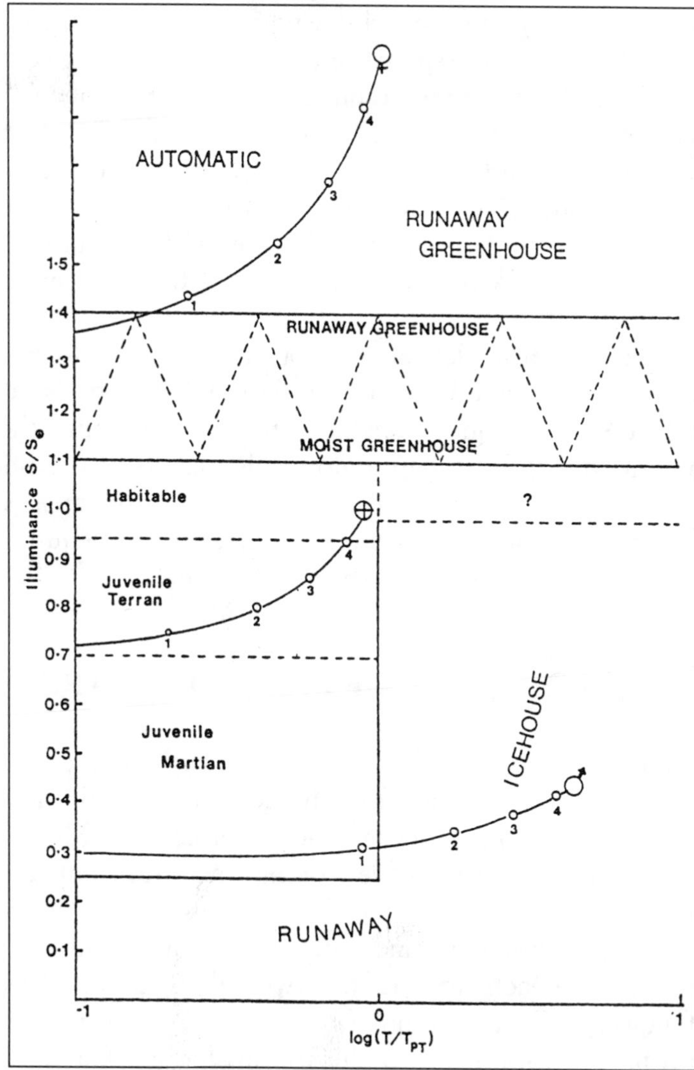

Figure 9.1. Climatic evolutionary tracks for Venus, the Earth, and Mars, comparing illuminance versus geological activity over time, marked in intervals of 1 billion years on the respective curves. The central dividing line at $\log(T/T_{PT}) = 0$ represents the point in a planet's geological evolution at which it can no longer sustain plate tectonics or a geochemical carbon cycle.

Now, what does Figure 9.1 tell us? Early in the history of the solar system, both the Earth and Mars were within the ecosphere and were warm and wet. Venus may have been in the wet greenhouse region, with oceans on its surface under a sweltering water vapor atmosphere. Shortly afterward, the seas of Venus evaporated permanently, the loss of water to space from the upper atmosphere desiccating the planet for good. At 1 billion years or thereabouts, Mars leaves the ecosphere for the "runaway ice house," being no longer able to recycle its carbon dioxide atmosphere and to prevent the onset of a permanent ice age. Only the Earth remains biocompatible. After 4 billion years it becomes habitable, and 600 million years later we appear to ask the questions about how it all happened in the first place.

Now we have a model robust enough to allow us to speculate in a reasonably sensible way concerning the situation about other stars. Figure 9.1 looks quite hopeful. After all, at one time the solar system contained *three* easily terraformable planets, instead of one. The habitable zone within the ecosphere, which is the approximate volume most other studies concentrate on, is seen to be just a small part of a much bigger *potentially* habitable zone.

EXPLORING AN EMPIRE OF STARS

In order to estimate the abundance of ETPs in our part of the galaxy, I embedded this model of the ecosphere within a broader astronomical framework. It became the centerpiece of a Monte Carlo computer simulation capable of generating random and unique planetary systems about stars of varying age and mass. The computer plays a kind of planet-building game, following a large number of steps and shaking dice each time. It starts with the creation of the star itself, followed by the formation of its planetary system and terminating with an evaluation of the climatic evolution of its terrestrial planets. The general strategy of the program is shown in Figure 9.2. The ultimate aim of the calculations is to determine the surface temperature range of a terrestrial planet to see if it qualifies as one of the three types of worlds, defined previously, which interstellar travelers might search for. The rules of the game cannot, of course, be based solely on rigorous theory as we have nowhere near a full understanding of planetology and have yet to detect an extra-solar planetary system. However, the laws of physics, empirical relations derived from observation, and current theory are blended together within the algorithms of the program such that the computer pro-

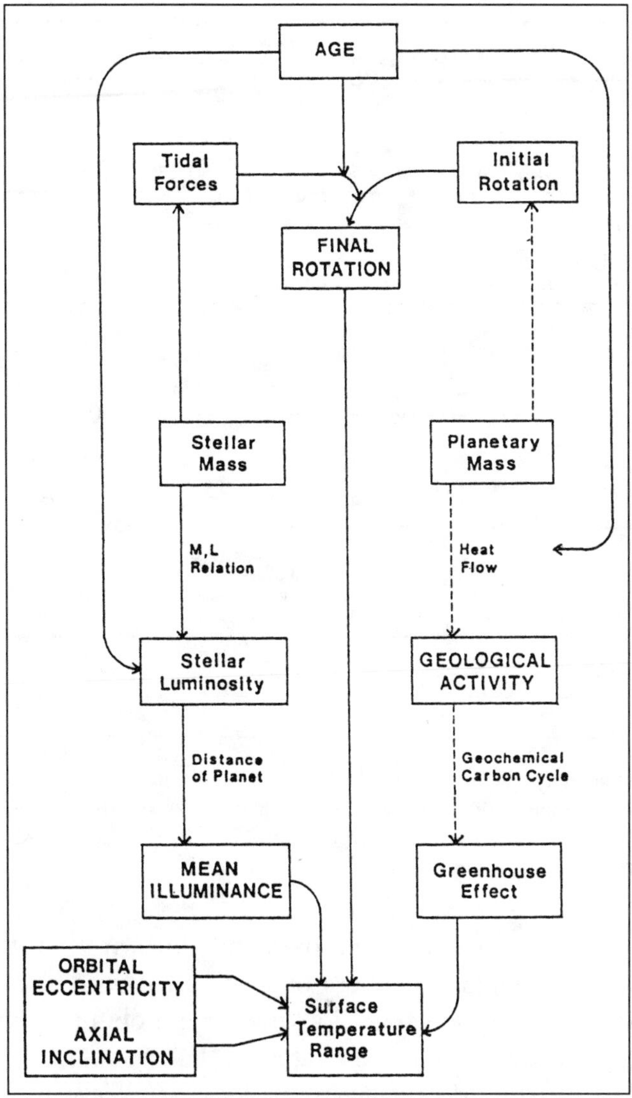

Figure 9.2. Stellar and planetary parameters that ultimately determine the range of planetary surface temperature. Dashed arrows represent speculative linkages.

duces physically realistic, "sensible," although not necessarily stereotypical, planetary systems (see Figure 9.3).

I'm not going to cover the technical aspects of the simulation here; those of you who are interested and want more details can obtain it from the references listed at the end of this article. Suffice it to say that since the mass distribution and spatial density of stars

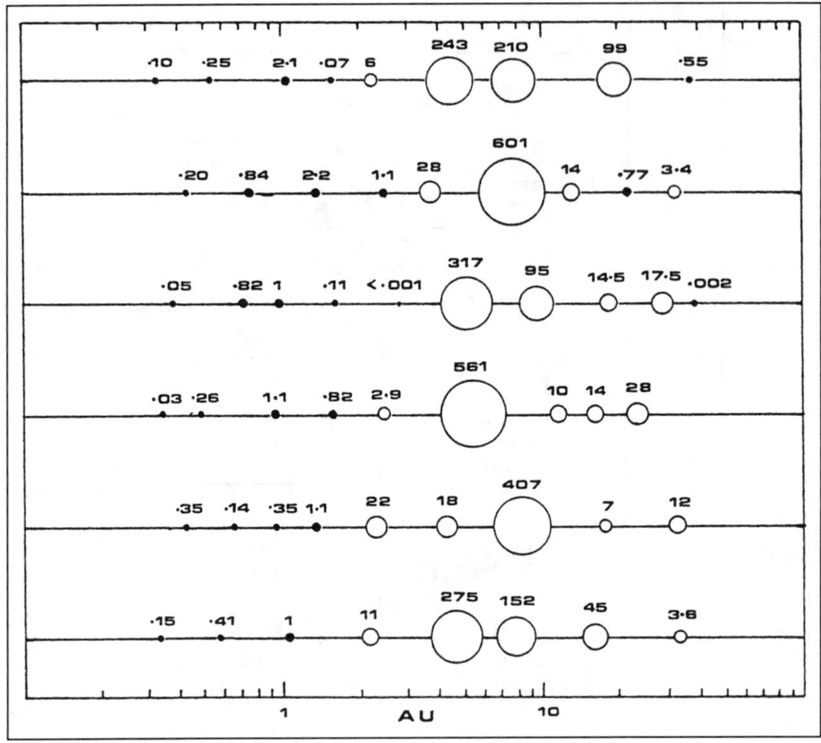

Figure 9.3. Planetary systems generated by the simulation, in this case about a primary star of 1 $M_{\odot}$. The masses of planets are given in Earth units and the horizontal axis is a logarithmic scale of distance from the primary, in AU. The solar system is included third from top for comparison.

in the solar neighborhood is approximately known, then the model can be used to simulate a sphere of space filled with as many stars as desired. The answers we are looking for are obtained by analysis of all the planetary systems generated.

How many stars do you want to look at? We'll need a good sample to get decent statistics. How about 100,000 stars for starters? That would be sufficient to keep the human race occupied for a few millenia; in fact, at about one millionth of the total stellar population of the Galaxy, it would be quite a respectable empire. OK, 100,000 stars it is then. Let's explore!

At the number density of stars in the Sun's region of the galaxy, about 1 star per 300 cubic light-years, 100,000 of them are contained within an enormous spherical region about 380 light-years (ly) across. Most of our empire therefore is cold, empty, interstellar space. Let an actual run of the computer be our telescope, exploring each star system one by one. What does it find when its survey is completed?

For a start, not all stars are solitary like our Sun. In fact, most of them occur in pairs or triplets, orbiting each other in a variety of fashions, some close together, others separated by great distances. Of all the stars formed in our region, about 55,000 exist within multiple systems. It may be that gravitational perturbations within such systems may prevent planets from forming and so first we shall examine single stars only. A significant fraction of the older and more massive of these stars will have evolved off the main sequence, passing through a period as a red giant, ending up as a white dwarf. No previously habitable planets about such stars will have survived; millions of years of being roasted to red heat followed by an eternity of the encroaching cold of interstellar space will have left them unfit for any sort of life. Other stars may be too young for any of their planets to be classified as being suitable for our purposes. The surfaces of these newly formed worlds may only have recently solidified from the inferno of creation. The pangs of birth persist for perhaps 1 billion years as a declining rain of giant planetesimal impacts, the last remnants of the swarm of debris from which the planets accumulated.

Having eliminated these stars from our survey, our computer-telescope searches the ecosphere of each remaining star for the sorts of planet we are interested in. From the huge sample of stars we started with it locates 210 habitable planets—warm and wet worlds with atmospheres mostly of nitrogen—prime targets for our explorers. Almost as attractive are the 490 juvenile terran and the 1940 juvenile martian planets that are found—planets with seas and oceans of Perrier kept warm by an atmospheric blanket of carbon dioxide. Only 52 wet greenhouse worlds are found that retain enough water to be easily terraformed, nonetheless these would be welcome additions to the list of potential sites for settlement.

Our final tally therefore is 210 HPs, 2640 BPs, and 2692 ETPs. Thus, about 1 in 476 stars possesses a habitable planet, a result generally in line with the more optimistic of the estimates produced by previous studies. You would have to travel an average of 32 ly to reach a star system containing such a world. However 1 in 37 stars possess an easily terraformable planet, *a ratio 13 times higher than for habitable planets*. Stars possessing ETPs would therefore be much easier to find and reach. Such planets would be separated by an average of 14 ly, a distance that is within the designed range of a number of proposed interstellar propulsion systems. Thus, we are able to make a very important point: If the above described model of the ecosphere is correct, then *there exists a substantial population of extra-solar planets that, while not habitable for man, could be rendered so relatively easily*. Past studies, with their narrower focus, may thus have missed out on a large category of potentially habitable planets.

The stellar mass range over which this expanded set of planets occur is also greater. HPs were found about stars of 0.8–1.8 solar masses (M_0), and BPs and ETPs about stars in the range 0.5–1.8 M_0. Since more massive stars age more quickly, the upper mass limit is determined by the star leaving the main sequence just at the point where its planets are ceasing to be influenced by the more violent aftereffects of formation. Since less massive stars are proportionately a lot less luminous, there reaches a point where the ecosphere is situated so close to the star that any planets in this zone suffer excessive tidal forces. This rapidly slows down the planet's rotation period so that its day equals its year, one hemisphere being roasted in an eternal daytime and the other plunged into everlasting night. HPs thus occur about a more restricted range of stars since they inhabit the warmer inner region of the ecosphere which is strongly influenced by tides. ETPs similar to early Mars can survive about stars of much lower mass since they orbit farther away. However, below 0.5 M_0 all of the ecosphere lies within the tidal danger zone, and conventional ETPs are not possible.

We cannot yet rule out the possibility that planets can form in multiple star systems, orbiting each component separately, or revolving about both. If this is the case then, ruling out the small proportion of multiple stars which are situated in such a way that stable planetary orbits within their ecospheres are impossible, we find that about 1 in 226 stars might possess habitable planets and an enormous 1 in 18 stars an ETP. What a change from previous gloomy predictions! Some of the Sun's nearest neighbors may be orbited by planets just waiting for life from Earth.

Statistics produced by the computer model allow us to assign the probability of the existence of a planet of a particular type about a star of a given mass. Which stars should we be looking at to find the first extra-solar planets to be settled by our descendants? To answer this, let's shrink the scale of our view from hundreds of light-years to a mere 22 ly from home, a volume that contains just 100 known stars in 75 star systems (see the map in Figure 9.4). Table 9.1 lists the stars within this distance which have a non-zero probability of possessing an easily terraformable or habitable planet. Perhaps surprisingly, there are 14 candidates, 28 if we include members of multiple systems. Some of these stars you will have heard of, some you may not. Epsilon Eridani, Epsilon Indi, Tau Ceti, Sigma Draconis, Delta Pavonis, 82 Eridani, Beta Hydri, and HR 8832, being single and more than 0.7 M_0 are the best candidates, all having a greater than 10% chance of being accompanied by an ETP. All except Epsilon Indi and HR 8832 may also be accompanied by a

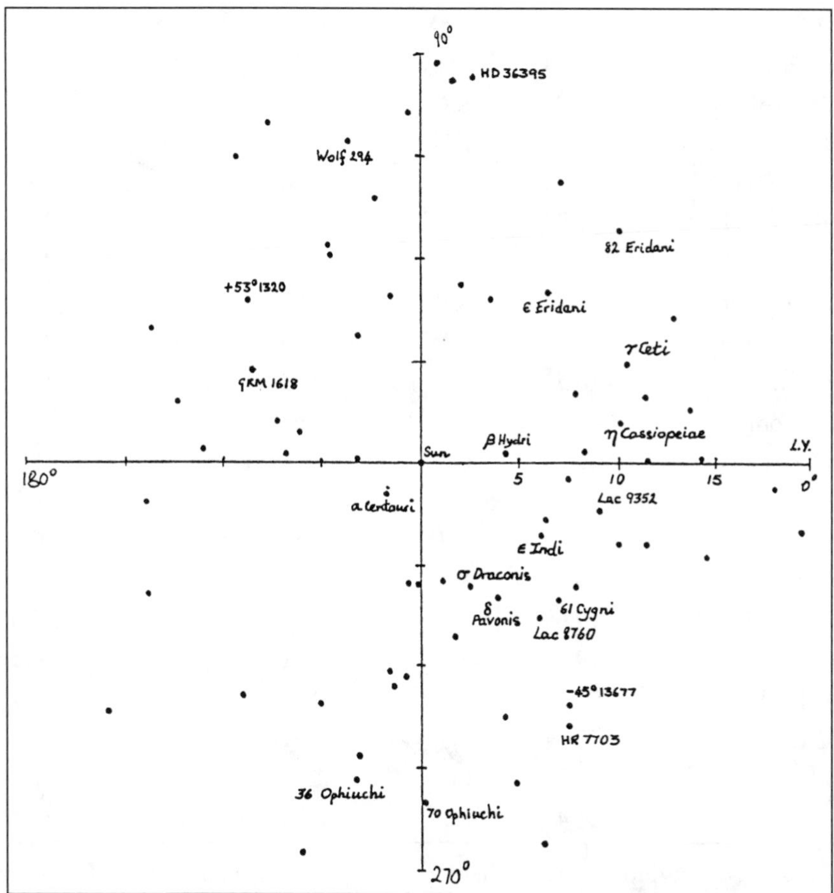

Figure 9.4. A two-dimensional map of stars within 22 ly of the Sun looking down on the plane of the celestial equator. A distance scale in light-years is marked on the positive x-axis. Named stars all have a nonzero probability of possessing an ETP.

Table 9.1. Star systems within 22 light-years which might possess suitable planets for colonization

Star	*Distance*	*Spectral Type*	*Mass/Solar Units*	P_{HP}(%)	P_{ETP}(%)
α Centauri A	4.38	G2V	1.1	7.8*	44*
α Centauri B	4.38	K6V	0.89	4.4*	38*
ϵ Eridani	10.69	K2V	0.8	0.6	34
61 Cygni A	11.17	K5V	0.59	0	5.8*
61 Cygni B	11.17	K7V	0.50	0	0.3*
ϵ Indi	11.21	K5V	0.71	0	18
Lac 9352	11.69	M2	0.47	0	<0.3
τ Ceti	11.95	G8V	0.82	1.5	35
Lac 8760	12.54	M1V	0.54	0	1.5
Grm 1618	15.03	K7	0.56	0	2.5
70 Ophiuchi A	16.73	K1	0.89	4.4*	38
70 Ophiuchi B	16.73	K6	0.68	0	16*
36 Ophiuchi A	17.73	K0V	0.77	0	28*
36 Ophiuchi B	17.73	K1V	0.76	0	27*
36 Ophiuchi C	17.73	K5V	0.63	0	9.0*
HR 7703 A	18.43	K3V	0.76	0	27*
σ Draconis	18.53	K0V	0.82	1.5	35
δ Pavonis	18.64	G5	0.98	5.1	39
η Cassiopeiae A	19.19	G0V	0.85	3.9	38*
η Cassiopeiae B	19.19	M0	0.52	0	0.7*
HD 36395	19.19	M1V	0.51	0	0.5
Wolf 294	19.41	M4	0.49	0	<0.3
+ 53° 1320 A	19.65	M0	0.52	0	0.6*
+ 53° 1320 B	19.65	M0	0.51	0	0.5*
− 45° 13677	20.6	M0	0.48	0	<0.3
82 Eridani	20.9	G5	0.91	4.4	38
β Hydri	21.3	G1	1.23	7.5	35
HR 8832	21.4	K3	0.74	0	23

Notes: P_{HP} = % probability of the occurrence of a habitable planet; P_{ETP} = % probability of the occurrence of an easily terraformable planet. Probabilities marked * only apply if planets form and have stable orbits in binary star systems.

habitable planet, although Epsilon Eridani (one of the most famous of the Sun's neighbors) is borderline, massing about 0.8 M_0. All the multiple star components listed in Table 9.1 have stable orbits within their respective ecospheres. Thus, if planets have formed in these regions, then those world-hunting interstellar travelers of the future, people like you and me who prefer untamed planets to tin cans, will have even more choice of sites. Alpha Centauri, 70 Ophiuchi, and 36 Ophiuchi have significant probabilities of possessing ETPs about each component; 36 Ophiuchi being triple actually has about a 0.6% chance of possessing *three* ETPs! The primaries of 61 Cygni, HR 7703, and Eta Cassiopeiae also merit serious consideration. As for habitable planets, the model predicts that the star with the highest chance of having such a world is Alpha Centauri A—a sun that is right on our cosmic doorstep!

COLONIZATION STRATEGY

With the possible presence of easily terraformable worlds on our cosmic doorstep, our next question is how they might be explored, visited, and made into a new planetary home. The standard scenario of interstellar travel and settlement goes something like this: A starship is launched at a point of light in the sky, about which almost nothing is known, in the hope that when it reaches its destination decades later, the target system proves to be suitable for settlement. We get the same message from both scientists and science fiction authors alike. For instance, the British Interplanetary Society's proposed *Daedalus* probe, designed to be able to perform a flyby mission to Barnard's Star in 50 years, would be capable of detecting giant planets a few hundred days, and terrestrial planets just fifty days, from closest approach. In *The Mote in God's Eye* by Larry Niven and Jerry Pournelle, Admiral Kutuzov's flotilla jumps the 35-ly trip to the Mote knowing nothing about what lies ahead, leaving all the exploration to be done after arrival. The implicit assumption common to both these scenarios, and a host of similar ones, is that missions to other stars will be dispatched in near total ignorance of what is to be found at the end of the journey. Since it is an assumption that is rarely stated it is rarely questioned. It is in fact completely wrong.

Any civilization wealthy and advanced enough to construct starships will have long before built large aperture telescopes in space. We're not talking about the Hubble Space Telescope here, which would have been hard put to detect an extra-solar planet even without its dodgy mirror, but instruments much more ambitious. Extra-solar planetary systems within our region of the galaxy will one day be extensively explored from right here in the solar system! One can imagine large arrays of telescopes on the Moon acting together as an interferometer achieving resolutions many orders of magnitude better than present astronomers' highest hopes. An array several *kilometers* across could detect terrestrial planets over vast distances and could even resolve coarse details of the discs nearest to them. Thus, contrary to the view commonly held, *interstellar travelers will know quite a lot about their future destination even before they have left home*.

One way to transport large populations over interstellar distances is to send them via worldship, a space colony modified by essentially attaching a propulsion system and a power plant. British scientists Alan Bond and Tony Martin have produced one of the most recent worldship designs, the vessel having enormous impact fusion motors capable of imparting a cruise velocity of 0.5% the speed of light. It could transport a population of 100,000 people, their ecosystems, industries, towns and countryside, their entire scaled-down world in fact, to another star 14 ly away in about 2800 years. However, since easily terraformable planets may be quite common and detectable from the solar system, then a detailed colonization strategy could be planned from the outset. Smaller and faster unmanned vessels containing an automated factory and sophisticated robots might be dispatched first to commence terraforming before the arrival of the settlers. Unburdened with the need to carry fragile ecosystems these ships might be launched with ten times the velocity of the worldship arriving in the target system about 2500 years in advance. Once the necessary industrial infrastructure has been constructed, terraforming could begin by positioning mirrors or shades in orbit about the planet to change its illuminance and by introducing forms of life, such as algae and bacteria which can start to generate atmospheric oxygen, if a suitable partial pressure is not already present. About 0.05% of the Earth's total illuminance is used by the biosphere for the purposes of photosynthesis. In the absence of processes that remove oxygen,

0.2 bars worth would be produced in about 6000 years. Thus we are talking about a time scale of millennia to convert the atmosphere of an ETP to a state where it is breathable. Since the colonists will arrive two and a half millennia after the robot precursor ships, terraforming would already be at an advanced stage. A habitable planet would be awaiting them at the end of their long journey.

POSTSCRIPT

Thus, those reactionary planet lovers among you should not despair! If interstellar travel ever becomes a reality, then searching for suitable planets to settle will not be like looking for a needle in a haystack. If the modern view of the ecosphere and planetary evolution is correct then there could be as many as *3 billion* planetary colonization sites in the galaxy. Ultimately, once a circumstellar civilization becomes more established, the terraforming of much more stubborn planets, such as extra-solar versions of Mars and Venus, would be feasible. This would increase the number of worlds occupied by a galactic civilization to perhaps over *100 billion*.

There's a future for us planet dwellers yet!

Chapter 10

Martyn J. Fogg

Astrophysical Engineering and the Fate of the Earth

Do not go gentle into that good night,
Old age should burn and rave at the close of the day;
Rage, rage against the dying of the light.

Dylan Thomas

We have all heard the doom-ridden pronouncements that human activities are on the brink of causing an ecological catastrophe. *Homo sapiens* have already exterminated a large number of species through hunting and destruction of their habitats. However, this damage to the biosphere may be slight compared with the potential harm caused by the man-made climate changes forecast for the next century. It is improbable, though, that mankind yet has the power to wipe out all life on this planet, from the most majestic whale to the lowliest virus. However, the astronomers among you will know that the Earth as an abode for life will not last forever. The Earth's biosphere, and perhaps the planet itself, is doomed to destruction by a natural process—the aging of the Sun.

Doomed? Members of a terrestrial civilization existing in those far distant times may not like the sound of that word, or its implication, but would there be anything they could do about it?

Analog readers will be familiar with the concept of terraforming, a process whereby the environment of a planet is artificially modified toward a state of Earth-like habitability. Such planetary engineering projects are vast and ambitious in terms of what human civilization is presently capable. But consider now *astrophysical engineering*, a term that invokes even grander visions of what a truly advanced civilization might be capable of. The subject matter of astrophysical engineering projects would not be just planetary surfaces, but entire planets, stars, and maybe even galaxies.

An arbitrarily advanced civilization would be able to achieve anything not ruled out by the laws of physics—they would have the capability to be astrophysical engineers. Would their astronomers think Earth doomed, or might they consider a bolder plan to save not just the population of Earth, samples of its biosphere, and artifacts of its culture, but to preserve the entire planet?

THE SUN'S ADVANCING SENILITY

The Sun is a well-behaved middle-aged star on the *main sequence*, where thermonuclear reactions in its core, the fusing of hydrogen into helium, provide a steady flow of energy that has maintained life on Earth over a period of billions of years.

As a star ages, helium accumulates in the core, as a sort of inert "ash." It is the slow accumulation of this "ash" and the gradual contraction of the core that causes main-sequence stars to gradually brighten with age. The Sun is thought to be about 30% more luminous now than it was 4.5 billion years ago when newborn. This increase in energy output, imperceptible over the length of human history, does not appear to have caused any major problems for terrestrial life so far. However, much more drastic changes characterize stellar evolution, and will affect the Sun, when the core has used up all its hydrogen. Thermonuclear reactions cease there, but continue in a shell surrounding the core. As the mass of the inert core grows, it contracts, heating up the hydrogen-burning shell above, greatly increasing its energy output. There comes a point when the mass of the core reaches about 12% of the mass of the star, the so-called Schönberg–Chandrasekhar limit, when the star can no longer adjust to this extra energy production by making small changes in its radius and surface temperature. Within a few million years, the star alters its structure drastically. It swells up to become a huge, distended red giant. Five billion years in the future, the Sun may be 100 to 1000 times more luminous than it is now, and its surface may lie somewhere in the vicinity of the orbit of Venus. At the very least, Earth's atmosphere will be stripped away and its surface melted to slag. More probable, perhaps, is that it will be engulfed by the Sun's outer layers and vaporized—a whiff of silicate gas into the surrounding inferno. Now that's a real ecological catastrophe!

Five billion years is a long way off. However, Earth may not just be at risk from the Sun when it reaches its red giant phase. NASA planetary scientist James Kasting has calculated that in a billion years' time, when the Sun is a mere 10% brighter than it is now, Earth could be at risk from a runaway greenhouse effect.[1] The climatic feedback mechanisms that have kept comfortable conditions on the planet since shortly after its formation will be put under such strain they might start to falter and break down. The oceans will start to evaporate, increasing the amount of water vapor in the atmosphere, which absorbs more solar energy, warming the planet still further, causing more evaporation and so on. Earth's climate will be driven toward a radically new equilibrium. Surface temperatures will soar, baking carbon dioxide out of carbonate rocks, leaving Earth resembling a second Venus. This climatic cusp catastrophe would occur quite rapidly, at least when measured on geological timescales. There is no biosphere we know of that could flourish, let alone survive, under those conditions; and if one were possible, it would have no time to evolve.

A billion years is only about a quarter of the time for which Earth has been in existence, which means that the time alloted to life on this planet could be four-fifths, rather than half, through. However, the exact timescale, 1 billion years, 5 billion, or somewhere in between, is of secondary significance to the fact that the final day when the curtain comes down remains very distant. In light of this, "Who cares?" you may ask. *Homo sapiens* will be long extinct and maybe Earthlife will have been scattered throughout the galaxy by then, so what does it matter? Well, I suppose it doesn't really matter, but nonetheless, I have a sentimental attachment to my home planet. So let us speculate how an advanced future civilization of astrophysical engineers, maybe distant descendants of humanity, or springing from some other origin altogether, might pluck Earth from the Sun's flames and preserve the planet intact as an abode of life long after its parent star has died.

EARTH SHIFT

One obvious way to protect Earth from the Sun's growing luminosity would be to expand its orbit so that it remains within the Sun's habitable zone. For the next 5 billion years such orbital tampering need only be modest. However, once the red giant phase commences and the luminosity of the Sun increases by several orders of magnitude, Earth would have to be relocated in the distant reaches of the outer solar system to be safe.

In 1982, the Swiss physicist M. Taube wrote a paper in which he outlined just such a scheme.[2] He named it "Earth Shift," where an advanced future civilization maneuvers the Earth a safe distance from the swollen Sun. In fact, he went further and speculated how Earth might be maintained far beyond the red-giant phase when the Sun had truly died and had become a shrunken black dwarf.

Using rocket propulsion, it is feasible, in principle, to alter the trajectory of a planet, just as it is with much smaller bodies such as spacecraft. Taube envisaged a 1 billion-year period commencing with the construction of enormous, 20-km high fusion rocket motors, ringing the Earth's equator. These engines would be arranged in 24 clusters of ten and designed to fire for 1 s each at intervals of 10 s as Earth's rotation brings them into the correct position. He estimated that the shift would require a peak power output of 8.3×10^{17} W, which could be produced by the fusion of 2.4 tonnes of deuterium per second. Rocket thrust would be obtained by using the deuterium to energize 15000 tonnes per second of hydrogen propellant. The total amount of fuel and propellant required for this planet-sized rocket motor would be enormous, about 8% of the mass of Earth itself! Acquisition of this material would be an enormous undertaking in its own right, involving a continuous mining of hydrogen from Jupiter and its transportation to the Earth.

By the end of 1 billion years of continuous use of this rocket system, Earth would have become a satellite of Jupiter, but Taube admits that this would not be far enough from the Sun to withstand its maximum luminosity. He speculates that, during the time of peak brightness, Earth's albedo (its reflectivity) would have to be artificially enhanced, but does not suggest how this might be done. Obscuring Earth behind a large occultation disc, like an enormous sunshade, is one idea that springs to mind.

Once the Sun's fires begin to fade and it collapses into a white dwarf star, the Earth now has the opposite problem to being overheated. Now it would be in danger of being deep frozen. It would not do any good to move Earth back in toward the remnant of the Sun. For a start, young white dwarfs, whilst small, are very hot and thus emit most of their energy in the dangerous high-frequency regions of the electromagnetic spectrum. Sunlight that consists mostly of far ultraviolet would not be beneficial. Moreover, to receive enough illumination Earth would have to be moved so close to the Sun that the effects of tidal forces slowing down the planet's rotation would also pose a serious long-term problem. Taube suggests instead that an artificial sun be constructed close to the Earth, fueled by deuterium mined from Jupiter. Perfectly efficient burning of deuterium and perfectly efficient focusing of the resulting energy onto Earth could provide Earth with illumination for over 100 billion years. Again however, Taube does not elaborate on the design for such a wondrous device. It is merely a concept, based on simple arithmetic and even simpler assumptions.

The only design for an artificial sun that I know about and which would be capable of warming an entire planet was presented by myself in a previous article in *Analog*. It was an idea for stellifying Jupiter—an astrophysical engineering process whereby the planet as a whole might be converted into an artificial star by seeding it with a primordial black hole. As the hole grows by accretion, enormous quantities of energy are released, giving Jupiter the appearance of a red dwarf star. Unfortunately, however, after a few tens to a few hundreds of millions of years, Jupiter would have disappeared down the hole, rendering the scenario in this case rather pointless, as this period of time is shorter than that required to move Earth into the vicinity of Jupiter in the first place.

The Earth Shift concept, as outlined by Taube, can be objected to in a number of areas. First, the rocket power required is about five times the total solar power input to the entire Earth! I have my doubts that Earth would remain habitable for long under the glare of enormous thermonuclear explosions, one every second, being released a mere 20 km above the surface. It would not do if the Earth was a charred and lifeless cinder by the time it had retreated a comfortable distance from the Sun! However, let us assume that it were possible to safely shift Earth into orbit around Jupiter, and that the planet could be protected during the Sun's violent death throes. Earth would then be in the unsatisfactory position of requiring an eternity of artificial illumination and would depend entirely for its continued habitability on the persistence of an advanced civilization, capable of feeding the fires of the artificial sun.

STAR LIFTING

An alternative approach to relocating Earth into the outer solar system might be to tamper with the Sun itself, in some way that increased its life span.

Now, the two major characteristics of a star that are of interest to us, namely its luminosity and life span, are sensitively dependent on its mass. As a rule of thumb, the luminosity of a star is proportional to between the third and fourth power of its mass. The life span is proportional to the mass divided by the luminosity; that is, it is proportional to the mass raised to the power minus two to minus three. Thus, a star of half a solar mass, for instance, would remain on the main sequence for between four to eight times as long as the Sun. For a planetary system about a star of this mass, the red giant disaster would be tens of billions of years more remote. Would it be possible to reduce the Sun's mass to extend its lifetime?

David Criswell, a consultant to the California Space Institute, has outlined a number of ideas for extracting mass from stars, a process he has termed "Star Lifting."[3] One of them, with the delightful name of the "Huff-n-Puff" method, involves a ring of ion accelerators orbiting the Sun and exchanging two counter-directed beams of oppositely charged ions. A circum-solar current is set up producing a powerful magnetic field, leaving two polar holes through which plasma can escape. Criswell suggests that the upper atmosphere of the Sun in the polar regions could then be heated and expelled like the gas from a rocket exhaust using solar powered lasers or particle beams. He estimated that if 10% of the Sun's energy were to be utilized for this purpose, then the star lifting rate would be about 3×10^{-9} solar masses, equivalent to about 0.1% of the mass of Earth, per year.

Efficient use of solar energy was Criswell's intent behind the Star Lifting concept. The aim was to reduce the mass of the Sun to 8% of a solar mass, the minimum mass of a star that can still sustain hydrogen burning. He estimated that the life span of this stripped down Sun, now transformed into a tiny, dim, red dwarf, would be extended to a colossal 23,000 billion years, over 1,000 times the present age of the Universe! The mass lifted from the Sun would be used for the construction of a number of other miniature long-lived stars. Thus, the solar system would be replaced by a cluster of 12 red dwarfs, each orbited by clouds of space habitats and whichever planets had been allowed to persist undemolished.

However, there are difficulties with this scenario as well. One of the curious things about stars is that both adding and *subtracting* mass tends to accelerate their evolution. The reason for the former is obvious, but for the latter it is more subtle. If material is stripped off the outer layers of a star then, true, we have a star of lower mass and therefore a star that should burn its fuel more slowly and last longer. However, the ratio of core mass to the mass of the whole star has been increased and so we have a lighter weight star that "thinks" it is older, or more evolved, than it really is. Removing 92% of the mass of the Sun would leave just the core behind, which would then rapidly evolve into something resembling a hot, dense, white dwarf star, not the placid lower main sequence red dwarf that Criswell suggests. A more modest reduction in the Sun's mass might indeed extend the Sun's lifetime, but not to the extent that the simple mass/luminosity proportionality indicates. If too much of the Sun's envelope were to be removed, driving the core/star ratio beyond the Schönberg–Chandrasekhar limit, then disastrous changes within the Sun might be triggered, such as the creation of a premature red giant.

Another problem is that a large modification of the Sun's mass and luminosity would require large alterations in Earth's orbit, with all the difficulties described in the previous section. Theoretical studies of extrasolar planets have also shown that there is a minimum mass for a star commensurate with the existence of a habitable planet in its system. Below about 0.7–0.8 solar masses, the habitable zone is so close to the star that tidal forces rapidly despin any potential Earth so that one hemisphere always faces the star. A star of 8% of the mass of the Sun could certainly support a cloud of artificial space habitats, but not Earth.

What hope then is there for Earth in 5 billion years' time; is the choice incineration or an eternity of artificial maintenance? Maybe not, for there is another way: to replace the Sun with another star entirely.

SOLAR EXCHANGE

The notion of swapping the Earth's sun for a much younger star seems, at first, even more improbable and outrageous than the scenarios I have described previously. However, this was suggested, as an aside, in a paper written by Los Alamos astronomer J. G. Hills in 1984.[4] Hills has published a large amount of research based on his computer simulations of close stellar encounters. In the paper in question, he was examining the outcome of simulated encounters between a one solar mass star, orbited by a single planet, with an intruding star of one solar mass. He found that if the closest approach of the intruder is two to three times the radius of the planetary orbit or less, then the encounter tended to expand the orbit of the star/planet system, or even to dissociate it. A large proportion of the encounters that did not result in dissociation resulted in the intruder capturing the planet into an orbit of average eccentricity about 0.7. (The eccentricity of an ellipse, e, is measured between zero and one, and represents how elongated an orbit is. To give some examples, Halley's Comet has an eccentricity of $e = 0.967$; the planets, except for Pluto, have $e < 0.2$). However, Hills noted that out of the 4496 simulated encounters with parameters appropriate to the Sun/Earth system, two encounters resulted in capture into an orbit of $e < 0.1$ and seven in which $e < 0.2$. This led Hills to speculate that any "advanced terracreatures," as he termed them, who might exist in the distant future might plan a carefully phased encounter with a new sun which would capture the Earth into a stable, near-circular orbit. He noted that a problem might be caused by the high eccentricities of other planets perturbed by the encounter, but this might be overcome by using careful timing.

I decided to look at this process in more detail and eventually published a paper on "Solar Exchange," in *Speculations in Science and Technology*. Planning the replacement of the Sun could be done millions of years ahead of the red giant catastrophe. There would be ample time in the last billion years of the Sun's life to select the right star, alter its course, and determine its time of arrival exactly with the configuration of planets most likely to result in an acceptable postencounter situation.

There would be plenty of nearby sun-like stars from which to choose the Sun's successor. Stars pass by the solar system at a velocity of about 30 km/s. If we take a minimum timescale of a million years to carry out the Solar Exchange, then such stars would travel, relative to the Sun, about 100 ly in one million years. With the local stellar number density being about 0.0028 stars per cubic light-year, this gives a total number of 12,000 stars within 100 ly, about 300 of which would be solar-type single stars. Many of these would be less than half the age of the Sun and thus possible candidates for exchange. Should a star be given an impulse while still far off, the course alteration neccessary to bring it on a collision course with the central solar system would be quite low.

However, didn't I elaborate above just how difficult it would be to maneuver a planet? What hope therefore would there be for moving stars? Stars also might be propelled by rocket propulsion, but this time using some of their own substance as reaction mass. The Star Lifting concept of Criswell might easily be adapted to this purpose. If mass is just ejected from one pole, instead of both, then the star would receive an equal and opposite reaction and can indeed be said to possess rocket propulsion (see Figure 10.1). If this method is to be used, though, it would be important, for the reasons already discussed, that the mass lost from the star's outer layers be as small as possible. The Earth's new sun would have to be stable and similar in mass to the aging star it is to replace.

Table 10.1 shows the results of calculations presented in my paper, in which it is assumed that the exhaust velocity of the stellar rocket would be 620 km/s, the same as the escape velocity from the Sun. The headings in the table are explained as follows: Δ V is the amount by which the star's velocity is altered; Θ is the direction

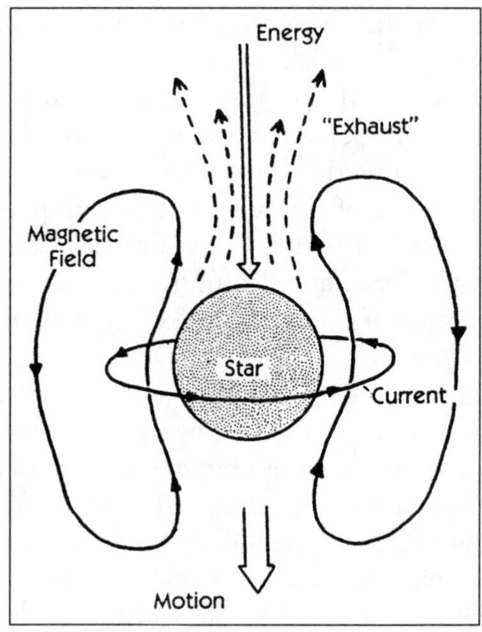

Figure 10.1. The Stellar Rocket redrawn from Reference 5.

change achievable by thrusting at right angles to the direction of the star's initial velocity of 30 km/s; M is the proportion of the star remaining after completing the maneuver; P is the proportion of the star's mass used as propellant; and T is the total time elapsed in millions of years. Since there would be numerous stars to choose for the exchange, it is likely that there would exist a candidate for which only a small velocity increment would be required to bring it on collision course with the solar system. Table 10.1 shows that the amount of reaction mass required, in terms of the mass of the star,

Table 10.1. Sample parameters for stellar rocketry

Δ *V (km/s)*	Θ°	M	*P*	*T (Myr)*
1	1.9	0.998	0.002	0.7
2	3.8	0.997	0.003	1.0
5	9.5	0.992	0.008	2.7
10	18.4	0.983	0.016	5.3
20	33.7	0.967	0.032	10.7

is very modest and that the time to carry out the maneuver would be between 1 and 10 million years.

THE STARS IN THEIR COURSES

Of all the astrophysical engineering techniques considered in this article that might be used to extend the Earth's habitability, Solar Exchange seems to present the fewest conceptual problems. Earth Shift has a project duration estimated to be 100 to 1000 times longer and would probably damage the Earth severely in the process. Star Lifting, if overdone, would probably destabilize the Sun and reduce, rather than extend, its stay on the main sequence.

Since Solar Exchange has no present practical use for us, and is far beyond present technology, it is easy to dismiss the concept as pure science fantasy. However, there may be other civilizations in the Galaxy who might consider it relevant to their own near future: civilizations based in planetary systems about a star, either far older than the Sun, or more massive and short-lived, who may be facing the red giant catastrophe right now. Should some of them have decided not to evacuate their homeworlds, but to take their homeworlds with them, then their rescue efforts might be something we can observe from the Earth. A careful statistical study of relative stellar motions, particularly between stars of similar mass, may reveal the galaxy not to be as wild as it looks.

Maybe 4 to 5 billion years from now a tropical Earth will bask under the heat of a warmer Sun. The length of day will be several hours longer, the sea level higher, and the map of the planet will have changed out of all recognition. The ice caps will have gone and mountain ranges will be less frequent and more eroded. Earth's crust moves more sluggishly, reflecting the dwindling of its internal fires. The land is green to the poles. There is life in the old planet yet, but the battle between the living biosphere and nonliving external influences for control of the climate of the planet is soon to be lost. Even the use of terraforming technology, such as artificial ring systems and orbiting sunshades, cannot stave off a drastic change in climate for much longer. The balance between precipitation and evaporation of water will soon be upset, the oceans will boil, sterilizing the planet. Life on Earth is close to its end.

However, in the last few centuries a star has been growing steadily brighter in the night sky. Diverted from its course 1 million years ago, it has only recently become a truly spectacular sight. For a while it has been visible in the daytime and some say they can discern a tiny disc, though as yet it gives no perceptible heat. Crossing the orbit of Neptune, the intruder has less than 5 years to go before it reaches closest approach to the Sun, just inside one astronomical unit. Then, there will be a short period when two suns, of almost equal brilliance will shine in the skies of Earth. Tides, the like of which would never have been seen before, will grip the planet, reflecting the two star's competing gravitational influences. There will be a year of unprecedented heatwave and hurricane, flood and earthquake. However, from the time of closest approach, it will not be the intruding star that will recede, waning in brilliancy until it becomes nothing more than another dot in the night sky. This will be the fate reserved for the Sun. For the Earth, recovered from the trauma of its exchange, will now be orbiting a new sun, one that will allow life to continue for billions of years into the future.

Part Four

Advanced Drives and Interstellar Travel

Chapter 11

Gordon R. Woodcock

To the Stars!

"Space travel is utter bilge"—thus spake Sir Richard van der Riet Woolley, Astronomer Royal of England, in 1956.

This quotation is, in some respects, astonishing. By that date, the United States had announced intentions to launch an Earth satellite in 1957. Dozens of engineering studies of space flight had been published. There was no serious doubt as to eventual technical feasibility of flights to Earth orbit and to the Moon and planets. There was only doubt as to when they might be accomplished.

But Dr. van der Riet Woolley was, after all, an astronomer. To an astronomer, then even more than now, "space" meant stars and galaxies. I don't agree with his sentiments, but if he meant that *starflight* is utter bilge, his remark is more understandable.

Astronomers are familiar with the vast, dark gulfs of deep space between the stars; they deal routinely with inconceivable distances. Although casual observers of the space travel scene may view starflight as only a modest step beyond trips to the planets in our solar system, it will in fact be inordinately more difficult.

The farthest we have ventured from Earth in manned ships is to our Moon, about 400,000 km. This distance, although great compared to the distance we travel on the surface of the Earth, is insignificant compared to interstellar space. The distance to Alpha Centauri, the nearest bright star, is a little more than 40,000,000,000,000 (40 trillion) km. If we make a celestial scale model, with the distance to the Moon as 1 cm (about 2/5 of an inch), the distance to Alpha Centauri will be about 1000 km (62 miles). On this scale, the distance to the Sun is about 4 m (13 feet), and the distance to Saturn, 40 m (130 feet). At Voyager speeds it would take some 50,000 years to reach the nearest star. Skepticism is understandable.

But skepticism is almost certainly wrong. As recently as 1926, rocket flight to the Moon was pronounced impossible. A futurist view more consistent with history is that, since starflight is not physically impossible, it is inevitable.

Our star quest clearly must begin with finding a place to go. A few years ago, it was thought that places had already been found. But the extrasolar planet discoveries of the 1960s seem to have been premature, probably the result of instrument errors. In light of demonstrations that the suspected perturbations were instrumental in origin, it may be said that *there is no unequivocal evidence for the existence of planets outside the solar system*. (Project Orion [a NASA study of means of detecting extrasolar planets], NASA SP-436, 1980). The question of places to go, of course, is related to processes of star formation. Again from Project Orion, "An equivalent way of expressing present cosmogonic hypotheses is to say that planetary system formation seems to be a natural, if not inevitable, aspect of the star formation process. The important distinction between the [old] catastrophic and [new] nebular cosmogonic hypotheses is that, if the former is correct, planetary systems are the exception rather than the rule, whereas if the latter is correct, planetary systems are the rule. A systematic study of the frequency of occurrence of planetary systems would thus provide a valuable observational check on present theories of star formation."

Finding a place to go is thus likely to be a byproduct of astrophysical research and need not be justified solely as a prelude to an interstellar flight venture. The question remaining is, "Just how difficult is it?"

There are two ways to find planets orbiting other stars. The first is astrometry: observing the very slight irregularity of motion of a star due to the gravitational effect of its planet(s). The motion to be observed is indeed slight! The irregularity in the Sun's motion, influenced by Jupiter, as seen from the nearest star, would present a perceived waviness in the motion no greater than the width of a softball in New York as observed from Los Angeles.

"With one exception, the telescopes presently used in astrometry . . . are about 60 years old, and only two were designed for high precision astrometric observations. . . . None of the existing instruments are designed . . . for successful detection of very small perturbations" (Project Orion). Project Orion concluded that ground-based astrometry could be improved by more than an order of magnitude and that such improvement would make possible the detection of large (Jupiter-size) planets around stars out to about 100 light-years' distance. This volume of space takes in thousands of stars. The results of such a search would be very significant, both to the theory of star and planet formation and to questions of intelligent life in the universe.

The second way of finding planets is direct observation—that is to say, imaging—with some sort of telescope. Observation will tell us the size or color of an extrasolar planet. Astrometry, however, will tell us its mass and orbital period. The two schemes are complementary.

It is quite easy to calculate the brightness of a planet circling a distant sun. The result, for stars within 10 or so light years from Earth, is on the order of 25th magnitude, a brightness about 100 million times fainter than the faintest stars seen by the unaided eye, but easily discerned by the largest Earth-based telescopes. "So what's the problem?" one might ask. The problem is the brightness of the parent star. It will be something like 1 billion times brighter than its planets. Its faint planets will be entirely lost in the blazing glare of the star's image. This is why Earth-based telescopes have never seen extrasolar planets.

If we put a telescope in space, the chances of direct observation improve because the scattering effects of our Earth's atmosphere are avoided. Still, the image of a star in a telescope is not a point, but a smear of light surrounded by rings that become gradually fainter as one looks farther from the central image. At distances expected for planets, the brightness of these surrounding rings will overwhelm the faint planetary images.

Consequently, sophisticated ways to defeat the brightness of the rings have been proposed. One way is apodization: tailoring the reflectivity of the telescope's mirror to minimize the brightness of the rings. Although apodization is theoretically capable of major improvements in the sensitivity of a space telescope for faint planetary images, it requires extreme precision in telescope optics. Alternative schemes include the use of interferometry and of distant occulting disks. These seem to be more practical approaches.

In infrared light, an extrasolar planet will be much brighter relative to its parent star than in visible light, because the planet emits infrared light from its own warmth, while the visible light is merely reflected. Infrared wavelengths for best detection, however, are about ten times longer than those of visible light. Consequently, by the laws of optics, ten times greater aperture is needed for the same resolution.

An interferometer simulates a great aperture by simultaneously analyzing the images from two or more smaller apertures coupled together. An interferometer for extrasolar planet detection would spin about its boresight, aimed at the parent star. Images from the two apertures would be combined to null the bright image of the star while expressing the images of any faint planets as oscillating electronic signals at the frequency of rotation of the interferometer. Sophisticated computer analysis methods would yield very high sensitivity for this instrument.

The planetary interferometer space telescope is a rather specialized instrument, ill-suited for other purposes. The occulting disk, however, is an augmentation of an otherwise general-purpose telescope.

One occulting disk concept was proposed by this author about 5 years ago. The idea is to fly a disk-carrying spacecraft to a great distance from a general-purpose space telescope, in order to blot out the image of a star and make its planets more easily visible. If we select a suitable disk size and distance, the disk will not block the planet's image. Positioning of the occulting disk could be controlled by a laser beam launched from the telescope. Navigating by sensing the laser beam, the disk spacecraft could interpose itself between the star and the space telescope.

One might imagine this to be a nearly foolproof scheme, but because of the diffraction of light it only offers an improvement factor on the order of 100. This, however, is enough to make extrasolar planets eminently detectable. We should even be able to detect smaller, Earth-like planets orbiting the nearer stars.

On balance, the finding of planets orbiting the nearer stars doesn't seem so difficult. Several methods have been studied, and all would apparently work. Moreover, there is a strong scientific motivation, unrelated to interstellar travel, to attempt detection of extrasolar planets.

Detection schemes, as presently understood, will be able to distinguish between gas-giant planets and Earth-like planets. They will tell us something about mass, size, color, orbital period, and temperature. But we will see no surface detail. The greatest telescopes imaginable will show us less than we can see of Mars with the naked eye.

However, a technical civilization able to accomplish interstellar travel will be able to survive in any system with Earth-like planets, whether or not they are able to harbor indigenous life. We now imagine ourselves nearly able to eke out a survival in the asteroid belt. Surely, interstellar colonists could do as well.

Places to go, according to present scientific theories of star formation, are plentiful. The progress of space research can be counted on to find a few long before we are ready to engineer a starship.

"It is certainly out of the question, at our present level of technology or, indeed, at any level we can foresee, to mount an interstellar search [for intelligent life] by spaceship" (*The Search for Extraterrestrial Intelligence*, NASA SP-419, 1977). At any level we can foresee? Let's try some foreseeing:

First, just how tough is it? Science fiction long ago created the three themes presently known for starflight: fly slow (the generation ship), fly fast (the relativistic ship), and fly tricky, invoking some sort of spacewarp or fifth-dimensional "jump." The third scheme relies on a physics presently unknown, but the first two depend only on our ability to apply energy and power to surmount the barriers of time and distance.

We need *both* high energy and a high power-to-weight ratio to travel to even the nearest star in a "reasonable" time. High energy will give us enough rocket jet velocity to attain the speed needed to cross interstellar distances in reasonable time. Only with high power-to-weight can we accelerate to our speed in a reasonable time.

"How high is high?" is the obvious question. Ordinary rockets powered by chemical fuels have plenty of acceleration but far too little energy (specific impulse). Nuclear-powered electric rockets could achieve enough jet energy, but are limited to low acceleration by the complexity and weight of their power conversion cycles. The nuclear energy, released as heat, must be changed into electrical power to operate an ion engine. Electric rockets, however powered, confront us with the old nemesis of space propulsion engineering: power conversion cycles. Always heavy and complex, they are usually inefficient as well. I once read an article describing an electric ion engine as "The Star Engine." Maybe, if one accepts a trip time of 1000 years or more!

We have to find a way to express nuclear energy directly as jet energy. Fusion reactor concepts offer fascinating possibilities (Figure 11.1). A magnetic-containment fusion reactor (assuming we can get one of these to work) will be a magnetic "bottle" of very hot plasma. All we must do is provide a controlled leak in the bottle, so that the plasma gradually leaks out in a particular direction, producing a high-energy jet. The leaky bottle is replenished by fresh fusion fuel. Specific impulses ranging from a few thousand to as much as a million seconds have been projected by various investigators. Power-to-weight ratios as high as 10 to 100 kW/kg might be reached, but we must first resolve a twofold problem.

The typical magnetic-containment fusion reactor concept begins with an evacuated chamber, usually doughnut-shaped, in which the reaction takes place. The wall of this chamber, the "first wall," must be vigorously cooled so that it will not be vaporized by the storm of radiation emanating from the reaction. This wall is surrounded by a "lithium blanket," actually a container filled with liquid lithium metal. Part of the reaction—the fusion of deuterium and tritium atoms into helium—occurs in the evacuated doughnut. About three-fourths of the energy released comes off as very high-energy neutrons. These are absorbed in the blanket, converting its lithium into tritium and helium. The blanket is necessary because natural tritium is very scarce; tritium used inside the reactor must be replenished from the blanket.

Outside the blanket are superconducting magnets that create the magnetic bottle. These must be refrigerated to about 5 K (about 450° below 0 F). If the fusion reactor is to be used for utility electric power generation (the present objective of the fusion power research program), the energy from the reactor will be taken from the lithium blanket as heat to make steam to run generators.

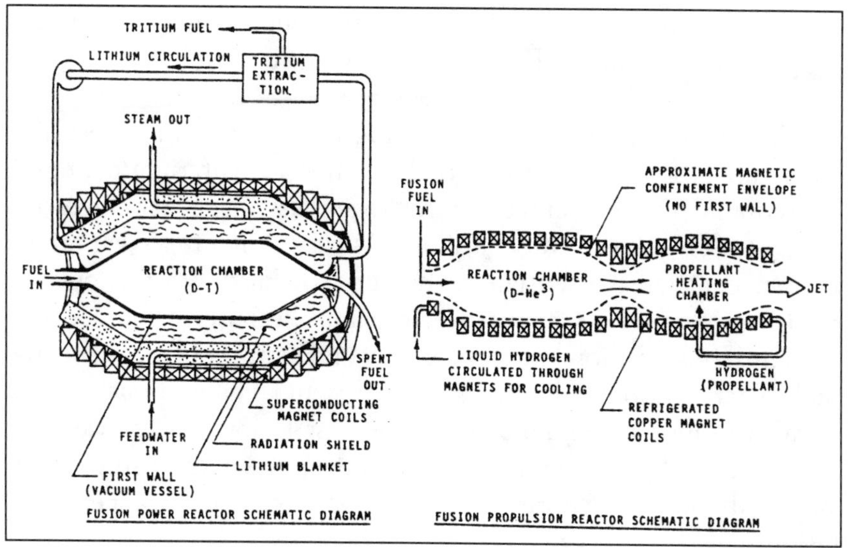

Figure 11.1. Fusion power reactor concepts. Fusion power reactor concepts for power and for propulsion are contrasted in this diagram. For simplicity, I have used a magnetic mirror geometry, although actual reactors will probably use a more complex geometry such as the Tokamak.

The power reactor includes a "first wall" vacuum vessel that maintains the high vacuum needed for the reaction; a lithium blanket in which tritium is regenerated; and superconducting magnets for confinement of the reaction. Power is extracted as heat from the lithium blanket. The heat boils water to run steam generators.

A rocket reactor may employ copper magnets cooled to cryogenic temperatures by liquid hydrogen. The hydrogen, after cooling the magnets, would be used as reaction mass for the rocket. It is assumed that this reaction runs on deuterium and helium-3. No blanket is needed. Neither is a first wall, because the natural vacuum of space will suffice.

The energy of particles leaking from the reaction may be too high, depending on the mission. If we want to trade jet velocity for higher thrust, a second magnetic bottle can be used to redistribute the energy of the reaction products to hydrogen propellant.

So we are still confronted by our space-propulsion nemesis: power cycles. The first generates electricity from the heat of the fusion reaction; the second cools the superconducting magnets. We have to get rid of these if we are to have a useful fusion star drive.

For a star drive, we can remove the lithium blanket. This gets rid of a major heat source. We could make tritium on Earth in fusion reactors to fuel our starship. The short half-life of tritium, 12 years, is a problem for a starship whose travel time may be several times this, but the decay of tritium into helium-3 may be a blessing in disguise.

We should also get rid of the superconducting magnets and, as proposed by Dr. Robert Bussard, use magnets cooled by the engine's fuel flow.

We could do even better by using a different fusion reaction. There are at least three from which to choose: deuterium/helium-3, deuterium/deuterium, and boron/hydrogen, listed in order of ignition difficulty. The first of these is almost as easy to ignite as deuterium/tritium, but there is essentially *no* helium-3 on Earth. It will, however, be a byproduct of a fusion power program because of the decay of tritium. Thus, a fusion energy economy on Earth could make starship fuel. There is doubt, however, that it could make enough. If we began to save up helium-3 when the first fusion reactor went on line, there still might not be enough for even the first starship. These ships will generate enormous power and have a great appetite for fusion fuel.

That is why the British Interplanetary Society, in its study of a fusion-powered star probe, proposed that helium-3 be obtained from the atmosphere of Jupiter. Unlike Earth, Jupiter still has its primordial atmosphere of hydrogen and helium; about 0.006% of the primordial mixture is helium-3, according to astrophysicist Fred Hoyle. This seemingly small amount is enough to make scooping up Jupiter's atmosphere from an orbiting ship very profitable. The power available, from fusion of scooped-up helium-3 and deuterium, to a "Jupiter scoopiter" would be something like 30 times that needed to maintain its orbit in the face of the scooping drag.

The deuterium/helium-3 reaction produces relatively few neutrons, and would greatly reduce neutron heating. The deuterium/deuterium reaction produces about one-fourth as many neutrons as the deuterium/tritium reaction, but is roughly ten times harder to ignite. The boron/hydrogen reaction produces no neutrons, but may be too hard to ignite ever to be used in a magnetic bottle reactor. Deuterium, boron, and hydrogen, of course, are all plentiful.

Star-drive reactors will have to be far more powerful than any yet conceived. At very high powers, new reactor types might be contemplated. One such is a pellet-collision scheme. Electromagnetic accelerators would fire small pellets of boron hydride at one another, at speeds of hundreds of kilometers per second. The high temperatures and densities produced by the collision would ignite the fusion reaction. A magnetic rocket nozzle would direct the jet. Maybe the now-defunct program of the 1950s to develop boron hydride missile fuels was strangely prescient!

Still more powerful star drives might be contrived from matter–antimatter engines. Antihydrogen can be made from positrons (anti-electrons) and antiprotons. The former were discovered in the 1930s, and antiprotons were first isolated in 1955. Plans are now being discussed for containment of up to a trillion antiprotons in a storage ring for physics experiments. One fine day, we will undoubtedly be able to create and store antihydrogen, or antihelium, or whatever. This, of course, will be sporty, inasmuch as any form of antimatter will annihilate ordinary matter upon contact! We will have to find a storage scheme that somehow suspends the antimatter fuel without its coming into contact with anything.

The payoff is that the matter–antimatter reaction will be able to convert mass into energy at more than 50% efficiency, whereas fusion is less than 1% efficient. This is the best star drive that presently known physics can prescribe: an annihilation engine, powered by a matter–antimatter reaction. Such a drive might approach lightspeed. Built large enough, an annihilation engine might attain high thrust and yield a star drive able to shorten star trips by relativistic time dilation. We are now speculating rather than forecasting, of course. No one has published a design for an annihilation star drive, but this is clearly the ultimate that presently understood physics has to offer.

What might a starship be like? Probably rather like one of Gerard K. O'Neill's space colonies. Imagine that we have found a planetary system orbiting a suitable nearby star. We know there are some Earth-size planetary bodies, but we don't know much about them. Colonies and bases on the Moon, Mars, and some of the moons of Jupiter and Saturn have taught us to survive on inhospitable worlds. We are confident that if we can get there, we can survive.

Survival, however, depends on perpetuation of a high-technology society. We must take along enough skills and knowledge to operate, repair, rebuild, replicate, and improve all of the machinery and equipment we need to live and prosper, perhaps on a moon-like body. And our raw materials are likely to be undifferentiated rocks, not high-grade ores. How many people do we need to embody all the skills? Remember, no help from home! Today, my guess is about 10,000. In the future, developments in robotics might reduce the number, but it will still be large.

One thing we will surely do is listen before we leap. We would not wish to arrive in a distant planetary system only to find we were not welcome. If indigenous intelligent civilization is present, careful listening with large radio telescopes will reveal it by detecting "leakage" of electromagnetic signals such as radio or radar, even if these are not meant for interstellar communication. And we should not chance that an apparent welcome at departure time will last until arrival. Imagine a Japanese expedition to the United States departing in 1903 for arrival 40 years later. Things change.

Our starship will probably gross on the order of 1 million metric tons and be something like 1000 m (11 football fields) in length. A triangular wedge shape similar to the empire ships in *Star Wars* will minimize the damage from hitting anything at high speed. Let's hope we don't hit anything bigger than a grain of sand. At 0.1c, a collision with a pea-sized pebble would release as much energy as a small atomic bomb.

The star drive will provide artificial gravity, perhaps one tenth of a "g," onboard the ship. Our program will be to accelerate until we are halfway there, then turn around and decelerate the rest of the way. If we are to travel 10 light-years, accelerating at 0.1g, our maximum speed will be about 0.15c and the trip will take 130 years. If our star drive has a specific impulse of 1 million s and a billion newtons (about 200 million lb) of thrust for our 0.1g, its power will be several billion megawatts. This is about 1000 times the present total energy consumption of the United States (see Figure 11.2). Such huge numbers sound like they come from a government budgeteer, but these are the awesome statistics of starship engineering as we now know it. Ah, for even the glimmer of an idea how to pull off the spacewarp trick!

If we have some ideas as to "how," then we are surely allowed to ask "when." The "when" of starflight may be more an economic question than a technical one. If we had the technology to build it, our million-ton ship would likely cost a trillion dollars. Such a proposal will never get by Senator Proxmire.

Further, when starships first become possible, the expected trip time will be 20 to 100 years. The return on an investment, that is, to Earth, will be nil. What will motivate the spending of huge sums on such an enterprise?

Our society today is willing to make huge investments only if a near-term payback is expected or if some urgent need, such as "war on poverty" or national security, is served. What the U.S. government spends on social causes, including social security, would pay for a trillion-dollar starship in 3 years; what it spends on defense, in about 5. At the present NASA spending rate, however, it would take 160 years to pay for the starship!

This short-sighted attitude toward investment in scientific or cultural advancement seems to stem from a "Harvard Business School" outlook. If one evaluates investments with a discount rate of 10% or more, anything that takes more than 10 or 15 years to mature is worthless. (Yet, for some reason, we keep on having children.) As usually practiced, the Harvard Business School approach is not even good economics, since it ignores indirect benefits such as technical advancements; these are often of more value than the direct benefits.

Ever since discounting became popular for investment analysis in the mid-1960s, our technological and cultural advancement has been slowed. But it was not always thus. The great cathedrals of Europe were constructed over generations. The U.S. interstate highway program has taken about 30 years. One wonders how long the pyramids of Egypt took, and what percent of Egypt's gross national product they consumed.

We shouldn't be too pessimistic. Starship technology is probably at least 50 years in the future. It may be as far in the future as the clipper ships are in the past. Our ability to fund epic projects continues to advance as our economy grows. At an annual growth rate of 3%, our economy will multiply by a factor of 20 in 100 years. A starship project will not be too staggering to contemplate. It will, in fact, be less of a fiscal challenge than was Project Apollo in 1961.

Some will argue about "limits to growth" and all that. Indeed, the finiteness of Earth's resources will force us into space if we are to maintain economic progress. The industrialization and colonization of the solar system will surely bring about great cultural changes in our society. It's difficult to guess exactly what they will be, but I would bet they will improve the social acceptability of a starship project.

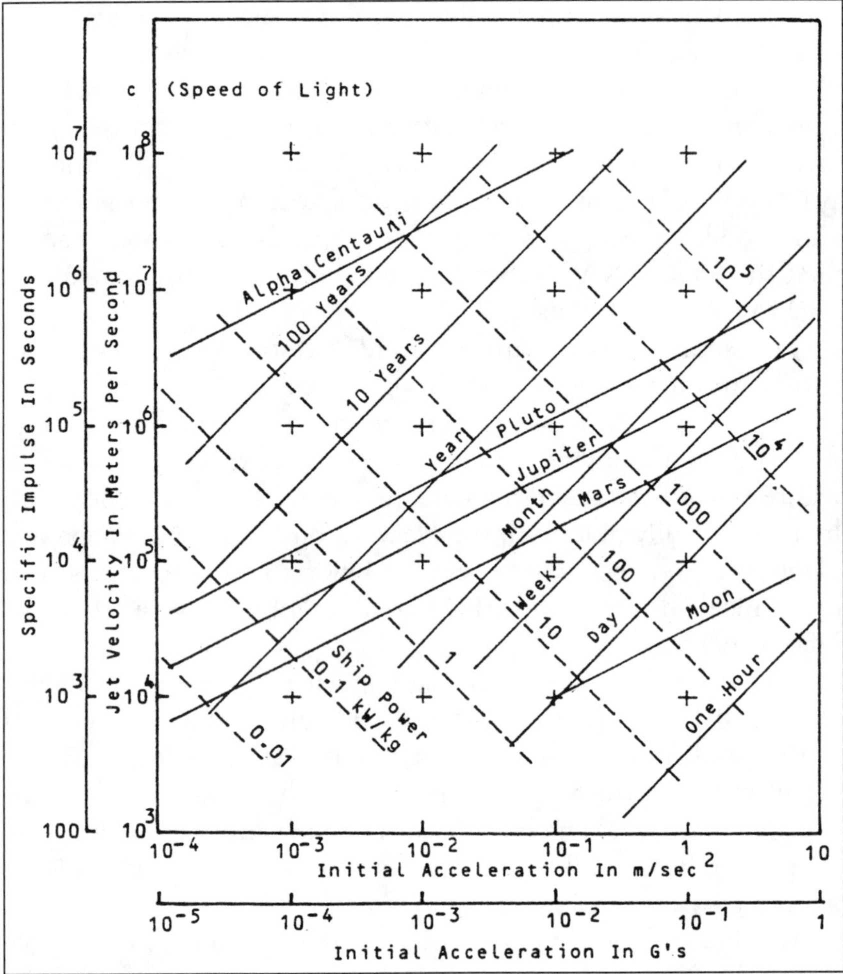

Figure 11.2. Spaceship performance map. Calculating the performance of a spaceship can be complicated. But if the ship is powerful enough, we can ignore gravity fields. It is then fairly easy. The ship will accelerate to a maximum speed and then turn around and slow down at its destination. Fusion or annihilation-drive ships will probably do this. They will apply power all the time, speeding up and then slowing down.

In this simple case, all the important performance parameters can be expressed on a single graph. This one is drawn for the case when 90% of the starting mass is propellant. Jet velocity and starting acceleration are the graph scales. Distances for several bodies are shown. Mars varies greatly; I used 150 million km. Trip times and specific power levels are also shown. "Specific power" expresses how much power the ship generates for each kilogram of its mass, that is, its total power divided by its mass. The propellant the ship will carry is not included in the mass value.

An example: Suppose your ship can produce 100 kW/kg of jet power. You wish to fly to Jupiter. Where the 100 kW/kg and Jupiter lines cross on the graph, read a jet

Now that we can begin to sketch the outlines of engineering starships, we are naturally drawn to questions about alien interstellar travelers. In the 1950s, and especially in the 1960s, the popular scientific view held that the universe was teeming with life, presumably intelligent. Radio telescopes listened for artificial signals from planetary systems of other stars. Discovery was announced of one or more planets orbiting Barnard's Star. Primitive life on Mars was almost accepted as fact. Enrico Fermi, anticipating a later view by about 20 years, asked, "Where are they?"

The United States once regarded the Atlantic Ocean as a protective barrier. Similarly, the great gulfs between the stars have been viewed until recently as a barrier to starflight. Discovery of intelligent life elsewhere in the universe, even though of enormous philosophical and scientific importance, was seen strictly as an academic matter and not one of practical concern.

In the last few years, all this has begun to change. The key development has been Gerard O'Neill's proposals for self-sufficient space colonies. Fitted with a fusion propulsion system, such a colony might become a "generation starship," that is, a ship capable of reaching the stars in a few generations of life aboard. Starflight by this means is no longer merely fanciful science fiction but technically conceivable.

Has intelligent life arisen somewhere else in the galaxy? Even if it spread only at a speed of 0.01c, such an intelligence could colonize the entire galaxy in 2 to 3 million years. This is about the length of time that man-like hominids have lived on Earth, an exceedingly short time in the history of the galaxy. 0.01c is one one-hundredth the speed of light. A fusion-propelled ship should easily exceed 0.01c; 0.04 to 0.05c is a more likely estimate. If we presume that hundreds of years are spent at each new stellar beachhead, to regroup and gather strength for the next leap across the dark reaches of interstellar

---

velocity of 300,000 m/sec (Isp = 30,000) and an initial acceleration of nearly 0.01g. Your trip will take about two months.

The upper area of the graph shows that high performance is needed to reach the nearest stars. Even generation ships will need, in addition to very high jet velocities, power on the order of 100 kW/kg. The space shuttle orbiter produces about 100 kW/kg with its three engines. The high power needed for starflight precludes its attainment with means such as electric propulsion.

space, a spreading velocity of 0.01c is quite believable. Indeed, where are they?

Recognition that construction of a starship may be possible with foreseeable extensions of our technology, coupled with a distinct lack of alien visitors, seems to be swinging scientific opinion toward doubting the occurrence of life elsewhere in the universe. Perhaps we are alone! Recently it has been speculated (*Science News*, June 20, 1981) that supernova explosions within the galaxy, or its central core, have prevented intelligent life from developing by spraying lethal doses of radiation throughout space. Earth is imagined to have escaped by fortuitously having been in the protective envelope of a galactic spiral arm during each lethal period.

Indeed, "Where are they?" If we can, why haven't "they"—some other intelligent civilization—achieved starflight? And why aren't they here or, at least, why haven't they been here and left some record? Of course, many people believe they *are* (UFOs) or have been (ancient astronauts). But the evidence for either of these views is hardly convincing. At least, I am not convinced!

One can think of dozens of reasons why an advanced civilization, spreading through the galaxy, would have bypassed Earth. Even so, current scientific opinion is veering away from the "teeming with life" views of the 1960s.

If starships are big and expensive, as I suspect, it is likely that they don't pass this way very often. Perhaps every few million years. And why didn't "they" land here and colonize? "Star Trek" had an answer: the "prime directive." Don't interfere with indigenous life or cultures. Maybe the spaceship phase of technical and cultural development is only transitory. How about teleportation? Or some sort of supersensory means of communication such that there simply is no reason to travel? For that matter, maybe "they" will land tomorrow. The fact that we do not have alien visitors proves neither (1) that aliens don't exist, or (2) that star travel is impossible.

I don't suppose I can avoid some sort of speculation on the spacewarp trick. Of course, it has no basis in known science. And scientists are forever acting as if they know all there is to know about the universe. That was certainly true about 1890. There was actually serious scientific opinion back then that no more basic science remained to be discovered. We knew all there was to know! There have been, since then, about three revolutions in physics.

Relativity and quantum mechanics are the biggies, and solid-state physics has had a profound impact on almost everyone's life. The pocket calculator lying on my desk could only have been explained as "magic" as recently as the 1940s.

We are apparently in the midst of another revolution in physics. The "gauge theories" of particle physics are coming close to Einstein's dream of a unified field theory, a single theory that explains all of the forces of nature. They even offer an explanation as to why antimatter is apparently very scarce in the universe.

These theories, in their present state, with all the stuff about colored and charmed quarks, are mainly mechanistic. They are like Kepler's elucidation of planetary motion. He discovered that planets move in ellipses, and that an imaginary line between the planet and the sun sweeps equal areas in equal times, and so forth. But it remained for Newton to propose gravity as an explanation and interpretation of Kepler's facts.

Similarly, the trappings of relativity, the constancy of lightspeed, the Lorentz–Fitzgerald contraction (it isn't named for Einstein!) were mostly known before Einstein offered his profound philosophical interpretation, with its awesome insight to the equivalence of matter and energy.

We await another great philosopher-interpreter, to transform the multitude of discoveries in particle physics and cosmology of the last 20 or so years into a new synthesis, a new and deeper explanation of the mysteries of nature. Out of his or her work may emerge the secret of star travel without strain and pain. Otherwise, we will just have to use brute force and high-energy propulsion.

If our human civilization does survive its near-term crises of militarism, nationalism, and resource exhaustion, we will soon move out into the solar system. And, we will eventually build starships. Our first starship will not be our last. ". . . several bright sources such as quasar 3C273 are famous for having high-speed jets protruding out one side" (*Science News*, August 15, 1981). It sort of makes you wonder.

Chapter 12

Robert M. Zubrin

The Magnetic Sail

Two of the most fundamental axioms of exploration are that it is necessary to have mobility, and that true mobility can only be obtained if the resources required to support it can be obtained from the environment whose exploration is desired. This was the great strength of the sailing ships of the age of exploration, which derived their motive power from the very air through which they moved, and thus were free to travel at will across the vast distances of the world's oceans. Indeed, had Columbus been equipped with a coal-fired steamer, or even a ship driven by advanced diesel engines, instead of his simple caravels, it is clear that he could never have made his great discovery. With such systems it would have been unthinkable to cut loose from his European fueling stations for a speculative voyage into the great beyond. Again, during the nineteenth century, small teams of explorers traveling the Arctic by dogsled and living off the herds of caribou were able to accomplish much more useful exploration, at much lower cost and risk, than fleets of steam-powered warships dependent on fuel and supplies they had hauled from home. To take a third example, Lewis and Clark would hardly have been able to cross the Appalachians, let alone a continent, had they decided to pack all the food, fodder, water, and air they and their animals needed for a transcontinental trip, rather than picking up what was necessary along the way.

These same axioms that have held true throughout human history for the exploration of Earth also hold true for the exploration of space. To travel on, off, or around planetary bodies, we need to make use of the indigenous resources those bodies afford to provide rocket propellant whose transportation from Earth would drive mission mass and costs through the roof. To travel through space most efficiently, we need to make use of those resources found in space itself.

Interplanetary and interstellar space do not appear at first glance to be rich in resources, but they do have some. First of all, in interplanetary space, there is sunlight, which we already use to supply electric power to spacecraft by means of photovoltaic panels, and which can also be used to provide propulsion through the use of large ultrathin solar light sails. Planetary and stellar gravitational fields are also available, and these can and have been used to provide spacecraft propulsion through clever gravity-assist maneuvers. In both interplanetary and interstellar space there is also matter, to the tune of about 5 million hydrogen atoms in plasma form per cubic meter in interplanetary space, and about 100,000 per cubic meter in the interstellar environment. The interplanetary plasma is streaming outward radially from the Sun at a velocity of about 500 km/s, a phenomenon which is termed the *solar wind*, while motion of the interstellar medium is unknown but generally presumed to be rotating with the rest of the galaxy, and thus static with respect to the Sun and its near neighbors. Space also contains magnetic fields, of planetary, stellar, and galactic origin. To date, the plasma winds and magnetic fields of space have not been used effectively to drive spacecraft. In order to capitalize on these unused resources, in 1988 Dana Andrews (of the Boeing Aerospace Co.) and I (of Martin Marietta Astronautics), working in close collaboration, introduced a new kind of space propulsion device, which we call the magnetic sail,[1–6] or magsail.

The magsail is a device that can be used to accelerate or decelerate a spacecraft by using a magnetic field to deflect the plasma naturally found in the solar wind and interstellar medium. It also can enable a spacecraft to push out of low orbit around a planet into interplanetary space by interacting with the planet's magnetic field. The magsail is not the first device that anyone has proposed to make use of space plasma for propulsion, and owes its origin in some degree to the conceptual prior art. The story of how it came to be is quite interesting.

In 1960, physicist Robert Bussard introduced one of the most beautiful concepts in speculative astronautics, the interstellar ramscoop.[7] In this concept, a spacecraft moving through interstellar space used a ramscoop to gather the interstellar hydrogen as it flies, which it then reacted in a thermonuclear fusion reactor to produce thrust. The concept was terrific because it required no onboard supply of propellant, and the faster the ship went, the better the scoop worked, allowing the spacecraft to asymptotically approach the velocity of light. Unfortunately, the realization of the Bussard interstellar ramscoop faces two formidable obstacles. The first is that the interstellar medium is composed predominantly of ordinary light hydrogen, not the heavier and much more reactive isotopes deuterium and tritium that would burn easily in a fusion reaction. Ordinary hydrogen would probably burn much too slowly to produce useful thrust, although means have been suggested[8] that might allow us to catalyze its reaction with a carbon-nitrogen-oxygen thermonuclear fusion cycle that could increase the rate of reaction substantially. The second problem is the need for a scoop with a vast cross-sectional area, so as to allow the effective gathering of the very diffused interstellar medium. With foreseeable materials, a scoop composed of physical matter would weigh so much that accelerating the spacecraft to useful interstellar velocities would be impossible. The remedy that has frequently been proposed to address this difficulty is to collect the interstellar matter not with a physical scoop, but with a magnetic field with a large radius of effective action.

In 1988, Dana Andrews was researching a concept of his that involved using a Bussard type magnetic scoop to provide propellant for an ordinary ion thruster which would be powered by an onboard nuclear reactor power source. This concept thus avoided the need for accomplishing the very difficult light hydrogen fusion reaction required by Bussard's original suggestion. Although potential performance was thus reduced far below levels that would be useful for interstellar flight, the system would be a knock-out for interplanetary travel as the freedom from dependence on ship-carried propellant would give the craft unlimited run of the solar system. The problem was, as best as Dana could calculate it, that the magnetic scoop employed by the system was generating more drag against the interplanetary medium than the ion engines were producing thrust. The ship was going nowhere.

Since I have a pretty good background in plasma physics, Dana told me about his concept and the problem he was running into, and asked me if I could figure out a way to remedy the situation. At first I thought there might be a way, because Dana was using certain approximations to calculate the plasma drag that were very rough for the situation he was dealing with. Perhaps, I thought, if a computer program were written that could calculate the drag more accurately, the revised estimate for the drag might be low enough that the system could function. So we worked together writing such a program, only to discover, once it was operating, that the actual drag was much greater than Dana had originally estimated. At that point I suggested that we abandon the ion thrusters entirely, and rather than seek to minimize the drag, try to maximize it; to use the magnetic field not as a scoop, but as a sail, and derive the spacecraft's motive force from the dynamic pressure of the solar wind itself. Dana concurred, and we went back to the drawing board with a new approach. The magsail was born, and what a baby it was! For when the smoke cleared, we found that we had invented a system that could move payloads from low Earth orbit to any destination in the solar system without using propellants and without regard to the usual launch windows that constrain conventional interplanetary ballistic flight. Furthermore, the same system could be used as a highly effective shield to protect space travelers from solar flares, or as a propellant-free brake for an interstellar spacecraft flying at relativistic velocities.

HOW A MAGSAIL WORKS

The magsail's principle of operation is as follows: A loop of superconducting cable tens of kilometers in diameter is stored on a drum attached to a payload spacecraft. When the time comes for operation, the cable is played out and a current is initiated in the loop. Since the wire is superconducting, the current once initiated will be maintained indefinitely without further power. The magnetic field created by the current causes a pressure which imparts a hoop stress to the loop, aiding the deployment and eventually forcing it to a rigid circular shape. The loop operates at low fields strengths, typically 0.00001 Tesla, or T (about 1/3 Earth's magnetic field at its equator), so little structural strengthening is required. The loop can be positioned with its axis at any angle with respect to the plasma wind, with the two extreme cases examined for analytical purposes being the axial configuration, in which the dipole axis is parallel to the wind, and the normal configuration, in which the dipole axis is perpendicular to the wind. A magsail with payload is depicted in Figure 12.1.

In operation, charged particles entering the field are deflected according to the magnetic field they experience, thus imparting momentum to the loop. If a net plasma wind, such as the solar wind, exists relative to the spacecraft, the magsail loop will always create drag, and thus accelerate the spacecraft in the direction of the relative wind. The solar wind in the vicinity of Earth is a flux of several million protons and electrons per cubic meter at a velocity of 400 to 600 km/s. This can be used to accelerate a spacecraft radially away from the Sun and the maximum speed available would be that of the solar wind itself. While inadequate for interstellar missions, these velocities are certainly more than adequate for interplanetary missions.

However, if the magsail spacecraft has somehow been accelerated to a relevant interstellar velocity, for example, by a fusion rocket or

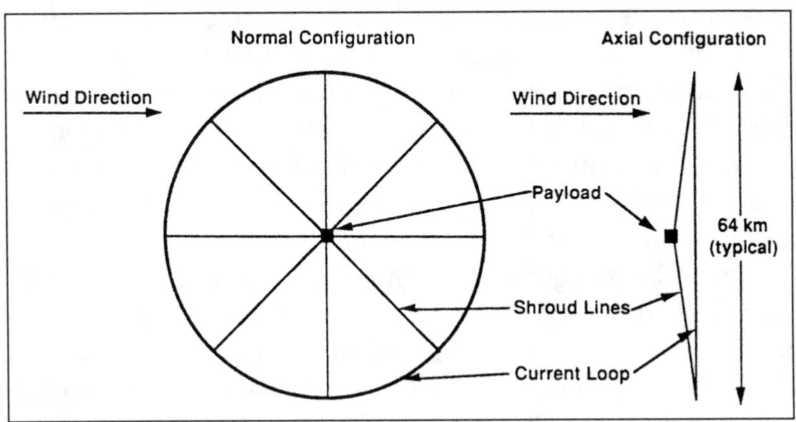

Figure 12.1. Magsail deployed with payload.

a laser-pushed lightsail, the magsail can be used to create drag against the static interstellar medium, and thus act as an effective braking device. The ability to slow spacecraft from relativistic to interplanetary velocities without the use of rocket propellant results in a dramatic lowering of both rocket mass ratio and total mission time.

If the magsail is utilized in a nonaxial configuration, symmetry is destroyed and it becomes possible for the magsail to generate a force perpendicular to the wind, that is, lift. Lift can be used to alter the magsail spacecraft's angular momentum about the Sun, thus greatly increasing the repertoire of possible maneuvers. In addition, lift can be used to provide steering ability to a decelerating relativistic interstellar spacecraft.

The magsail as currently conceived depends on operating the superconducting loop at high current densities at ambient temperatures. In interstellar space, ambient is 2.7 K, where current low temperature superconductors NbTi and Nb_3Sn have critical currents of 1.0×10^{10} and 2.0×10^{10} A/m^2 respectively. In interplanetary space, where ambient temperatures are above the critical temperatures of low temperature superconductors, these materials would require expensive and heavy refrigeration systems. However the new high-temperature superconductors such as $YBa_2Cu_3O_7$ have demonstrated comparable critical currents in microscopic samples at temperatures of 77 K or more, which would make them maintainable in interplanetary space using simple multilayer insulation and highly reflective coatings. Assuming that this performance will someday be realizable in bulk cable, we have chosen to parametrize the problem by assuming the availability of a high-temperature superconducting cable with a critical current of 10^{10} A/m^2, that is, equal to that of NbTi. Because the magnets are operating in an ambient environment below their critical temperature, no substrate material beyond that required for mechanical support is required. Assuming a fixed magnet density of 5000 kg/m^3 (copper oxide), our magnet has a current-to-mass density (J/ρ_m) of 2.0×10^6 A-m/kg.

It might be thought that a magsail could not operate effectively within the Earth's magnetosphere, because the solar wind is excluded from that region by Earth's magnetic field. However, by interacting with Earth's magnetic poles, the magsail can generate sufficient force to drive both itself and a substantial payload up to escape velocity via a series of perigee kicks. Once escape has been reached, the magsail will find itself in interplanetary space where the solar wind is available to enable further propulsion.

The contrast between the mode of propulsion of a magsail operating within a magnetosphere as opposed to one within a plasma wind is depicted in Figure 12.2.

THE MAGSAIL OPERATING IN A PLASMA WIND

The operation of a magsail within the solar wind can be approximated by a dipole field (or a collection of dipoles) compressed within a boundary created by a perfectly conducting plasma. Within the boundary, there is a magnetic field but no significant plasma pressure; outside the boundary there is a plasma stream with significant dynamic pressure ($q = \rho V^2/2$) but no magnetic field. The boundary is taken to be the surface in space at which the magnetic pressure $B^2/2\mu = q\cos^2\omega$, where ω is the angle between the free stream solar wind direction and the normal to the boundary surface.[9]

The derivation and analysis of this fluid model was first presented in reference 2. It was found that, assuming a drag coefficient of unity

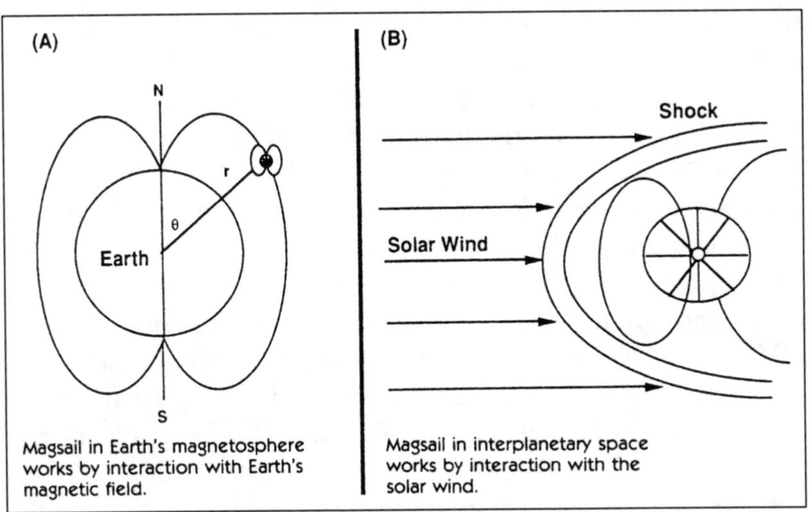

Figure 12.2. Magsail operating within a magnetosphere (A), and within the solar wind (B).

for the area defined by the magsail's magnetospheric boundary, the self-acceleration of the magsail, D/M, is given by

$$D/M = 0.6(\mu \rho^2 V^4 R_m/I)^{1/3}(J/\rho_m) \quad (1)$$

(Note: The definitions of all mathematical variables used in this article are listed in the appendix. Don't be intimidated by the equations. Feel free to skip over mathematical details to the summaries of what they mean.)

If we substitute into this expression typical solar wind values of $V = 5 \times 10^5$m/s, $\rho = (8.35 \times 10^{-21}\text{kg/m}^3)/R_s^2$, where R_s is the distance of the magsail from the Sun in astronomical units, $J/\rho_m = 2 \times 10^6$ amp-m/kg, and $\mu = 4\pi \times 10^{-7}$ N/A^2, equation (1) reduces to

$$D/M = 0.02(R_m/(IR_s^4))^{1/3}\text{m/s}^2 \quad (2)$$

From expressions (1) or (2) it can be clearly seen that it is advantageous to construct a plasma wind interacting magsail with a small current (i.e., thin wire) but a large radius. Using equation (2) we find a sample magsail ($B_m = 10^{-6}$ T, R_m = 31.6 km, I = 50 kA, wire diameter d = 2.52 mm) sailing at 1 AU has a mass of 5 metric tons and a self-acceleration of 0.0172 m/s^2. This performance would be degraded on an actual spacecraft in proportion to the weight factor W. The total magnetic energy contained in this sail is about 80 MJ, and the hoop stress is 11,760 psi. Thus, this magsail can be "inflated" (i.e., have its current built up) by a 10-kW$_e$ solar panel power array in about 2.2 hours, and the magsail material can probably react the hoop stress without additional mechanical support. However, even if the ceramic superconductor had a tensile stength of zero, this hoop stress could be reacted by a reinforcement of high-strength aluminum that would only add about 10% to the sail mass. Adopting this worst-case assumption, the reinforced magsail self-acceleration is found to be 0.015 m/s^2. A 10-kW$_e$ (at 1 AU) solar power source can be built for a mass as low as 300 kg, and so could easily travel with the magsail, allowing the magsail to be recharged if for any reason it is shut off during the mission. For missions to the outer solar system, a dynamic isotope power system (DIPS) would be more appropriate. Such systems, massing 800 kg and generating 6 kW$_e$, are currently under development by the U.S. Department of Energy.

Lift can also be generated if the dipole is situated with its axis at some orientation intermediate between the axial and normal configurations. Using a hypersonic aerodynamics code, we have found simple dipole configurations with L/D as high as 0.14. If compound magsails were adopted, consisting of two or more loops connected by a spar along their axes, more desirable magnetospheric boundary shapes could be obtained yielding a much higher L/D.

THE MAGSAIL OPERATING WITHIN THE MAGNETOSPHERE

While the idea of using a magnetic field to sail on the solar wind is original with Dana Andrews and me, the concept of using the interaction between an onboard magnet and the Earth's magnetic poles to generate spacecraft propulsion is much older, and in fact was first proposed by J. Engleberger[10] in 1963. There was a significant error in Engleberger's derived equation, but the larger problem with his concept was that it could not be made practical due to the nature of then state-of-the-art superconductors, and the concept appears to have received no further consideration after a 1971 Air Force review.[11] The invention of high-temperature superconducting materials by Chu in 1987, however, has changed this picture dramatically. In 1989, Robert Forward suggested to me that the possibility of useful interaction between a high-temperature superconducting magsail and Earth's magnetic field should be investigated. In carrying out this investigation, I encountered the work of Engleberger, and derived a corrected version of his magnetic propulsion equations. The derivation was presented in reference 6 and results in the following equations:

$$\mathbf{F} = -3(B_e/r_o)IA(r_o/r)^4(R(\Theta)\mathbf{r} + T(\Theta)\Theta) \tag{3}$$

where

$$R(\Theta) = (3\cos^2\Theta + 1)^{1/2} \tag{4}$$

$$T(\Theta) = (1/2)(\sin 2\Theta)/(3\cos^2\Theta + 1)^{1/2} \tag{5}$$

and r and Θ represent the radial and polar angle directions in spherical polar coordinates, with the poles placed at the Earth's magnetic poles (see Figure 12.2(A)). There is no azimuthal component to the force.

The values of the magnetic propulsion functions $R(\Theta)$ and $T(\Theta)$ are shown in Figure 12.3.

If we substitute values of $B_e = 3.05 \times 10^{-5}$ T and $r_o = 6.378 \times 10^6$ m, equation (3) can be written as

$$\mathbf{F} = -1.46 \times 10^{-11} IA (r_o/r)^4 (R(\Theta)\mathbf{r} + T(\Theta)\Theta) \qquad (6)$$

Equations (3), (4), and (5) fully characterize the behavior of a self-stabilized magsail orbiting in an ideal dipolar geomagnetic field. There are several consequences that stand out immediately. First of all, the dependence of F upon r^{-4} yields a rapid fall-off of thrust with altitude. This means that escape and orbit-raising maneuvers will be carried out by using a series of perigree kicks, or thrust arcs, in which the portion of the orbit during which thrust occurs is kept at a low altitude. Second, the dependence of F upon IA indicates that the maximum system thrust to weight will be obtained using a magsail of large radius and small B_m. This drives system optimization

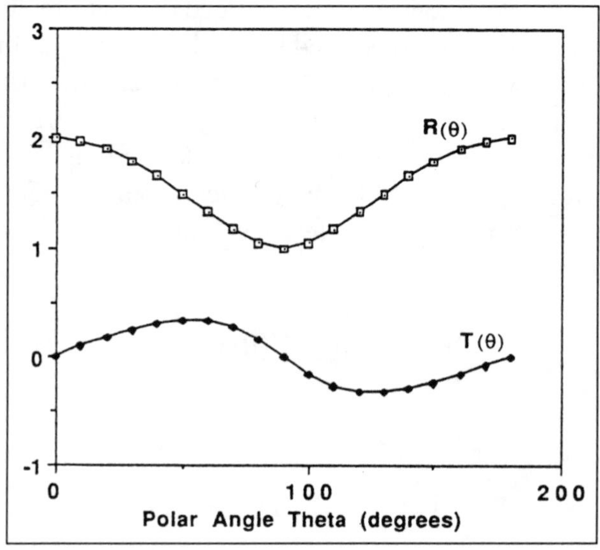

Figure 12.3. Magnetic propulsion functions R(θ) and T(θ).

in the same direction as that indicated by the plasma fluid model for a magsail in the solar wind. Third, there is no azimuthal force. Finally, the negative value of the constant in equation (3) combined with the values of R(Θ) and T(Θ) imply that the radial force is always inward, attracting the magsail to the center of the Earth, while the theta force always attracts the magsail toward the nearest pole. (If the magsail can be maintained in its unstable equilibrium position directly opposite the self-stabilized position, the sign of the force can be reversed.)

UTILIZATION OF THE MAGSAIL TO ESCAPE FROM LEO

Let us now analyze the case of our sample magsail being used to lift a 14-metric tonne payload from a low Earth polar orbit into a geosynchronous polar elliptical orbit with an apogee altitude of 71,090 km and a perigee altitude of 638 km. Such a satellite would be very useful for supporting communication in polar regions, as it would spend over 80% of its 24-hour-orbit traveling over the arctic. The magsail has a mass of 5 tonnes, and we assume 1 tonne for supplementary systems such as shrouds, solar panels, avionics, and so on, so the total initial mass in LEO is 20 tonnes. This can be lifted into a polar LEO orbit by a Titan IV.

The magsail is switched on to generate thrust for an orbital arc between $\Theta = 80$ and $\Theta = 20$, with perigee kept at $\Theta = 50$ (south, magnetic) degrees. The spacecraft is orbiting in a true polar inclination, while the magnetic poles are traveling with the Earth's rotation and located at 76°N, 101°W (near Bathurst Island) and 65°S, 138°E (near the Adelie Coast of Antarctica), so we accept an estimated cosine loss term of 0.9 times the ideal thrust given by equation (3). The spacecraft starts with a 300-km perigee ($1.047\ r_0$), which in the course of the series of thrust arcs rises to 636 km, for a final perigee r value of $1.1r_0$. To be conservative we use the thrust level associated with a perigee of $1.08r_0$ for the entire transfer. For the thrust arc between 20 and 80°, T(Θ) has an average value of 0.272. We thus find, using equations (3) and (5), that the average useful thrust of the magsail during the arc in question is 413 N.

The magsail thus has a self-acceleration of 0.0826 m/s^2, and the entire magsail system plus spacecraft system has an acceleration of 0.0206 m/s^2. This is a much higher level of thrust than would be available from an electric propulsion system of the same mass. An ion engine, for example, with an I_{sp} of 5000 s would require about 17 MWe to produce an equal thrust, and assuming a mass/power ratio (alpha) of 5 kg/kWe (10 times better than the current state of the art) would weigh about 85 tonnes, or 17 times as much as our 5-tonne magsail. The relatively high thrust level available to the magsail in a geomagnetic field enables it to use a perigee kick strategy to achieve Earth escape.

A computer program was used to model our sample magsail mission. The results are given in Table 12.1. We see that 160 orbits are required with a total flight time of 34.3 days.

It is worth noting that if a cryogenic chemical stage with a specific impulse of 450 s and a dry stage mass fraction of 0.15 had been used to achieve this transfer, only 8.9 tonnes could have been delivered to the destination orbit off of our initial LEO launch capability of 20 tonnes. The magsail has thus increased the mass deliverable to the polar geosynchronous elliptical orbit by a factor of 14/8.9 = 1.573. While the use of low-thrust ion electric propulsion could also achieve a similar improvement in mass deliverable, the required transfer time would exceed 1 year.

Table 12.1. Computer simulation of magsail transfer from low polar orbit to polar geosynchronous elliptical orbit

Orbit #	*Time (days)*	*Perigee (km)*	*Apogee (km)*	*Velocity (km/s)*
0	0	290	310	7.7
20	1.33	325	1.778	8.09
40	2.94	355	3.645	8.42
60	4.90	383	6.076	8.75
80	7.35	409	9.492	9.08
100	10.6	431	14.301	9.39
120	15.0	451	21.723	9.70
140	21.7	471	35.229	10.0
160	34.3	521	67.265	10.3

If an interplanetary mission is to be launched, two alternative strategies can be followed. One is to use the magsail as an Earth-orbital tug to lift the payload spacecraft to an elliptical orbit and then kick out onto an interplanetary transfer by staging off of it with a single kick of a high-thrust chemical engine. Thus, in our example above, an interplanetary spacecraft staging off of the elliptical orbit to go onto direct trans-Mars injection would require a ΔV of about 1 km/s. With 14 tonnes starting out in the destination orbit, a cryogenic chemical stage (450 s I_{sp}, mf = 0.15) could then deliver 10,722 kg onto trans-Mars injection. This is compared to 6,430 kg deliverable by a cryogenic chemical stage firing directly out of LEO.

The more interesting method of launching into interplanetary space, however, is to simply continue the perigee kicks until most of the magsail orbit is outside Earth's magnetosphere. Once such a condition has been achieved, the magsail can begin effective interaction with the solar wind to provide propulsion for the remainder of the escape maneuver and thence onward towards the interplanetary destination.

The Earth's magnetosphere extends outward to about 11 Earth radii, or 68,000 km, so we are just reaching the boundary in our example of transfer to a 1-day period elliptical orbit. If instead we were to continue the series of perigee kicks until a 4-day elliptical orbit with a 638-km perigee, the apogee of the orbit would be at 200,000 km with the large majority of the time of each orbit spent outside the magnetosphere. Using our computer model, we have found that the sample magsail described above, pulling a 14-tonne payload, will reach the 4-day orbit after 181 perigee kicks and a total transit flight time of 76.6 days. The magsail plus spacecraft can now be kicked out into interplanetary space by a trivial 178 m/s chemical perigee burn. Alternatively, if the orbit is aligned so that the outward arc of the ellipse is roughly parallel to the solar wind, the magsail can catch the wind and in the course of 1.1 days of sailing can accelerate itself to escape velocity. The magsail is now independently orbiting the Sun in Earth's heliocentric track.

The planets Jupiter, Saturn, Uranus, and Neptune are all gifted with substantial magnetic fields, enabling magsail maneuvers in their vicinities utilizing the same technique as that employed in magsail maneuvers within Earth's magnetosphere. This capability could be quite valuable, enabling a mission in which a single spacegraft could make extended observations of each of the moons of Jupiter, for example, before moving on to examine the next. As no propellant is required for magsail maneuvers, the survey could continue almost indefinitely.

PROPULSIVE SIGNIFICANCE OF THE "R" FORCE

Equations (3), (4), and (5) show that the magsail exerts a radial force with respect to Earth, which for a self-stabilized magsail, has a magnitude about six times the Θ direction force and is always attractive. The magsail thus feels a self-acceleration (at perigee) toward Earth of about 0.5 m/s^2, and the magsail plus payload combination we have analyzed feels a self-acceleration toward the Earth of about 0.12 m/s^2. This is equivalent to increasing the apparent gravity felt by the spacecraft during its perigee pass by a factor of 1.012. The spacecraft will thus require an initial perigee velocity of 7.77 km/s in order not to lose altitude while it travels through its initial perigee thrust arc, which means that the spacecraft should be launched into an initial orbit with a 300-km perigee and a 425-km apogee.

While the radial force generated by a self-stabilized magsail is always attractive, the magsail has an unstable equilibrium (no torque) position rotated 180° opposite to its self-stabilized position where the radial force is repulsive. If a magsail can be maintained in such an orientation, and if the current density of the high temperature superconducting magsail cable can be increased by about a factor of 80 relative to that of existing low temperature superconductors (it will be recalled that throughout the present article we have assumed equal performance of low and high temperature superconductors), the *self-driven ground launch of the magsail* would become possible. For example, if our 5-tonne magsail can be made to carry 4000 kA (instead of the 50 kA assumed up to now), and it is launched from Bathurst Island near the north magnetic pole, it will exert a force at launch of 376,800 N. If it is carrying 1 tonne of spacecraft systems and a 3-tonne payload, it will self-accelerate upward at a rate of

41.9 m/s^2, or about 4.27 gs. Since it is pulling directly away from Earth's gravity, its net upward acceleration will therefore be 3.27 gs. The force is dying off as r^{-4}, so integrating the force from $r = r_o$ to r = infinity, it can be shown that the final velocity $v = (2a_o r_o/3)^{1/2}$, where a_o is the acceleration at ground level. In our present example this yields v = 11.68 km/s, which means that the magsail can launch itself and its 3-tonne payload off Bathurst Island onto a medium energy trans-Mars injection trajectory (C3 = 24 km^2/s^2), reaching the red planet in about 150 days.

MAGSAIL ORBITS IN HELIOCENTRIC SPACE

Magsail orbits in heliocentric space can actually be calculated analytically, and methods of doing so were first presented in reference 2. In heliocentric space the force generated by the magsail's interaction with the solar wind is much, much greater than that created by the interaction between the magsail and the Sun's magnetic field.

In order to calculate the orbit of a magsail spacecraft, we choose to parametrize the drag (thrust) generated by the magsail in the solar wind as a fraction of the Sun's gravitational attraction on the spacecraft. The Sun's gravitational acceleration $g_s = .006/R_s^2$ (in units of m/s^2), and the maximum magsail spacecraft acceleration $D/M = 0.015/(WR_s^{4/3})$ m/s^2, where W, the weight ratio, equals the mass of the magsail plus payload divided by the mass of the magsail. The apparent fraction, α, of the Sun's gravity operating on the spacecraft with its magsail operating at full current is then given by

$$\alpha = (1 - D/(Mg_s)) = (1 - 2.5R_s^{2/3}/W) \qquad (7)$$

If $\alpha = 1$, the magsail is not operating. If α is between 1 and 0, the spacecraft acts as a body moving about a star whose mass is the fraction of the Sun's mass represented by α. If $\alpha = 0$, the spacecraft feels no solar force and moves in a straight line; while if $\alpha < 0$, the spacecraft feels a new repulsion from the Sun and moves away in a hyperbolic orbit. In other words, because the magsail can exert a force against the Sun which can be comparable or even greater than the gravitational attraction that the Sun is exerting on the magsail spacecraft assembly, the magsail can be conceived to be a kind of variable antigravity machine, used to adjust the Sun's effective gravitational mass seen by the spacecraft to fractional, zero, or negative values. Once the effective mass of the Sun has been suitably adjusted, the magsail spacecraft orbit can be calculated using the well-established tools of standard orbital mechanics.

Let's say our 5-tonne magsail requires 1 tonne of additional mass for shrouds, solar panels, avionics, and so forth, and we wish to use it to transfer a 41.5-tonne payload ($W = 9.5$) from Earth to Mars. Assume that the magsail is co-orbiting with the Earth but outside of its gravitational well. Using canonical units[12] such that $R_{Earth} = V_{Earth} = GM_{Sun} = 1$, we can write:

$$E = V_{sc}^2/2 - \alpha/R = -\alpha/2a \qquad (8)$$

where E is the specific energy of the spacecraft, V_{sc} is its velocity about the Sun in canonical units, R is its distance from the Sun in AU, and a is the semimajor axis of its elliptical orbit. Since for a Hohmann transfer to Mars, $2a = 2.52$, we can solve equation (8) for the required value of α (V_{sc} initially $= 1$) to send the spacecraft onto such an orbit. The result is $\alpha = 0.8289$. Checking equation (7), we find our spacecraft with $W = 9.5$ can attain an α at 1 AU as low as 0.7368, so it is capable of doing this maneuver. Since in this zero-life trajectory angular momentum about the Sun is conserved, upon reaching Mars orbit, the ship will be moving with a velocity of V_{sc}(Mars arrival) $= 1/1.52 = 0.6579$. If we now wish to circularize the orbit, we use this value of V_{sc} together with $2a = 3.04$ in equation (8) and find that the required value of α to circularize at Mars is 0.6579. Checking equation (7), we see that our spacecraft at 1.52 AU is capable of generating an α as low as 0.652, and so it can circularize at Mars.

Our spacecraft is now moving in Mars' orbit about the Sun, but *at a different speed than Mars*. Mars is overtaking the spacecraft with a relative velocity of 4.564 km/s. This odd situation gives the magsail craft a very interesting capability. What it means is that the spacecraft can leave Earth for a Hohmann transfer to Mars' orbit, circularize, and then loiter at will in Mars' orbit until the red planet catches up to it. Thus, a magsail interplanetary transfer can be done *at any time;* unlike ballistic interplanetary transfer orbits, there are no limited launch windows.

When Mars approaches, the magsail can release its payload, consisting of cargo plus an aerobrake, allowing the payload to aerobrake into Mars orbit or land. Simultaneously, the magsail reduces its current partially so as to increase α back to 0.8289, sending it on a Hohmann transfer orbit back to Earth. Upon reaching Earth orbit, the magsail is turned off, and the spacecraft will circularize at 1 AU. If the timing of this maneuver is incorrect for Earth rendezvous, all the magsail has to do is make its initial Hohmann transfer back from Mars not to Earth, but to a circular orbit intermediate between Earth and Mars. The magsail can then waste as much time as required in that orbit to allow the Earth to attain the correct position for the final Hohmann transfer home. Since the intermediate orbit can be chosen at will, such return flights can be scheduled with great flexibility.

The time of flight of such magsail Hohmann transfers is given by

$$\tau = \pi(a^3/\alpha)^{1/2} \tag{9}$$

For our Earth-Mars Hohmann transfer, $a = 1.26$, $\alpha = 0.8289$, and thus $\tau = 4.88$ canonical units = 283 days—a time slightly longer than the usual Hohmann transfer ballistic flight time.

In Table 12.2, we show magsail requirements and capabilities for moving payloads to different planetary destinations in the outer solar system, assuming no magsail lift. In Table 12.2, α_{trans} is the value of α required to initiate the transfer ellipse to the given destination, α_{circ} is the value of α required at that destination to circularize

Table 12.2. Zero lift magsail payload capability

Destination	α_{trans}	α_{circ}	α_{circ0}	W_{trans}	W_{circ}
Mars	0.8289	0.657	0.741	14.60	9.66
Jupiter	0.5906	0.192	0.711	6.11	8.64
Saturn	0.5525	0.105	0.801	5.58	12.55
Uranus	0.5259	0.052	0.868	5.27	18.96
Neptune	0.5165	0.033	0.900	5.17	25.06
Pluto	0.5125	0.025	0.916	5.12	29.87
Escape	0.5000	0.000	1.000	5.00	infinite

the orbit, α_{circ0} is the value that α would have to have been at 1 AU to allow the spacecraft to attain α_{circ} at the destination, W_{trans} is the weight ratio (the mass of the magsail plus payload divided by the mass of the magsail) allowable to permit the attainment of α_{trans}, and W_{circ} is the weight ratio allowable to permit the attainment of α_{circ0}. The weight ratio actually attainable for any given destination is simply the lesser of W_{trans} and W_{circ}. We can see that a magsail without lift can move a payload amounting to four times the sail weight to any destination in the outer solar system.

Finally, if we do not desire to go anywhere in particular, but only wish to rapidly accelerate out of the solar system (as is required for the proposed Thousand Astronomical Unit probe, for example) we can set $W = 1.25$, and thus $\alpha = -1$ at 1 AU, becoming more negative as we move out.

Integrating the equations of motion, we find that the probe will be hurled out of the solar system with a terminal velocity of 95 km/s, reaching 1000 AU in about 50 years.

If lift can be generated, the magsail becomes capable of changing its angular momentum about the Sun, giving it both greater maneuverability and payload hauling capability. The mathematics of the orbit transfer becomes more complex. Methods of calculating such orbits are given in reference 2.

The use of lift allows the magsail to adopt much more flexible flight plans between planets. For example, let us say we send the spacecraft on a zero-lift trajectory toward Mars. We arrive in Mars orbit, and dally until Mars shows up, at which point we release the payload and set forth on a transfer orbit toward Earth, all as described in the discussion of zero-lift maneuvers. Now, however, we apply negative lift to decrease the spacecraft's angular momentum about the Sun. In this case, when we arrive at Earth orbit, we need a value of $\alpha < 1$ to circularize, which means that we can now circularize in *Earth* orbit with a different orbital velocity than the Earth, and loiter until the Earth catches up to us. We thus have the ability to move large payloads back and forth between the Earth and Mars with the knowledge that rendezvous can be achieved at each end of the orbit without regard to when the spacecraft sets forth. This solves the problem that derailed the concept of cycling interplanetary "castles," that is, the inability of these large manned habitats following ballistic interplanetary orbits to obtain a useful number of planetary encounters in their lifetime. In effect the magsail allows the castles to "cheat" against the laws of orbital mechanics by giving it the ability to adjust the effective mass of the Sun to that required to assure orbital rendezvous with the target planet at each end of the castle's commute. In addition, the use of negative lift allows the magsail to drop below Earth orbit to visit Mercury and Venus.

If lift is to be utilized, it becomes necessary to be able to control the orientation of the magsail. One way to accomplish this would be to connect the payload to the magsail loop with a set of tethers that can be either reeled in or out on a windlass. This would allow the magsail to shift its center of mass in either of the two dimensions within the plane of the loop. By moving the center of mass relative to the sail's center of pressure a torque can be induced, allowing the magsail to be swung into the desired attitude.

Above and beyond its propulsive capability, the magsail has an additional advantage as a system for manned interplanetary spacecraft, in that it shields the crew from the radiation dose they would otherwise receive from the solar wind and solar flares. Without such shielding, these hazards may well place a severe constraint on long-distance manned spaceflight.

THE MAGSAIL AS AN INTERSTELLAR BRAKE

In addition to its role as an interplanetary propulsion system, the magsail also offers great potential as the braking device for an interstellar spacecraft that has been previously accelerated to relativistic velocities by some other means, for example, by a fusion rocket or a laser pushed lightsail. In this case, the plasma wind is the apparent wind created by the relative velocity between the spacecraft and the interstellar medium. Using equation (4) with $V = V_{sc}$, $\rho = 1.67 \times 10^{-22}$ kg/m^3, $R_m = 100$ km, $I = 159$ kA, and $W = 2$ (a 50-ton magsail with a 50-ton payload), we obtain:

$$dV/dt = -1.66 \times 10^{-11} V^{4/3} \tag{10}$$

The solution of this equation is:

$$V = V_0/(1 + 3.68 \times 10^{-12} V_0^{1/3} t)^3 \qquad (11)$$

where V_0 is the velocity of the spacecraft at the beginning of the braking maneuver. If V_0 is 3×10^7 m/s (one-tenth the speed of light) and braking time t is given in years, (11) becomes:

$$V = (3 \times 10^7 \text{m/s})/(1 + 0.054t)^3 \qquad (12)$$

which will reduce V by a factor of eight in 18.5 years. In 55.5 years V will be reduced by a factor of 64 to 468 km/s, a velocity suitable for magsail or fusion rocket braking within the destination star system. For all intents and purposes, the magnetic sail has eliminated the propellant required for terminal deceleration, with the result being a massive reduction in mission mass ratio.

The above calculation is based on an assumed interstellar hydrogen number density of $10^5/\text{m}^3$. This is quite conservative. Some astronomers put the estimate ten times higher, which would shorten the time scales given above by a factor of 4.64.

It should be noted that while research into the magsail has proven that a Bussard ramscoop composed of a simple current loop or solenoid would not work, it has not ruled out the possibility that more complex ramscoop configurations may be functional. Recently, for example, Brice Cassenti[13] has proposed using two very large magnetic toroids oriented with their axis along the line of flight of the spacecraft. The first toroid, with its weaker field, would act as a magnetic lens to focus electrons down toward the center line. The second toroid would have a much stronger field, in the opposite direction to the first, which would act as a lens to focus the protons. There are major engineering problems associated with the construction and operation of such a device, but it does offer some hope for the ramscoop. Cassenti proposes reacting the matter his scoop gathers with an onboard supply of antimatter to produce thrust. Since antimatter is, and in all probability will remain, very, very, expensive, it would be useful to reduce the amount of antimatter that would be required to accomplish the mission. If a magnetic sail were employed to decelerate such a craft, the amount of antimatter required for any flight would be cut in half.

CONCLUSION

We have seen that, provided high temperature superconducting cable becomes available with current densities equal to that of existing low temperature superconductors, magnetic sail devices can be developed with the potential to move very large payloads from low Earth orbit to high orbits, and then on to anywhere in the solar system. Such magsails offer the advantage that they require no propellant, and can accomplish orbit transfer maneuvers without regard to the usual ballistic transfer launch windows. The required flight times are slightly greater than the usual Hohmann transfer ballistic flight times. Compared to a conventional solar lightsail, the magsail offers a thrust-to-weight ratio up to two orders of magnitude greater, as well as a system that is far more robust and simpler to deploy.

But the greatest promise of the magsail is as an enabling technology for interstellar missions. By providing a braking device which requires no propellant, this simple device brings us halfway to the stars.

Appendix: Nomenclature

A = Cross-sectional area enclosed by magsail loop (m^2)
a = Semimajor axis of magsail orbit (AU)
α = Fraction of Sun's gravitational attraction felt by magsail spacecraft
B_e = Magnetic field on the Earth at the equator (T)
B_m = Magnetic field at the magsail center (T)
B_o = Ambient interplanetary magnetic field (T)
D = Drag force exerted by plasma wind on magsail (N)
E = Canonical energy of magsail orbit
F = Force between magsail and Earth's magnetic field (N)
I = Magsail loop current (amp)
J = Magsail loop current density (A/m^2)
L = Lift force exerted by plasma wind on magsail (N)
M = Mass of magsail (kg)
R_m = Radius of the magsail loop
r_o = Radius of the Earth (km)
ρ = Density of the plasma wind (kg/m^3)
ρ_m = Magsail loop mass density (kg/m^3)
τ = Time of flight of magsail orbit (years/2π)

Θ = Polar angle in Earth's magnetic spherical coordinates
ω = Angle between plasma free stream and the normal to the magnetospheric boundary
V = Velocity of the plasma wind (m/s)
V_{sc} = Velocity of magsail spacecraft (2π AU/year)
W = Magsail-spacecraft weight ratio (mass of magsail plus payload divided by mass of magsail alone)

Chapter 13

John G. Cramer

The Tachyon Drive: Infinite Exhaust Velocity at Zero Energy Cost

We are told by the well-tested physics orthodoxy of special relativity that neither information nor material objects can travel faster than light speed, $\mathbf{c} = 3 \times 10^8$ m/s. If an object with rest mass **M** had a velocity equal to **c,** its mass energy would be infinite. Therefore, it would require all the energy in the universe and more to accelerate the object to a velocity of **c.** If the massive object could somehow be drop-kicked *over* the light-speed barrier so that its velocity was greater than **c,** then its mass-energy **E** would become *imaginary* quantities (like $\sqrt{-1}$). This, says physics orthodoxy, is Nature's way of telling us that such quantities have nothing to do with our universe, in which all measurable physical variables must have real (not imaginary) numbers as values.

"Not so!" said Gerald Feinberg, the eminent physicist and SF fan who died last year at the age of 59. In a 1967 paper, Feinberg postulated a type of hypothetical particle with a rest mass **M** that *also* has an imaginary value ($\mathbf{M}^2 < 0$). Then the observable mass energy **E** of these particles becomes real and positive and is compatible with other energies in our universe. Feinberg christened his hypothetical particles "tachyons" (from the Greek word for swift) for their characteristic that they always travel more swiftly than **c.**

A normal particle (or "tardyon" in Feinberg's terminology) has a velocity of zero when its mass-energy is smallest (when **E** is equal to **M**). Its velocity rises until it is slightly less than **c** when its mass energy **E** becomes large compared to its rest mass **M.** A tachyon (if such particles exist) would behave in an inverted way, so that when its mass-energy is smallest (equal to zero) it would have *infinite* velocity. When the mass energy **E** of a tachyon is made very large compared to the absolute value of its rest mass, it will slow down until its velocity is only slightly larger than **c.**

This can perhaps be seen more clearly by considering some equations of special relativity. When any particle (tachyon or tardyon) has rest mass **M** and mass-energy **E,** it has a momentum **P** (in energy units) given by $\mathbf{E}^2 = \mathbf{P}^2 + \mathbf{M}^2$. For tardyons (normal particles) it should be clear from this equation that **E** cannot be less than **M** and is always greater than **P.** For tachyons, however, we have the peculiarity that $\mathbf{M}^2$ is negative, so that the energy equation becomes $\mathbf{E}^2 = \mathbf{P}^2 - |\mathbf{M}|^2$ or $\mathbf{P}^2 = \mathbf{E}^2 + |\mathbf{M}|^2$. This means that, for tachyons, **E** can be as small as zero (when $\mathbf{P} = |\mathbf{M}|$) and that **P** is always greater than **E** and cannot be less than $|\mathbf{M}|$. These quantities are related to the relativistic velocity β by the equation $\beta = \mathbf{P/E}$. This tells us that when a tachyon has its minimum possible momentum $\mathbf{P} = |\mathbf{M}|$, it will also have its lowest possible mass-energy ($\mathbf{E} = 0$) and will have infinite velocity.

The theoretical work on tachyons in the 1960s by Feinberg and others, particularly Sudarshan and Recami, prompted a "gold rush" among experimentalists seeking to be the first to discover tachyons in the real world. They studied the kinematics of high-energy particle reactions at large accelerators, they built timing experiments that used cosmic rays, and they probed many radioactive decay processes for some hint of tachyon emission. Although there were a few false "discoveries" among these results, all of the believable experimental results were negative in the decade or so after the initial theoretical work. Some cold water was also thrown on the tachyon concept from the theoretical direction when it was demonstrated (by physicist and SF author Gregory Benford, among others) that tachyons could be used to construct an "antitelephone" capable of sending information backward in time in violation of the principle of causality, one of the most fundamental and mysterious laws of physics. Tachyons were therefore metaphorically placed on a dusty shelf in the museum of might-be particles for which there is no experimental evidence, and there they have languished for the past 25 years. But this may now be changing; a new and growing body of evidence from an unexpected direction supports the possible existence of tachyons.

There is great fundamental interest in the mass of the electron neutrino (ν_e), because it is a leading "dark-matter" candidate. Several very careful experiments have been mounted to measure its mass through its effect on the beta decay of mass-3 hydrogen—tritium. Tritium, with one proton and two neutrons in its nucleus, is transformed by the weak interaction beta-decay process into mass-3 helium (two protons and one neutron) by emitting an electron and an antineutrino ($^3H \rightarrow {}^3He + e^- + \overline{\nu}_e$) with an excess energy of 18.6 keV. This is the lowest energy beta decay known, and therefore the one which is affected most strongly by the mass of the electron neutrino.

If the kinetic energy of the emitted electrons is measured for a very large number of similar tritium decays, one finds a bell-shaped "spectrum" of energies ranging from essentially zero electron energy to a maximum of about 18.6 keV. This maximum-energy tip of the electron's kinetic energy distribution is called the "endpoint," and is the place where the neutrino is emitted with near-zero energy and where the neutrino's mass will make its presence known. When the endpoint region is made linear (using a plotting trick called a Kurie plot), then the straight-line dependence of the electron's kinetic energy takes a nose-dive just before it reaches zero, displaying the effect of neutrino mass.

Because of the relativistic relation of mass, energy, and momentum ($\mathbf{E}^2 = \mathbf{P}^2 + \mathbf{M}^2$) it is the mass-squared of the neutrino that is actually determined by the tritium endpoint measurements. The mass-squared is allowed to vary from negative values (too many electrons with energies near the endpoint) through $\mathbf{M}_\nu^2 = 0$ (the expected number of electrons with energies near the endpoint), to a positive mass-squared (too few electrons with energies near the endpoint), and this variation is used to fit the experimental data. The resulting fit is quoted with the measured value of $\mathbf{M}_\nu^2$ plus or minus the statistical error in the measurement plus or minus the estimated systematic error in the measurement.

At least five experimental groups have made careful measurements of $\mathbf{M}_\nu^2$, and several of these groups have published their results in scientific journals. The two most recent published values are

Zürich (Switzerland)
$\mathbf{M}_\nu^2 = -158 \pm 150 \pm 103 \text{ eV}^2$ (1986)
Los Alamos (USA)
$\mathbf{M}_\nu^2 = -147 \pm 68 \pm 41 \text{ eV}^2$ (1991)

As the numbers imply, both groups find an *excess* of electrons with energies near the tritium endpoint. There have also been recent informal reports (but no further publications) from these and other laboratories, particularly a group at a well-known weapons laboratory in California, of measurements which continue to give negative values to $\mathbf{M}_\nu^2$ with even more statistically meaningful error estimates. I was told by one of the experimenters that if a similar result had been found with the same errors but with the *positive* of the determined value for $\mathbf{M}_\nu^2$, there would have been much publicity, with press conferences announcing the discovery of a nonzero mass for the electron neutrino.

OK, this is an SF magazine, not a scientific journal. We are not scandalized by the possibility that $\mathbf{M}_\nu^2$ is negative, indicating that the electron neutrino is perhaps a tachyon. In fact, we rather like the idea that a well-known particle may routinely be breaking the light-speed barrier. Let us then suppose that the ν_e is a tachyon with an imaginary mass of say $i \times 12$ eV. What are the physical consequences of this? The answer is disappointing. The tritium endpoint measurement is so difficult precisely because assuming a small neutrino mass (real or imaginary) has very few observable consequences. The "dark matter" implications are also nil. Since tachyons can have any mass-energy down to zero and are never at rest they, like photons, cannot contribute to the excess of dark matter in the universe.

The previously mentioned "tachyon antitelephone" with its violations of causality is also essentially impossible to construct in practice. Neutrinos are fairly easy to produce (using an accelerator to create beta-decaying nuclei) but very difficult to detect. The only successful neutrino detectors use either neutrino-induced nuclear reactions (the Homestake and Gallex experiments) or hard neutrino-electron scattering (Kamiokande and SNO) to detect neutrinos with extremely low efficiency. But to use the possible tachyonic super-light speed of the electron neutrinos, ν_e's must have mass-energies comparable to or less than 12 eV. This is about 10^{-6} of the lowest neutrino energy ever detected, so neither of the above detection schemes can be used in this energy range, and there is no known alternative method of detection. Thus, even if the ν_e is a tachyon, the law of causality is safe from our tampering for the foreseeable future.

This brings us our second question: What new SF gimmicks are suggested by the possibility of easy-to-produce tachyons? I have a delightful answer. We can make a *tachyon drive*.

Consider the central problem of rocketry: How can one burn fuel at a high enough exhaust velocity to provide reasonable thrust without an unreasonable expenditure of energy? This is the dilemma that plagues our space program, and the solutions we have developed are not very good.

So let's consider a device that makes great quantities of $\mathbf{E} = 0$ tachyons and uses them as the infinite velocity exhaust of a "rocket." Within the constraints of the conservation laws of physics, we can make all the tachyons we want for free, provided we make them in neutrino-antineutrino pairs to conserve spin and lepton number. Momentum conservation is not a problem because we want and need the momentum kick derived from emitting the neutrino-antineutrino pair. This leaves us to deal with energy conservation.

The paradox here is that with a high-momentum exhaust of tachyons produced at no energy cost and beamed out the back of our space vehicle, the vehicle would seem to gain kinetic energy from nowhere, in violation of the law of conservation of energy. The solution to this paradox (as can be demonstrated by considering particle systems) is that the processes producing the tachyons must also consume enough internal energy to account for the kinetic energy gain of the system. Thus, a tachyon drive vehicle might be made to hover at no energy cost (antigravity!), but could only gain kinetic energy if a comparable amount of stored energy were supplied.

How could we arrange for an engine to produce great floods of electron neutrino-antineutrino pairs beamed in a selected direction? All I can do here is to lay out the problems and speculate. Neutrinos are produced by the weak interaction, which has that name because it is many orders of magnitude weaker than electromagnetism. Neutrino production of any kind is improbable. On the other hand, in any quantum reaction process the energy cost squared appears in the denominator of the probability, and if that energy is zero, it should make for a big probability. The trick might be to arrange some reaction or process that is, in principle, strong but is inhibited by momentum conservation. Then the emission of a neutrino-antineutrino pair to supply the needed momentum with zero energy cost would make the process go. A string of similar atomic or nuclear systems prepared in this way might constitute an inverted population suitable for stimulated emission (like light, correlated neutrino-antineutrino pairs should be bosons), resulting in a beam from a "tachyon laser" that might amplify the process and produce the desired strong beam of tachyons.

That's about the best I can do at the moment for providing the scientific underpinnings of a tachyon drive for SF purposes. I think it's a nifty idea to which I will devote more thought. I just hope it survives the ongoing experimental measurements of $\mathbf{M}_\nu^2$ for the electron neutrino. Watch this space for further developments.

Chapter 14

Dr. Robert L. Forward

The Negative Matter Space Drive

In the August 1975 issue of *Analog*, I published the science "fact" article "Far Out Physics."[1] (I since have expanded the article and turned it into the book *Future Magic*.[2]) The article was based on a talk I gave to the 1974 Science Fiction Writers of America meeting in Los Angeles. In the talk I described six different kinds of antigravity devices, three time machines, two space warps, and a number of other far out ideas that I had collected over the years. One of the more interesting ideas was a space drive based on the concept of negative matter. I was hoping that one of the writers would pick up the idea of the negative matter space drive and write a story based on it. They didn't, so now I have.

Negative matter is a hypothetical form of matter whose mass is opposite in sign to normal positive matter. Negative matter is not antimatter, which as far as is known, has normal (positive) mass just like regular matter. I will show later that the gravitational field of negative matter causes all forms of matter, including negative matter, to move away from it, while the gravitational field of positive matter causes all forms of matter, including negative matter, to move toward it. Thus, as is shown in Figure 14.1, if we take a ball of

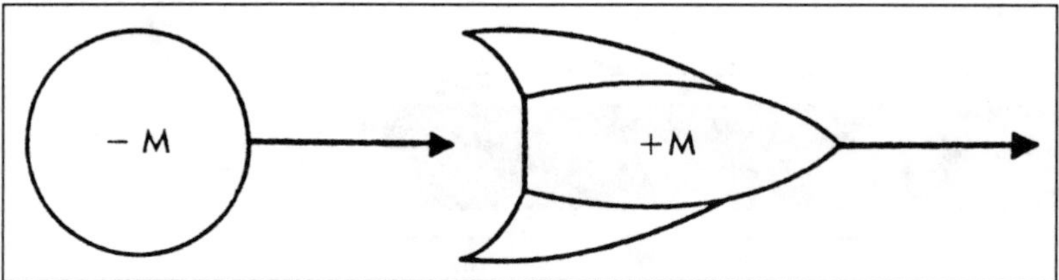

Figure 14.1. Negative matter gravitational propulsion.

negative matter of mass −M and place it near a rocket ship of positive mass +M of equal magnitude, then the negative mass will repel the positive mass, while the positive mass will attract the negative mass, and the rocket ship and the ball of negative matter will go off in the *same* direction with an acceleration equal to the gravity force between them. This truly miraculous negative matter space drive provides an *unlimited* amount of *unidirectional* acceleration *without* requiring either an *energy source* or *reaction mass!*

Now, at first glance, it seems obvious that this proves that negative matter cannot exist. The system starts out with two objects standing still, then after a while, the two objects are moving off in one direction with nothing going in the opposite direction. This *obviously* seems to violate the laws of conservation of linear momentum and energy. *Amazingly enough, it doesn't.*

When the two objects are at zero velocity, the total momentum of the system is zero. After the two objects have reached the velocity v, their combined momentum is still zero,

$$P_+ + P_- = (+M)v + (-M)v = 0$$

because the ball made of negative matter has *negative momentum*.

There is also no violation of the law of conservation of energy. When the two objects are at zero velocity, the total energy of the system is zero. After the two objects have reached the velocity v, their combined kinetic energy is still zero,

$$E_+ + E_- = 1/2(+M)v^2 + 1/2(-M)v^2 = 0$$

because the ball of negative matter has *negative kinetic energy*.

In addition, it requires no energy to make the negative matter ball to run our miraculous negative matter space drive. As long as positive matter and negative matter are generated in equal amounts during the fabrication process, the total energy needed to create the rest mass for the combined system is zero,

$$(+M)c^2 + (-M)c^2 = 0$$

because the negative matter ball has *negative rest mass energy!* (At this point the audience usually breaks into incredulous guffaws, or at least stifled giggles.)

Recently, I presented this concept once again at a lecture for novice science fiction writers. The next speaker, the famous science fiction author, Larry Niven, was in the audience. During the question and answer session after my lecture, he raised a question which seemed to lead to a logical contradiction that proved that negative matter was logically forbidden. Larry Niven's question was essentially this:

"Suppose the positive mass $+M_+$ is greater in magnitude than the negative mass $-M_-$ and the two are connected together by a stiff rod. The acceleration would, of course, be somewhat different than the case where the masses were equal in magnitude, but if they did reach any velocity v, then since the positive mass is greater than the negative mass, then a calculation of the total momentum would *not* produce zero:

$$P_+ + P_- = (+M_+)v + (-M_-)v = (M_+ - M_-)v \neq 0$$

In that case, wouldn't the law of conservation of momentum be violated?"

I couldn't answer him at the time. It took me many weeks of thinking and calculation before I got even a partial answer. Solely because of that single, simple question, I now have written and published a lengthy, tedious scientific paper.[3] The paper shows in excruciating mathematical detail that even if the positive and negative matter objects don't have the same magnitude of mass, and even if the coupling between the masses is mechanical or electrostatic instead of gravitational, the resulting behavior doesn't violate the laws of conservation of energy and momentum. In the process I found some interesting behavior when the two masses are different. I also found that for a "practical" negative matter space drive, you want to use elastic forces (e.g., a garage door spring) instead of gravitational forces.

NEGATIVE MATTER

The first modern scientific paper to discuss negative matter was by Bondi,[4] who gave a general discussion of the concept of negative mass in Einstein's theory of gravity, the General Theory of Relativity. Bondi showed that the concept of a negative mass chasing a positive mass with a constantly increasing velocity is consistent with general relativity. Bondi's work was later expanded by Bonnor and Swaminarayan,[5] who found an exact solution to the full Einstein field equations that accurately describe a uniformly accelerated pair of gravitationally interacting bodies with opposite masses as shown in Figure 14.1. The only difference between the Newtonian solution and the general relativity solution is that, in the general relativity solution, the two masses are not quite equal and opposite because they are being measured in an accelerating reference frame. For the two masses to keep a constant separation in the accelerated reference frame, the negative mass should be slightly larger than the positive mass.

There are three operationally distinct definitions of mass possible in Newtonian mechanics.[4] They are: active gravitational mass, passive gravitational mass, and inertial mass. The active gravitational mass of an object is that property that produces a gravitational field around the object. The passive gravitational mass of an object is that property that produces a force on the object when it is placed in a gravitational field produced by another object. The inertial mass of an object is that property that causes the object to accelerate when it is subjected to a force (of any kind).

In addition, the Einstein Special Theory of Relativity allows for an additional operational definition of mass, the rest mass. The rest mass M_0 of an object produces, upon conversion of the rest mass to energy, an amount of energy given by:

$$E = M_0c^2$$

where c = 300 Mm/s is the speed of light.

For normal positive matter, all the masses are equal and positive. It can be shown[4] that it is easy to violate the Newtonian laws of conservation of energy and momentum if the active and passive gravitational masses are not equal, but there is yet no reason why they cannot both be negative, or different from the inertial mass, or the rest mass. Speculation on these mixed-mass forms of matter is a topic for another article. For this chapter I will define negative matter as matter where all the different definitions of masses are equal and negative.

GRAVITATIONAL COUPLING OF TWO POINT OBJECTS

The first thing I did in my attempts to answer Larry Niven's question was to examine the case of the behavior of two objects made of opposite types of matter that did not have the same magnitude of mass and were coupled solely by their gravity fields. We all know that if the two point objects are made of positive matter, they will attract each other and fall toward each other. If one of the objects is much heavier than the other, the heavier one won't move much, while the lighter one will fall rapidly toward the more massive object. In actuality, of course, both move together toward their common center of mass.

Suppose we have two objects, one made of negative matter and one made of positive matter. They are separated by a distance r, where the positive sense of r is away from the negative object toward the positive object.

The negative matter object with an active gravitational mass of $-M_-$ will create a repulsive gravitational field A_- at the position of the positive matter object given by:

$$A_- = +GM_-/r^2$$

The direction of the gravity field is in the positive direction, away from the negative object, since its active gravitational mass is negative.

The positive object then responds to that gravitational field by producing a gravitational force F_+ proportional to its passive gravitational mass $+M_+$:

$$F_+ = +M_+A_- = +GM_+M_-/r^2$$

where the force is in the positive direction away from the negative object.

In a similar manner, the positive object creates an attractive gravitational field A_+ at the position of the negative object that points in the positive direction toward the positive object.

$$A_+ = +GM_+/r^2$$

The negative object responds to that gravitational field by producing a force F_- that is proportional to its negative passive gravitational mass:

$$F_- = -M_-A_+ = -GM_-M_+/r^2$$

where the force is in the negative direction away from the positive object.

The force F_- on the negative object causes it to move with an acceleration a_- that is inversely proportional to its negative inertial mass $-M_-$:

$$a_- = -F_-/M_- = +GM_+/r^2$$

where the acceleration is in the positive direction toward the positive object since the force F_- was away from the positive object and the negative inertial mass of the negative object acts perversely to the applied force.

In the same manner, the force F_+ on the positive object causes it to move with an acceleration a_+ that is inversely proportional to its positive inertial mass $+M_+$:

$$a_+ = +F_+/M_+ = +GM_-/r^2$$

where the acceleration is in the positive direction away from the negative object.

Note that since I assumed the passive gravitational mass and the inertial mass of each object are the same, even if they are negative, they drop out of the equations. The acceleration of an object in a gravity field is independent of the mass of the object and only depends upon the mass of the body generating the gravity field. This shows that a positive mass causes all other masses to accelerate toward it, while a negative mass causes all other masses to accelerate away from it. When I went through the detailed calculations, I found that if I assumed the magnitudes of the masses were equal, then I obtained the expected result that both objects moved off in the same direction at a constant acceleration.

If I assumed the positive matter object was larger, then the larger mass of the positive object attracted the smaller negative object more than the smaller mass of the negative matter object repelled the positive object, so the distance between the two objects decreased with time. On top of the motion closing the gap between the two objects, I found there was superimposed a unidirectional acceleration of both objects, the positive matter object leading the way. The velocity of the negative mass object was faster than the velocity of the positive mass object and it was catching up to the positive mass object, closing the distance between them. As the gap closed, the gravitational fields become stronger and the acceleration increased until the two objects collided.

If I assumed the positive matter object was smaller than the negative matter object, then the distance between the two objects increased with time since the large mass of the negative matter object was repelling the smaller positive matter object away. This motion was also accompanied by a unidirectional motion of both objects. In this case, however, the mutual gravitational fields and the acceleration levels decreased with time.

In all cases, when I calculated the net linear momentum of the system, it never changed from the initial value. Any increase in the positive linear momentum of the positive matter object was always balanced by the increase in negative linear momentum of the negative matter object.

When it came to conservation of energy, however, there *was* a difference. The positive kinetic energy gained by the positive matter object was different than the negative kinetic energy gained by the negative matter object. When I included the mutual gravitational *potential* energy of the two objects, however, I found that the change in gravitational potential energy was exactly equal and opposite to the change in the kinetic energy.

Thus, after many days of tedious work, I finally obtained a partial answer to Larry Niven's question. Even when the two gravitating objects of opposite mass have different mass magnitudes, there is no violation of the laws of conservation of linear momentum and energy. But Larry had also mentioned using a stiff rod to keep the two masses and constant distance apart. My investigation of the "stiff rod" led me to a detailed study of the behavior of two objects coupled by elastic forces, and the discovery of a more "practical" negative matter space drive that uses springs instead of gravitational forces.

NEGATIVE MATTER PROPULSION USING SPRINGS

It turns out that since the force we can apply to a negative matter object with a strong, stiff spring, like a garage door spring, is much greater than the force we can apply using gravitational or electrostatic fields, a simple spring coupling gives us a highly effective and easily controlled space drive that can take us anywhere we want—at any acceleration we can stand.

To make the ideal space drive, we just need a negative matter object in the "engine" room that has a negative mass equal in magnitude to the positive mass of the entire ship. If we want to go forward, we pull a spring from the back wall of the engine room and hook it to the negative matter object. Immediately, the perverse inertial reaction of the negative matter object will cause it to accelerate in the forward direction, pulling on the tension spring, which pulls the spacecraft forward with an acceleration that is proportional to the strength of the spring.

To stop acceleration, merely unhook the spring. To decelerate to a stop, replace the tension spring coming from the back wall of the engine room with a tension spring coming from the forward wall. How much simpler can you make a space drive that gives you an unlimited amount of acceleration with no expenditure of energy or reaction mass?

Preposterous, you say? But in my scientific paper,[3] I show that this negative matter space drive does not violate the classical laws of conservation of energy and linear momentum, even if the magnitudes of the masses are not the same.

ELASTIC COUPLING OF TWO OBJECTS

In the paper, I next studied in detail the case of two point objects coupled by an ideal, massless, tension spring. This was a more realistic version of "stiff rod" that Larry Niven had assumed could be attached between the two opposite mass objects to cause them to move at the same velocity. What we both had not considered was that the stiff rod would apply mechanical forces to the two objects in addition to their mutual gravitational forces. I found that it was the "springiness" of a realistic nonrigid rod that kept the conservation laws from being violated.

In my paper, I assumed that the spring had zero initial length (difficult, but possible, to achieve in practice with a complex reentrant spring design) and a tension force that was linearly proportional to the amount the spring had been extended. I first calculated the behavior when the two objects had positive masses. As expected, the two objects oscillated sinusoidally back and forth. If one of the objects was very massive, then the heavier object stood essentially still while the other object bounced back and forth with a frequency determined by the square root of the spring constant divided by the mass of the smaller object.

For the case where I assumed two objects of opposite mass, the force of the spring on the negative matter object caused the negative object to move *away* from the spring because of the perverse reaction of the negative inertial mass to the spring force.

EQUAL MASS MAGNITUDE CASE

If I assumed the magnitude of the positive mass was equal to the magnitude of the negative mass, then the accelerations of both objects were the same. This produced the expected but bizarre results that both the positive mass object and the negative mass object moved off at a constant acceleration that was proportional to the strength of the spring, the initial extension of the spring, and inversely proportional to the magnitudes (equal) of the two masses.

The total linear momentum of the system remained zero, even though both objects were moving off in the same direction at constantly increasing velocity. Because the magnitudes of the masses of the two objects were equal, the increased positive linear momentum gained by the positive matter object was compensated by the increased negative linear momentum gained by the negative matter object.

In the same manner, the law of conservation of energy was also not violated. The initial energy of the system was just the energy in the spring since the velocities of the objects were zero. The total energy of the system remained constant with time as the velocities of the two objects increased, since the increase in positive kinetic energy of the positive matter object was exactly compensated by the increase in negative kinetic energy of the negative matter object, while the extension (and therefore the energy) in the spring remained constant.

NEGATIVE MASS MAGNITUDE LARGER

If I assumed the magnitude of the negative mass was larger than the magnitude of the positive mass, then the equation of motion for the length of the spring changed. Instead of the spring staying at a constant length, the length of the spring oscillated sinusoidally. This is similar to the two positive mass case except that the frequency of oscillation of the spring now depended upon the difference of the masses instead of the sum of the masses. On top of the sinusoidal motion of the spacing between the two objects was superimposed a sinusoidal motion of the combined system, first off to one side, then the other side.

It is interesting to note that for the case where the magnitude of the negative mass was much larger than the magnitude of the positive mass, then the frequency of oscillation was the same frequency that would be obtained if the larger object were made of positive matter and were acting as a large, nearly motionless, inertial body, while the smaller mass oscillated back and forth at the end of the spring. Thus, from an inertial viewpoint, a large negative mass behaved like a large positive mass.

If I assumed that at the initial time, the objects were at zero velocity and the spring was at its maximum extension, then the objects were found to be at one of their maximum deviation points from their oscillation midpoint. As time proceeded, they moved toward the midpoint together, the negative mass leading the positive mass. The lighter positive mass, moving faster, caught up with the negative mass, which decreased the distance between them. This, in turn, decreased the spring force and the acceleration levels.

I found that the spring length and the spring force became zero at the midpoint and the two objects switched places (I assumed they were ideal point objects and could pass through each other without colliding). The spring started to stretch, the spring force went up, the positive mass (now leading the way) was decelerated and slowed, while the negative object pulled perversely in the opposite direction. The velocities of the two objects then decreased, both becoming zero when the end of the oscillation was reached. The spring had now reached maximum extension, and the spring forces and the acceleration levels were at their maximum again. The objects then started moving in the opposite direction.

If I assumed the magnitude of the two masses approached each other, the frequency of oscillation approached infinity, and the behavior of the system approached the unidirectional, constant acceleration case where the two masses were equal and opposite. I then calculated the total linear momentum and the total energy of the system for any point in time during the oscillation. As long as I included the energy stored in the stretched spring, there was no violation of the laws of conservation of energy and momentum.

POSITIVE MASS MAGNITUDE LARGER

If I assumed the magnitude of the positive mass was larger than the magnitude of the negative mass, I found the behavior was exponential instead of sinusoidal. After an initial transient which involved both an exponential growth and an exponential decay, the exponential growth took over. Both objects moved off in one direction, with the negative mass leading and the positive mass following. Since the less massive negative matter object moved faster than the positive matter object, the spring stretched. The increased spring length increased the spring force, and the system accelerated at an exponentially increasing rate. If the magnitudes of the two masses were almost equal, then the motions of the two masses were similar, the spring remained nearly constant in length, and the behavior of the combined system approached the constant acceleration case. Again, I found no violation of the conservation laws.

COUPLING OF MASSES USING ELECTROSTATIC FORCES

Although real negative matter particles (if they exist) may not have convenient "handles" to hook a spring to, and may not be dense enough to produce significant levels of gravitational forces, they may be massive enough to be useful and also have an electrical charge. The electrical charge would give us a "handle" on the negative matter particle that could be used to "push" and "pull" the particle at a distance using electrostatic forces. Electrostatic forces may also be used to build a computer-controlled active "trap" that can capture and collect large numbers of negative matter particles (provided they exist and provided they are charged).

I also carried out a detailed analysis of the interaction of a positive matter object and a negative matter object coupled by Coulomb electrostatic forces. I obtained the same results of unidirectional motion of the combined system at an acceleration proportional to the strength of the electrostatic force. Again, there was no violation of the laws of conservation of momentum and energy. You will have to take my word for it, as the analysis was far too long to include even in my scientific paper.

THE "NULLOR DRIVE"

In my next science fiction novel (tentatively entitled *Timemaster*), my hero will be using a "Nullor Drive." It is a gravitationally coupled device that combines the near-ideal propulsion capabilities of the negative matter space drive with the high acceleration capabilities of the spacecraft Charles Sheffield describes in his novel, *The McAndrew Chronicles*.[6]

The Nullor Drive uses two massive rings of circulating particles. One is made of ultradense positive matter, and one is made of ultradense negative matter. The positive matter ring is in the "forward" portion of the squat cylindrical spacecraft, while the negative matter ring is in the "rear." The positive matter ring causes the negative matter ring to accelerate toward it, while the negative matter ring causes the positive matter ring to accelerate away from it. Thus, the basic propulsion mechanism of the spacecraft is a gravitationally coupled negative matter space drive.

For the purposes of the story (to keep my hero young, to keep the reader from getting bored, and to bring in the relativistic time dilation effects I want to use later), I need to have my hero travel at significant fractions of the speed of light as he sets up his commercial empire between the various stars in the local solar neighborhood. If I limit the acceleration of the ship to one gee, it will take him a year to get to 70% of the speed of light. This is too long. To get him up to the speed of light in a hurry, I need to accelerate him at 100 gees so he can reach 90% of the speed of light in 1 week. Unfortunately, the human body can't take 100 gees for very long, which is where the other part of the Nullor Drive comes in.

The Nullor Drive uses gravity for both propulsion and high acceleration protection. If the two rings are made with a radius that is 1.414 times the separation distance, then it can be shown that the gravitational acceleration applied to a person in a cockpit near the center of the two rings is the same as the acceleration applied by the rings on each other. The positive mass ring pulls the pilot at 50 gees, the negative mass ring pushes the pilot at 50 gees, and these two forces combine to cancel the inertial reaction force to the 100 gee acceleration of the spacecraft.

To get 100 gees of acceleration while providing reasonable dimensions for the zero gee cockpit region (a few meters in diameter) requires that the positive and negative matter rings have a mass of about 10^{12} tons (an asteroid 10 km in diameter). In order to get that much mass concentrated in that small a region it will have to be collapsed into ultradense matter.

To attain lower acceleration levels, the rings are moved further apart and increased in radius. The zero gee region enlarges dramatically, until at 4 gees the room available approaches that of a large mansion, except this mansion has some strange floors. On the middle floor we have the zero gee pool surrounded by rooms for flying, acrobatics, and other zero gee sports. Above and below are the lunar gravity floors for easy living, while the next floors in each direction are at Earth gravity to keep you in shape. The direction of gravity on these floors is in the direction of the inertial reaction force.

If you are right in the middle of the two rings, the positive ring pull and the negative ring push just cancel the acceleration. If you move toward the positive ring, its pull actually decreases since you are getting closer to the center of the ring. (At the center of a massive ring of positive matter, the net gravity field is zero since the pull of the ring on one side is balanced by the pull of the ring on the other side.) Similarly, the push from the negative matter ring decreases since you are moving farther away from it. Since both the push and the pull are decreasing, they cancel less of the inertial force. The result is a net acceleration toward the rear of the ship.

If you move toward the negative matter ring and away from the positive matter ring, the negative ring push decreases because you are getting closer to the center of the ring, while the positive ring pull decreases because you are getting further away from it. This again produces a net acceleration toward the rear of the ship. I am having fun exploring the ramifications of life aboard such a spacecraft.

WHERE IS IT?

The purpose of my scientific paper was to emphasize to the scientific community that the concept of negative matter is not logically forbidden. In physics, there is an unwritten law that if something is not forbidden, it is compulsory. If negative matter is not logically forbidden, then where is it? There do exist some clues that may point to places where negative matter can be found.

One clue that there may be large amounts of negative matter in the universe can be found in papers discussing the huge voids found in large-scale 3-D "maps" of the universe.[7] As shown in Figure 14.2, these "bubbles" are 100 million light-years across (our Milky Way Galaxy is a mere 0.8 million light-years across). The bubbles are sharply defined by large numbers of galaxies that seem to lie on the surface of the bubbles. There are almost no galaxies *in* the voids, and those that are found there are very unusual galaxies characterized by strong, high-excitation emission spectra.

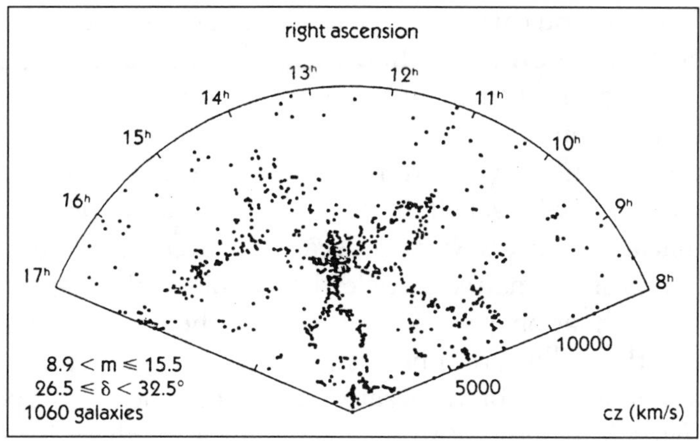

Figure 14.2. A slice of the universe. (Courtesy Valerie de Lapparent, et al. *Astrophysical Journal* © 1986.)

One possible explanation for this "frothy" structure of the present-day universe is that the universe was formed with equal amounts of negative matter particles and positive matter particles. (This has the nice feature that the net mass of the universe is zero.) The "voids" are full of the negative matter objects trying to keep as far away from each other as possible, meanwhile pushing the positive mass objects to the surface of the voids where they attract each other to form galaxies, stars, planets, and us. One way to test this hypothesis is to use some of the available computer models for universes to see if an equal mixture of positive and negative matter would separate into regions similar in size and shape to those observed.

In addition, if there are large numbers of negative matter particles in the universe, then positive masses, like our Sun, will attract those negative matter particles. As Terletskii[8] has pointed out, when the negative matter particles strike the positive matter particles in the Sun, they don't slow down, but continuously accelerate. In the process, they gain negative kinetic energy and put positive kinetic energy into the positive matter particles, heating the Sun up. Terletskii argues that because of the absence of the catastrophic heating of the Sun, then either there are very few negative matter particles (read none), or their interaction cross-section is low. It could be, instead, that there *is* heating of the Sun by an influx of negative matter particles and this is why the fusion neutrinos observed coming from the Sun are only one-third that calculated assuming all the energy in the Sun is generated by thermonuclear fusion plus gravitational contraction.

The reason negative matter particles have not been seen may be because a process called "nullification" is taking place. During the nullification process, when a negative matter particle physically contacts a positive matter particle they would both disappear, just like the annihilation process that occurs when antimatter meets matter. In the nullification process, however, no energy is released since the net rest mass of the negative matter particle and the positive matter particle is zero. With no energy released, there is nothing for scientific instruments to detect.

In my novel, I will have my hero discover and gather this postulated flux of negative matter particles so he can produce the negative matter space drive that I need to make the story work. It would be nice if the real world were as easy to manipulate as fictional worlds. But you never know, perhaps it is. What the space community really needs is a nonpolluting, infinite range, effortless propulsion system like the negative matter space drive. Maybe if someone will go out into space and look for negative matter, we will find just what we need to build one.

Chapter 15

Warren Salomon

The Economics of Interstellar Commerce

Why don't we have a vast literature of imagination that assumes, as a background concept, that there will be a mass transit system linking us to Antarctica? No doubt it's because such a transit system is fundamentally ridiculous. Travel to Antarctica is certainly possible, but there is no reasonably foreseeable demand for mass transit, and therefore tales of adventure on the "Antarctica Express" would be inherently unbelievable.

Yet it is a postulate of science fiction that one day there will be routine travel between the stars. And that means we're all assuming that interstellar travel (however it may be done) will be commercially viable, that it will be self-supporting—somehow.

But sooner or later reality must intervene, and whoever writes the checks (or the future equivalent) is going to say: "Starships are very nice to dream about, but if you want me to pay for a dozen-year voyage to who knows where, you'd better explain what's in it for me."

That might not match your heroic vision of the future, but it most definitely is the way of the world, so perhaps it's time to take a cold, hard look at economic realities, and ask ourselves the Big

Question—*Why* is anyone going to pay the price? Or, to put the matter bluntly, can we make a buck out there?

I'm going to ignore all those SF tales that are filled with ingenious ideas about *how* interstellar journeys will be made. Those ideas are certainly interesting, but most of them would be very expensive—some of those ships might cost the gross "national" product of our whole planet. Even if such ships are technically feasible, we're still faced with the Big Question—Is there money to be made in interstellar commerce?

Let's be clear about what's involved in this question. I'm not talking about whether anyone can profit from ship building, or supplying equipment for the crew, or providing fuel, or any of a thousand other peripheral activities. If someone is willing to pay for interstellar voyages, there will of necessity be a demand for ships, equipment, and fuel; and businesses will naturally spring up to fill those needs. What I'm getting at is a more fundamental issue—what makes the *whole venture* economically worth the bother? Where will the funds come from to pay for interstellar voyages?

Science fiction literature is filled with endless blather about the "sense of wonder," mankind's love of adventure, and our insatiable quest for knowledge. These motives exist, and no doubt some ships will be launched for those reasons. But what will keep the activity going on a continuing basis? Why will fleets of ships be built and launched decade after decade, generation after generation, century after century? Just for the sheer joy of it? I think not.

Our sense of wonder is very real. It's sufficient, for example, to keep this magazine in business. But magazines are considerably cheaper than starships. Obviously our quest for knowledge, by itself, is not the answer to the big question. If star travel is to be an ongoing affair, it's got to be profitable. So where are the profits in interstellar voyages?

To answer that question with our limited knowledge at this time, we need to make a few assumptions. We base our assumptions on human nature, which certainly won't change, on the probable likelihood of rapid technological progress, and on what we now know (or think we know) about how the universe works. And if we're wrong . . . well, an essay like this is an admittedly risky undertaking.

Our first assumption involves technology. Obviously, it's absurd to guess what technology will be available a century or two in the future—so we won't seriously try. Also, we shall ignore the possibility of "miraculous" discoveries. The invention of instantaneous (or at least faster-than-light) communications and transportation will profoundly alter the economic assumptions in this essay—as well as everything else in the world—but such a prospect now seems unlikely. We'll also ignore the possibility of technological shortcuts derived from encounters with star-faring aliens, eager to engage in trade. That could happen (eventually it's probably inevitable), but its timing is so unpredictable that it's outside the scope of this essay.

In the area of technology, let us (blithely?) assume that starships (or starliners, or plain old "ships," or whatever they'll be called) will be built. Don't ask me how they'll work; we're just assuming that somehow they will. They'll be expensive items of equipment—not nearly as expensive as our present-day moon rockets, but quite costly nevertheless—probably on the order of present-day supertankers, which are relatively conventional in terms of available technology (as starships presumably will be) but which are still quite costly. This means that if a cargo isn't extremely valuable and in great demand, it won't be worth the expense of transporting it.

And let us further assume that interstellar travel and communications will be limited by the speed of light—which as far as we know is a natural constraint. Also—optimistically—let's assume that starships will be able to travel at fairly close to light-speed, so that voyages won't require centuries of transit time.

All right then. We've made some technological assumptions, and they seem to be reasonable for the foreseeable future. Beyond that, by definition, we can't foresee. Now what?

Now let's consider our first problem, which is: Where are these expensive starships going to go? That shouldn't be a very big problem. There are approximately 300 stars within 35 light-years of the Sun. Few of them are Sun-like, and presumably fewer still will have Earth-like planets, but now that we've developed our starships, let's not get pessimistic. We shall make yet another assumption: Within a realistically achievable distance—the working lifespans of a starship's crew—there will be numerous destinations to choose from.

OK, we've got ships and places to go. Let's consider problem number two. Even traveling at near light-speed, interstellar trips take a long time, don't they? Sure, but SF literature has worked that out long ago. If your destination is 10 light-years away, and your ship is traveling at a reasonably good (and presently unattainable) clip, you won't age 10 years during the trip. For a ship moving at near light-speed, time dilation requires that in terms of your subjective, shipboard life span, the voyage won't be much more time-consuming than, say, one of Francis Drake's pirate raids.

For those who care about the actual numbers, I've got a few. If you could travel at about 99.49% of light-speed (ignoring lesser velocities involved during the beginning and ending phases of the voyage) the time aboard ship will pass at only 10% of Earth's time. At about 99.87% of light-speed, ship's time is only 5% of Earth's time. Therefore, a 10-light-year voyage at 99.49% of light-speed will age the crew only 1 year, and at 99.87% of light-speed, only 6 months. So if we assume that we'll have fast enough ships (and a fantastic energy source to power them), you could make quite a few interstellar voyages in a productive lifetime—if it were worth your while to do so. But would it be?

This brings us to problem number three: Assuming there are adequate ships and places to go, and the crew's lifespans aren't a problem, why would fleets of expensive vessels be launched to go there? That's another way of asking the Big Question, and we'll spend the rest of this essay trying to answer it.

But before continuing, let's be sure we're all together. I suspect that the Big Question may have taken some of you by surprise. After all, there are abundant examples of terrestrial, trans-oceanic trade, which at first glance seem to provide models for interstellar commerce. For example, the Japanese import raw materials to their resource-poor islands, transform the materials into automobiles, send the finished goods across the Pacific, and sell them in the United States—and they make a lot of money doing so. Couldn't the same kind of thing work among the stars?

Not necessarily. The times and distances (and therefore the costs) involved are not analogous—not even close. The distance to the Sun's nearest stellar neighbor is approximately *five billion* times the distance from Japan to California. Therefore, the model of trans-oceanic trade is virtually useless.

It's often been assumed that there would be interstellar freighters and ore ships based on the trans-oceanic model, but is this assumption realistic? Consider the importation of raw materials to the Earth. Sure, resources might vanish from the Earth or become unimaginably expensive, although this is doubtful. Still, we won't be using starships to import raw materials. We can always mine the asteroids, or Jupiter's moons. They're millions of times closer, and therefore far cheaper. So unless there are minerals out there we've never dreamed of, and that we can't synthesize closer to home, we can forget about interstellar ore boats.

It's not raw materials that we'll lack in the solar system, it's cheap labor. But the cost of labor on Earth would have to be incredibly high to justify an interstellar flow of manufactured goods. It's conceivable, of course. We can easily imagine a future political setup (the post office scenario) in which all nations on Earth are so bogged down with artificially high labor costs and archaic work rules that the "cheapest" Earth-made automobiles would cost, relatively, what a Rolls Royce costs now. But ask yourself—would even that kind of economic insanity justify an interstellar transportation system, with a 10- or 15-year (Earth viewpoint) transit time?

Probably not. The unions would take care (if they were clever) that terrestrial prices never got so high that the interstellar free-traders would have a competitive advantage.

Even if Earth was devastated by war (a common science fiction scenario), we could rebuild our factories faster than we could import finished goods from the stars. Remember, after the destruction of World War II, Western Europe was back in business within a few short years.

So we need to assume a really amazing manufacturing advantage that would make goods from the stars so valuable as to be worth the cost—and years of transit time—of shipping them to Earth.

Is that realistic? Maybe. Some goods are unique—like the products of newly created technologies. Ah, but would new colonies develop such technologies? And even if they did, there's always the risk of industrial espionage; and anyway, by the time the products got to their distant market (Earth), would they still be state of the art? A dozen years of transport time can dull a product's competitive advantage.

Besides, absent a new terrestrial dark age (another common SF scenario), interstellar shipments are going to be pretty much a one-way street. Earth will have technologies the new worlds need, at least in the early stages of our interstellar expansion. They (the colonies) will need goods from Earth, but not vice versa. In marketing terms, they're going to be like the natives of Bangladesh—we know they're out there, and they want what we produce, but what's in it for us? The problem for an interstellar merchant is finding something Earth can buy from the new worlds.

Well, what can the new worlds export? It'll be a long time until the new worlds are out-inventing Earth. All their technology will be old stuff, made with machines they took with them. But even old technology can be unique if it involves secret processes. Sure, but does Coke's secret formula justify the cost of interstellar freight? What else have they got?

Artwork is unique. Persian rugs are regionally specific, labor-intensive products. Havana cigars and French wines require special climatic conditions. Extraterrestrial analogs of such items could be traded. But it would take a lot of future Picassos, cases of Coca-Cola, bottles of Chateau Betelgeuse, Oriental carpets, and interstellar stogies to support a galactic merchant fleet. Anything else?

There's the possibility of Dune-like spice, or Star Trek's dilithium crystals, or some other wonder goods—but we can't count on their existence. For the moment, let's ignore this problem, and arbitrarily assume that something, say automobiles, will be worth shipping from one planetary system to another. This (the Toyota scenario) is our biggest, wildest assumption so far, but let's play with it for a while, and see how it goes.

If you were a star-faring merchant considering the purchase of a shipload of cars from, say, Epsilon Eridani, which is almost 11 light-years away from Earth, how would you know what market conditions were like on Earth? It'll take you 11 years (actually 10.8 or so, but let's not be fussy) to send a message to Earth ("Cars for sale. Want some?") and 11 more years to get a reply ("Yes, we'll take a few."). By the time you got that reply, the information would be 11 years out of date. Perhaps Marco Polo could operate like that, but things were somewhat different then.

Ah . . . let's assume that you don't need to send an inquiry to Earth. Instead, imagine that Earth is always broadcasting its needs, so you touch down on a manufacturing planet circling Epsilon Eridani (which we'll call "EE") and you get the latest info (11 years old) from Earth—"Hot market here for cars from EE." Fine. Now what?

Now you start thinking like a merchant. What kind of mark-up could you expect that would justify buying a starship-load of cars and tying up your capital (or paying interest on a loan) for the dozen years you would need to get those cars to your destination? I said a dozen years, because your ship will certainly be slower than the communications system. Bear in mind that you'd be making an investment in goods that might very well be obsolete when they finally arrived. And if Earth is dominated by strong labor unions (as they would have to be to make scarce, extraterrestrial labor a bargain) they'll have a full range of protectionist legislation to keep out cheap imports. And what kind of import duties would you have to pay in order to clear your cargo through Earth customs?

The only way your venture could work is if you could know, a dozen years in advance of your arrival on Earth, what your sales price and other costs would be. Could you? Maybe.

It's possible for that broadcast of Earth's needs to be some kind of continuing offer, containing price and terms, and by acting on it you could be assured of selling your cargo at those prices—even though your cargo would be a dozen years old when your ship arrives on Earth. That would require an automobile dealer on Earth to commit himself, years in advance, to pay a healthy price for cargo he hoped would be arriving—some day. Maybe his broadcast offer would say, "Irving's Interstellar Imports needs 100 cars, as of the year 2200. Will pay 30 Heinleins each, plus all import taxes, if they get here by the year 2224 (that's 11 years for Irving's offer to get to EE, and 13 more for the goods to be produced and sent from EE to Earth). This offer guaranteed by irrevocable letter of credit from Bank of Terra."

The "offer" would have to be officially registered somewhere at EE, and if you accepted it, that too would be registered, so the next interstellar entrepreneur arriving at EE wouldn't duplicate the order. Irving only wants 100 cars, not 100 million. A message would then be sent to Earth saying that the goods were on the way.

Would that do it? Perhaps, if there were strict laws that made that kind of deal a binding contract, if the Bank of Terra were still in business when you arrived, if there were no currency depreciation, and perhaps a thousand other things. Maybe a local branch of the Bank of Terra on EE would use that broadcast offer as collateral, and make you a loan equal to the cost of your cargo and the cost of the loan, plus some profit. Nice deal. Then you pay for the cars, leave the profit on deposit (with interest compounding) and you head for Earth to deliver your cargo to Irving.

The bank should do quite well, too. The loan is secure (it's backed by the Bank of Terra on Earth, and your ship is insured by Interstellar Lloyds). Your profit deposit is going to sit on EE, waiting about 24 years until you return. With a loan portfolio and a deposit base like that, interstellar banking should be a super-profitable industry.

When you arrive on Earth with your cargo in good condition, the Bank of Terra (on Earth) broadcasts to its branch (on EE) that everything's fine, and you can withdraw your funds. (We've just described how a "letter of credit" works today in international trade.) And observe, future bankers, that it can take decades for funds to clear. That's one hell of a profitable float. Faster-than-light communications would probably be a banking disaster!

Now you dash back to EE, most likely with an outward bound cargo arranged in the same manner. Both the trip to Earth and the return to EE take a short time, subjectively (about 2 or 3 years altogether, depending on how much beyond 99% of light-speed you're traveling), and when you get back to good old EE, you're a rich man—depending on the tax laws that have been enacted on EE during the 24 or so years of your absence.

That sounds like it could be workable, but does this Toyota scenario make any sense? Would an automobile dealer on Earth (or any other interstellar destination) offer to pay for a shipload of cars (or whatever) which wouldn't arrive for two dozen years?

It's unlikely, but not impossible. A deposit of 20¢ now, compounding annually at only 7% per year, grows to $1 in 24 years. At an interest rate of 10% per year, you only need to deposit about 10¢. So our terrestrial auto dealer only has to put up a small deposit now with the Bank of Terra to have the payment guaranteed in 24 years. And, if the deposits come from his customers, the auto dealer isn't even investing his own funds. The only risks are structural ones—the bank may fail, the laws may change, the currency may depreciate, there may be war, plague, and so on. But these are risks that could be faced, and gladly—if the lure of huge profits were there.

It makes even more sense if the customer doesn't have to wait 24 years, which is possible. He makes his 10% deposit, then goes off on an interstellar trip, and returns to Earth a couple of subjective years later, while 24 Earth-years have passed, and . . . ta da! His car is waiting for him, all paid for. Of course it's an old-style car, but that's OK. He's technologically like Rip Van Winkle. Unlike Rip, he's still young, but he's hopelessly out of date, and not trained to use new vehicles. (We're assuming rapid technological progress, remember?) Interstellar travelers need old-style goods (and probably live in behind-the-times communities with their contemporaries) so the years of transit time your cargo requires turns out to be a desirable feature.

The Toyota scenario makes more sense now than it did when we (in our desperation) first invented it.

But we're getting ahead of ourselves. Before you can import cars from the stars, you'll need flourishing settlements out there. If you're going to make a living as an interstellar merchant, you'll need lots of settlers with lots of equipment to make the inventory you'll be hauling off to Earth—or wherever. And those interstellar settlers will be your market for whatever goods you'll bring back on the return leg of your trading voyage. So they need to be not only productive, but rich enough to pay for goods hauled in from other systems.

I realize that factories could be automated, but why would anyone build automated factories on an unpopulated EE? Certainly not to place the factories near EE's raw materials—we've got the asteroids, remember? So there won't be factories (or markets) on EE unless people are there.

I don't know (and can't even guess) the figures, but it's a safe bet that it will cost a bundle to set up a successful interstellar (extrasolar) community. Setting up a new world, years of traveltime away from Earth, requires a whole lot of talented, highly trained people so we can end up with a productive, self-sustaining society at the other end—and there are no guarantees of success. In case you doubt that, remember that after many costly attempts, Spain was *never* successful in planting a self-sustaining settlement in Florida—and it tried for 300 years!

So we have another problem: Where do all the people come from?

Finding settlers will be no problem. I'd probably volunteer myself. But who will pay for the settlement's equipment and transportation? And even after the pioneers arrive at their destination, it's probably the work of a generation or two just to get things up and running. So we're back to the big question: Why is anyone going to bankroll this operation?

Earth won't tax itself for centuries to sustain a colony on EE, just for the thrill of it all. Governments will finance a few voyages, sure, and maybe a quasi-permanent science colony, like Antarctica. But beyond that, forget it. If we're going to have thriving interstellar settlements, it will have to be the result of private, voluntary activity.

But won't that happen more or less automatically? I don't think so.

We should recall that the great transoceanic explorations on Earth were undertaken for the purpose of finding a quicker, cheaper route to the Orient—a place where traders were already going by overland routes—in pursuit of goods for which there was already an established market (the Dutch East India Company scenario). Those incentives don't exist where the stars are concerned, so unless we can come up with some good ideas, it won't be private investors using their own funds who first go to the stars.

After the first few interstellar exploration voyages, presumably financed by governments or universities, what comes next? What is the next step that will keep the ships being built, and crewed, and—financed?

Consider examples from Earth's history. After the explorations of Columbus (a government-financed project), several early follow-up voyages were made—to secure territory and trade routes (originally presumed to lead to the Orient) which Spain's maritime rivals might otherwise grab, and to carve out great estates for land-hungry pioneers. By the early 1500s, government-chartered agricultural settlements (using indigenous slave labor) had been established throughout the Caribbean.

Agricultural ventures (and the lure of free land and slaves) alone were sufficient to cause adventurers and would-be grandees to cross the Atlantic, but if that were all there was, the "winning" of the New World would have been a very slow process, like the gradual colonization of North America. What caused the immediate glory, the gunships, the pirates, and the huge fleets of Spain's early transoceanic empire?

The real payoff was gold. Cortez's conquest of the Aztecs in Mexico and Pizarro's conquest of the Incas in Peru yielded sudden, incredibly vast quantities of gold, silver, and gems—which flooded back to Spain in a profitable stream that continued for almost 200 years. Ultimately, Spain's trans-oceanic empire was financed by plunder.

But neither agriculture nor plunder (the Spanish scenario) will be a likely incentive for interstellar travel. We won't find any Aztecs, and agriculture is absurd. A settlement on an Earth-like planet may swiftly become self-sufficient, but no set of circumstances that would make it worthwhile to grow sugar or tobacco on a distant planet, and then transport it for years in an expensive starship, and finally sell it profitably to consumers on Earth. It would probably be cheaper—by far—to irrigate the Sahara!

So the Big Question rears its head again: Who would finance a settlement on another planet, in another system?

At this point, it's difficult to imagine a group of private investors pooling their funds to develop and build the first starships, and then launch them on a voyage of decades—unless they know something we don't know (and therefore can't consider) about what they're going to find when they get there. People don't make investments unless they can see a reasonable possibility of earning a return. Where is the profit from the first ship to the stars? Or from the tenth ship, for that matter?

Tourism has been suggested as a possible free-enterprise method of financing space travel ("Space Tourism—The Door into the Space Age," by Patrick Collins, *Analog*, June 1988). But hotels in near-Earth orbit are one thing, and hotels on EE are quite another. As with all other interstellar schemes, the Earth-bound investors might not live long enough to get a return on their investment. So the Big Question appears again—Why would any sane Earthman invest his money in a tourist complex (or anything else) on EE?

It's starting to look grim. We've already gone and figured out a (fairly rickety) system for buying celestial Toyotas on EE and selling them on Earth; but now we can't figure out how to get a colony going on good old EE in the first place. Maybe you can't get there from here.

But let's not give up. Rome wasn't built in a day either. But, of course, building Rome was easy compared to an interstellar common market—not to mention Trantor! How do you get "over the hump" of getting it all started? And we keep coming back to the Big Question: Why would anyone pay the bills?

Let's go back and consider a few more possibilities suggested by Earth history: Maybe extraterrestrial (no, extrasolar) settlements could start out as military posts, perhaps to protect trade routes (uh, what trade?) or claims to valuable resources (uh, valuable to whom?—we've still got the asteroids). Hmmmm. No good.

Let's start again. As a result of terrestrial, international rivalry, the superpowers of the future start sending out interstellar explorations. That could happen. Governments traditionally do expensive things with taxpayers' money that individuals would never do voluntarily, or universities (spending government funds) send out exploration ships to do research. This could happen, too. We've already assumed that the early voyages may be financed by these methods. But either way (via government or academia) what you end up with is Antarctica—not Boston Harbor. Now what?

How about using the Vikings or the Polynesians as a model? They just built their ships and went exploring. Period. Probably pushed by population pressures. But that won't work for the stars. Their ships didn't cost very much, but starships do. And besides, there are cheaper ways to keep the population down than building enough starships to make a difference.

Well, we can do what the Portuguese did to encourage exploration, and the Spanish. There could be a system of land claims, where whoever gets to a world first can own it—forever. Maybe even with a fancy title to go with it. That might work (although, as the descendants of Columbus will attest, such promises are rarely kept). Lots of the early settlements in North and South America started out as proprietary colonies. A well-financed corporation might invest the funds necessary in order to own a whole world. If some land were then made available to settlers, they might come—eventually.

I can make it even more interesting. We can set it up like one of those multilevel distributorship deals. The owners of the first ship get a claim on their planet, and their colony pays a perpetual percentage of its profits to the homeworld proprietors who financed the deal. Then, as the new world launches ships of its own, they repeat the process, and a small percentage from these secondary ventures is skimmed off for the homeworld, too. In commercial terms, the original proprietors get an "override" commission on all future worlds settled by their colony.

You can keep this kind of thing going forever. As long as there are new worlds to conquer, there will be an endless profit stream flowing back down the pipeline, with each parent world in the discovery chain taking its cut and passing on a dividend to the world before it, all the way from the far periphery of the galaxy to the original homeworld. And then there are other galaxies . . . growth without end—forever. Talk about pyramid schemes!

But for the investors at any stage in the drama, it's a huge, long-term gamble—one that might not pay off for generations. And if you know your history, you'll recall a phenomenon known as revolution. By the time things started to look rosy for the investors, the settlers they've bankrolled will no doubt change the rules of the game. Goodbye, empire; hello, people's republic of whatever. Pyramid schemes are never a very sound investment.

Here's another possibility: How about penal colonies? Remember Australia? Remember Georgia? But why build a starship for that purpose? It's a lot cheaper to build prisons on Earth.

Have we run out of ideas? Not yet. There's another group of possibilities we'll lump together as the libertarian scenario. It's well known that people will abandon their homes and migrate to the most inconvenient places in order to escape silly government regulations. Las Vagas exists in the middle of a desert merely because of an absence of gambling prohibitions. Switzerland prospers (without resources) because of its neutrality, and its liberal banking laws. Other unlikely places are densely populated and prosperous, not because of any natural advantage, but because of an absence of restrictive laws—Hong Kong, for example. You can name a dozen off-shore banking centers, tax havens, and so on, that would likely be impoverished backwaters, but for the congeniality of their legal systems. It's possible that inhospitable interstellar locations could develop as libertarian refuges, for immigrants seeking nothing more than freedom from excessive governments. After all, that's pretty much how the United States was populated.

Once such a world was established, settlers would find their way. People escaping conscription, smugglers, fugitives, people running away for any of a thousand personal reasons. Some of these would be excellent settlers, some would not. There'd be no way to pick only the best and brightest. The very existence of an agency screening out undesirables would contradict the *laìssez faire* nature of the destination. Probably the hardships inherent in surviving in a new world would quickly weed out those who were unfit. You can't run away from mother nature. The libertarian scenario is a bit messy, but freedom is an inherently sloppy condition.

Once we have extrasolar worlds as centers of outlawed, black market (i.e., free market) activities, all sorts of ideas come to mind: Illegal drugs could be grown on the new worlds—which conjures up cliché images from old pulp magazines of swift interstellar clippers running contraband past Earth's cumbersome, bureaucratic blockades.

The libertarian scenario has its dark side. Off-world populations could be used for organ banks and baby farms. Wealthy but aging travelers from Earth could travel to EE (requiring only a few short years of subjective travel time), get fixed up with a new set of insides, maybe have a child (carried by a sturdy EE peasant woman), and then return to Earth, rejuvenated, replicated, and reaping the results of a compound-interest deposit left behind.

Maybe we're getting somewhere now, with a concept of extrasolar worlds which is both fascinating and repulsive—worlds which specialize in black market goods and services, worlds offering commerce both free and sordid, populations both liberated and degraded, distant worlds of rejuvenation and degeneration.

Consider this example of what interstellar travel agencies might advertise: "Take a few years (subjective) out of your life, earn a few decades (Earth time) interest on your money, and travel to exotic EE, where your every wish can be fulfilled." Attractive or not, is it plausible?

No, because we still can't figure out how to finance the early ships! This is just as impossible as the Toyota scenario (although the libertarian "products" make trade with Earth much more likely). So the libertarian scenario—fascinating though it is—will have to wait.

We're getting desperate now. We've got ships, we've got places to go. Time and distance are no problem. Compound interest makes long voyages worthwhile, and we've worked out a system of interstellar finance. We can even imagine some kind of commerce going on. But how can we get interstellar colonies organized and self-sufficient? Where will the funds come from? The Big Question looms as large as ever. Can it be done?

Maybe. Remember the tremendous profits to be made from the banking system, if only we could think of a way to get it started.

Surely, with wealth like that waiting to be made, someone will think of a way. How about this: Our venturers might not have to wait decades for a return on their investment. Remember time dilation—a round trip to EE takes about 24 years, Earth time, but only about 3 years, ship's time. Investors could get a much quicker payoff (subjectively) if they go along for the ride. Not that they'd have any desire to become settlers. All they want is to stay alive long enough to reap the rewards of their enterprise. A rich man could put part of his portfolio at interest on Earth, invest the rest in an exploration company, and then climb aboard ship. After 24 years have passed on Earth, he returns only 3 years older, finds a potful of money waiting for him in the bank (his left-behind deposit has multiplied five or ten times, depending on interest rates) and he also owns the beginning of a thriving business on EE. After another trip or two, he's incredibly rich, still relatively young, and now his investment on EE should be starting to pay off.

This is the scenario of star-traveling investors, who become centuries old by Earth's reckoning, with fortunes (and maybe families) established on several worlds. It's quite possible that something like this will happen. In fact, this scenario is so tempting that it may be the answer to the Big Question!

All right. Star-traveling investors and bankers will pay for the first ships. But we still have a problem: What about the settlers, the workers, the pioneers? Who buys their tickets? Can we realistically expect our star-hopping venture capitalists to pay for everyone's passage? Not likely. We need people who can pay their own way. And we need a lot of them.

How about religious settlers? That's happened before—the Puritans, the Quakers, the Mormons. The outcast sects of the future would go to the stars (if they could afford it) because they had no realistic alternatives, and in time their settlements would flourish—and produce those cars (if not the illegal services) that Earth might one day want to buy. Maybe—but where will they get the money for the voyage?

How about this one—welfare costs money, lots of it. Consider someone who is 20 years old, on welfare, and who is also having a kid every year—kids who (alas) are likely to be future welfare candidates. This fruitful but impoverished individual is going to cost the taxpayers plenty as long as we have the kind of setup we do now.

I imagine such a person costs the taxpayers (in today's dollars) at least $25,000 per year (factoring in the cost of bureaucratic overhead for the welfare system, plus schools, health care, police, and so on), and if our welfare recipient lives a normal life span, these costs will go on for about 50 years. Plus the costs of the next generation, and the next, ad infinitum.

If the government borrowed $400,000 at 6% interest, payable annually for 50 years, they could pay off that debt at a cost of $25,377.71 a year—which is our estimated first-generation welfare person's annual cost. We don't know what a one-way ticket will cost on a colony ship, but (assuming these figures are translated into future currency) if it's anything less than $400,000, a "welfare buyout" resulting in a ticket to EE looks like a worthwhile investment for the taxpayers.

Not only that, but if the government (i.e., the taxpayers) paid the fare, it would also be a way to subsidize the fledgling starship companies. This is how mail-carrying contracts once helped our infant airlines. Provided the people don't mind paying subsidies for someone else's business, it could work.

Remember, if the government pays for the "settlers" to be transported to good old EE, we're free of their welfare burden forever. As much as I'm opposed to paying taxes, I like this idea—the Liberia scenario. It would be cheaper to halt welfare and forget about the stars, too, but the former won't happen any time soon, and I don't want to do the latter.

So after exploring numerous scenarios, here's the model we've finally arrived at: Ships paid for by star-traveling investors, who finance the banks and the infrastructure. Settlement by interstellar fanatics (as they will seem to their contemporaries) and relocated welfare folk (a source of good, cheap labor), plus a scattering of refugees from the libertarian scenario. It sounds rather scruffy, but who do you think the North American settlers were? That rough, exotic mixture is what starts the whole thing going.

Then, to make their efforts pay off, we need the post office scenario—Earth turned into a market for interstellar goods and services because of government restrictions, prohibitions, and rab unionism. Services outlawed on Earth will be available on far worlds, the trips made painlessly affordable by compound interest piling up during (subjectively) swift voyages. Commerce will be financed with interstellar letters of credit issued by branches of fabulously wealthy interstellar banks. Products will be paid for years in advance by departing star-travelers making small deposits, which will swiftly inflate (via compound interest) over the time-dilated decades. Interstellar goods will be shipped to Earth and bought by wealthy, returning Rip Van Winkles with a need for affordable, off-world, obsolete goods. And, after a few centuries, when it all comes to pass, the banks' star-traveling founders may still be alive to enjoy their much deserved dividends.

And that's the way the future works. It's rich, raucous, various, and vulgar. It's wonderful and strange and profoundly complex. And if the assumptions are accurate, then it might just happen. Someday. But it's not the way you thought it would be, is it?

References

Chapter 1: Comes the Revolution . . .

1. Dr. Arlan Andrews, "Single Stage to Infinity," *Analog Science Fiction and Fact*, June 1993, Vol CXIII, No 7.
2. G. Harry Stine, and Paul C. Hans, "Economic Considerations of Hypersonic Vehicles and Spaceplanes," AIAA-90-5267, AIAA Second International Aerospaceplanes Conference, Orlando, FL, 29–31 October 1990.
3. G. Harry Stine, and Paul C. Hans, "Air Cargo, 1988 Traffic and Assessment," *Distribution* magazine, February 1989.
4. G. Harry Stine, *The Third Industrial Revolution*, New York, G. P. Putnam, 1975.
5. G. Harry Stine, Hearings before the Committee on Science and Technology, U.S. House of Representatives, Ninety-fifth Congress, Second Session, January 24, 25, 26, 1978, U.S. Government Printing Office, Washington, DC.
6. G. Harry Stine, *The Space Enterprise*, New York, Ace Books, 1980.
7. *Op.cit*. "Air Cargo, 1988 Traffic and Assessment."

8. Walter R. Dornberger, *V-2*, New York, The Viking Press, 1954.
9. G. Harry Stine, *ICBM: The Making of the Weapon That Changed the World*, New York, Orion Books, 1991.
10. *Ibid.*
11. P. C. Hans and G. H. Stine, "Spaceplane Contributions to the Hydrogen Economy," *International Journal of Hydrogen Energy*, Vol 16, No 6, pp 427–431, 1991.
12. "Treaty on Principles Governing the Activities of States in the Exploration and Use of Outer Space," Article 7, 1967.
13. Lee Correy, *Shuttle Down*, New York, Ballantine/Del Rey, 1981.
14. Lee Correy, *Manna*, New York, DAW Books, 1983.

Chapter 2: The Hypersonic Skyhook

1. Y. Artsutanov, "V Kosmos na Electrovoze," *Komsomolskaya Pravda*, July 31, 1960. Described by Lvov in *Science*, Nov. 17, 1967, Vol *158*, p 946.
2. J. D. Isaacs, A. C. Vine, H. Bradner, and G. E. Bachus, "Satellite Elongation into a True 'Skyhook,'" *Science*, Feb. 11, 1966, Vol 151, p 682, and May 6, 1966, Vol *152*, p 800.
3. J. Pearson, "The Orbital Tower: A Spacecraft Launcher Using the Earth's Rotational Energy," *Acta Astronautica, 2*, Sept.-Oct. 1975, p 785.
4. H. Moravec, "A Non-Synchronous Orbital Skyhook," *Journal of the Astronautical Sciences* Oct.-Dec. 1977, Vol 25.
5. R. Hyde, "Earthbreak: Earth to Space Transportation," *Defense Science 2003+*, 1985, Vol 4(4), pp 78–92.
6. J. Pearson, "Low-Cost Launch System and Orbital Fuel Depot," IAF-86-128, published in *Acta Astronautica*, 1989, Vol 19, No 4, pp 315–320.
7. J. E. McCoy, *Advances in the Astronautical Sciences*, 1987, Vol 62.
8. R. Forward, "Failsafe Multistrand Tethers for Space Propulsion," NAS8-39318, SBIR 91-1 Phase 1 Research Study.

Chapter 3: Mars Direct: A Proposal for the Rapid Exploration and Colonization of the Red Planet

1. R. Zubrin, "The Large Scale Colonization of Mars," Presented to the Ninth International Space Development Conference, Anaheim, CA, May 28, 1990.
2. D. Baker and R. Zubrin, "Combining Near Term Technologies to Achieve a Two Launch Manned Mars Mission," AIAA 90-1896, 26th AIAA/ASME Joint Propulsion Conference, Orlando, FL, July 1990.
3. S. K. Borowski, "Nuclear Propulsion—A Vital Technology for the Exploration of Mars and the Planets Beyond," AAS-87-210, Proceedings of the Case for

Mars III conference, Published by the American Astronautical Society, San Diego, CA, 1989.

4. R. Zubrin, "Nuclear Rockets Using Indigenous Martian Propellants," AIAA 89-2768, 25th AIAA/ASME Joint Propulsion Conference, Monterey, CA, July 1989.
5. R. Zubrin, "Nuclear Rocketry Using Indigenous Propellants: The Key to the Solar System," *Analog Science Fiction/Science Fact,* March 1990.
6. R. Zubrin, "The Engineering of a Nuclear Thermal Landing and Ascent Vehicle Utilizing Indigenous Martian Propellant," AIAA 90-1995, 26th AIAA/ASME Joint Propulsion Conference, Orlando, FL, July 1990.
7. D. Koenig, "Experience Gained from the Space Nuclear Rocket Program (Rover)," Los Alamos National Laboratory Report LA-10062-H, May 1986.
8. J. Powell, Private communication, July 1990.
9. P. J. Boston, "The Case for Mars," American Astronautical Society Science and Technology Series, Vol 57, Univelt Publishers, San Diego, CA, 1984.
10. C. P. McKay, "The Case for Mars II," American Astronautical Society Science and Technology Series, Vol 62, Univelt Publishers, San Diego, CA, 1985.
11. C. R. Stoker, "The Case for Mars III," American Astronautical Society Science and Technology Series, Vols 74 and 75, San Diego, CA, Univelt Publishers, 1989.
12. B. M. Cordell, "A Preliminary Assessment of Martian Natural Resource Potential," AAS 84-185, Presented to the Case for Mars II Conference, Boulder, CO, July 1984.
13. L. Friedman, "Starsailing: Solar Sails and Interstellar Travel," New York, John Wiley & Sons, 1988.
14. R. M. Zubrin and D. G. Andrews, "Magnetic Sails and Interplanetary Travel," AIAA 89-2441, Presented to the 25th AIAA/ASME Joint Propulsion Conference, Monterey, CA, July 1989.
15. C. P. McKay, "An Assessment of the Habitability of Mars," Presented at the Case for Mars IV Conference, Boulder, CO, June 1990.
16. C. P. McKay and C. R. Stoker, "The Early Environment and its Evolution on Mars: Implications for Life," Reviews of Geophysics, May 1989, 27, 2.

Chapter 4: Inward Ho!

1. C. Pellegrino and J. R. Powell, *Analog,* Sept. 1986.
2. R. L. Forward, *Flight of the Dragonfly.*
3. William Shakespeare, *Troilus and Cressida,* Act II.
4. Jerry Oltion and Lee Goodloe, *Analog,* Oct. 1988.
5. J. M. A. Danby, *Fundamentals of Celestial Mechanics*, New York, Macmillan, 1964, pp 1–348.

6. Greeley. *Earthlike Planets: Surfaces of Mercury, Venus, Earth, Moon, Mars.* W. H. Freeman & Co., 1981.

7. S. L. Gillett, "Mining the Moon." *Analog*, Nov. 1983.

8. Freeman Dyson, *Disturbing the Universe*, New York, Harper & Row, 1979.

Chapter 6: Islands in the Sky: Human Exploration and Settlement of the Oort Cloud

1. Freeman Dyson. "The World, the Flesh and the Devil," Third J. D. Bernal Lecture, May 1972; Reprinted in Sagan (ed.): *Communication with Extraterrestrial Intelligence*. Cambridge, MA, MIT Press, 1973.

2. Ben R. Finney and Eric M. Jones, editors. *Interstellar Migration and the Human Experience*. Berkeley, University of California Press, 1985.

3. Eric M. Jones and Ben R. Finney. "Interstellar Nomads" in *Space Manufacturing 1983; Advances in the Astronautical Sciences 53*, 1983, pp 357–374.

4. David G. Stephenson. "Comets and Interstellar Travel" in *Journal of the British Interplanetary Society, 36*, 1983, pp 210–214.

5. Gregory L. Matloff and Kelly Parks. "Interstellar Gravity Assist Propulsion: A Correction and New Application" in *Journal of the British Interplanetary Society, 41*, 1988, pp 519–526.

Chapter 7: Alien Life Between Here and the Stars

1. Robert L. Forward, *Camelot 30K*, New York, Tor Books, 1993.

2. Robert L. Forward, "Exploring Infrastellar Space," *Analog Science Fiction/Science Fact*, 1977, Vol 97, pp 43–56.

3. Carl Sagan and E. E. Salpeter, "Particles, Environments, and Possible Ecologies in the Jovian Atmosphere," *Astrophysical Journal Supplement Series*, 1976, Vol 32, pp 737–755.

Chapter 8: Terraforming Mars

1. C. McKay and W. Davis, "Duration of Liquid Water Habitats on Early Mars," *Icarus*, 90, 214–221, 1991.

2. M. Fogg, "A Synergistic Approach to Terraforming Mars," *Journal of the British Interplanetary Society*, August 1992.

3. P. Birch, "Terraforming Mars Quickly," *Journal of the British Interplanetary Society*, August 1992.

4. R. Forward, "The Statite: A Non-Orbiting Spacecraft," AIAA 89-2546, AIAA/ASME 25th Joint Propulsion Conference, Monterey, CA, July 1989.

5. J. Pollack and C. Sagan, "Planetary Engineering," in *Near Earth Resources*, J. Lewis and M. Mathews, eds, University of Arizona Press, Tucson, 1993.

Chapter 9: A Planet Dweller's Dreams

1. M. J. Fogg (Editor), Terraforming: *Journal of the British Interplanetary Society*, special terraforming issues, April 1991.

Chapter 10: Astrophysical Engineering and the Fate of the Earth

1. J. F. Kasting, "Runaway and Moist Greenhouse Atmospheres and the Evolution of Earth and Venus," *Icarus*, 1988, 74, 472–494.
2. M. Taube, "Future of the Terrestrial Civilization over a Period of Billions of Years" (Red Giant and Earth Shift), *J. Br. Interplanet Soc.*, 1982, 35, 219–225.
3. D. R. Crisell, "Solar System Industrialization: Implications for Interstellar Migrations." In: Finney, R. & Jones, E. M. (eds.) "Interstellar Migration and the Human Experience," pp 50–87, University of California Press, 1985.
4. J. G. Hills, "Close Encounters Between a Star/Planet System and a Stellar Intruder," *Astr. J.* 1984, 89, 1559–1564.
5. M. J. Fogg, "Solar Exchange as a Means of Ensuring the Long Term Habitability of the Earth," *Specul. Sci. Technol.*, 1989, 12, 153–157.

Chapter 12: The Magnetic Sail

1. D. G. Andrews and R. M. Zubrin, "Magnetic Sails and Interstellar Travel," 39th Congress of the International Astronautical Federation, IAF-88-553, Bangelore, India, Oct. 1988. Published in the *Journal of the British Interplanetary Society*, 1990.
2. R. M. Zubrin and D. G. Andrews, "Magnetic Sails and Interplanetary Travel," AIAA-89-2441, AIAA/ASME 25th Joint Propulsion Conference, Monterey, CA, July 1989. Published in *Journal of Spacecraft and Rockets*, April 1991.
3. D. G. Andrews and R. M. Zubrin, "Use of Magnetic Sails for Mars Exploration," AIAA-89-2861, AIAA/ASME 25th Joint Propulsion Conference, Monterey, CA, 1989.
4. D. G. Andrews and R. M. Zubrin, "Progress in Magnetic Sails," AIAA 90-2367, AIAA/ASME 26th Joint Propulsion Conference, Orlando, FL, 1990.
5. G. Vulpetti, "Achievement of Rectilinear Trajectories in the Solar System by Non-Rocket Propulsion," IAF-90-303, 41st Congress of the International Astronautical Federation, Dresden, Ger, Oct. 1990.
6. R. Zubrin, "The Use of Magnetic Sails to Escape from Low Earth Orbit," AIAA-91-2533, AIAA/ASME Joint Propulsion Conference, Sacramento, CA, June 1991.
7. R. Bussard, "Galactic Matter and Interstellar Flight," *Acta Astronautica*, 1960, Vol VI, pp 179–195.
8. D. Whitmire, "Relativistic Spaceflight and the Catalytic Nuclear Ramjet," *Acta Astronautica*, 1975, Vol 2, pp 497–509.

9. J. R. Spreiter and A. Y. Alksne, "Plasma Flow Around the Magnetosphere," Proceedings of the International Symposium on the Physics of the Magnetosphere, Washington, DC, Sept. 1968.
10. J. Engleberger, U.S. Patent 3,504,868, granted April 7, 1970.
11. F. Mead, et al, Air Force Rocket Propulsion Lab Report AFRPL-TR-72-31.
12. R. R. Bate, D. D. Mueller, and J. E. White, "Fundamentals of Astrodynamics," New York, Dover Publications, 1971.
13. B. N. Cassenti, "Design Concepts for the Interstellar Ramjet," AIAA 91-2537, 27th AIAA/ASME Joint Propulsion Conference, Sacramento, CA, June 24–26, 1991.

Chapter 14: The Negative Matter Space Drive

1. Robert L. Forward, "Far Out Physics," *Analog Science Fiction/Science Fact*, August 1975, Vol 95, No 8, pp 147–166.
2. Robert L. Forward, *Future Magic*, New York, Avon Books, 1988.
3. Robert L. Forward, "Negative Matter Propulsion," *Journal of Propulsion and Power*, Vol 6, No 1, Jan/Feb 1990, pp 28–37. (For a free reprint of this paper, send a large 45¢ SASE to P.O. Box 2783, Malibu, CA 90265).
4. H. Bondi, "Negative Mass in General Relativity," *Reviews of Modern Physics*, Vol 29, 1957, pp 423–428.
5. W. B. Bonnor and N. S. Swaminarayan, "An Exact Solution for Uniformly Accelerated Particles in General Relativity," *Zeitschrift für Physik*, 1964, Vol 177, pp 240–256.
6. Charles Sheffield, *The McAndrew Chronicles*, New York, Tor Books, 1983, pp 72–112, 234–235.
7. Valerie de Lapparent, Margaret J. Geller, and John P. Huchra, "A Slice of the Universe," *Astrophysical Journal*, 1986, Vol 302, L1–L5.
8. Yakov P. Terletskii, "Negative Masses and the Energy-Sources of the Universe," *Experimentelle Technik der Physik*, 1981, Vol 29, pp 331–332.